Tilling Sacred Grounds

Emerging Perspectives in Pastoral Theology and Care

Series Editor: Kirk Bingaman, Fordham University

The field of pastoral care and counseling, and by extension pastoral theology, is presently at a crossroads, in urgent need of redefining itself for the age of postmodernity or even post-postmodernity. While there is, to be sure, a rich historical foundation upon which the field can build, it remains for contemporary scholars, educators, and practitioners to chart new directions for the present day and age. Emerging Perspectives in Pastoral Theology and Care seeks to meet this pressing need by inviting researchers in the field to address timely issues, such as the findings of contemplative neuroscience, the impact of technology on human development and wellness, mindfulness meditation practice for reducing anxiety, trauma viewed through the lens of positive psychology and resilience theory, clergy health and wellness, postmodern and multicultural pastoral care and counseling, and issues of race and class. The series will therefore serve as an important and foundational resource for years to come, guiding scholars and educators in the field in developing more contemporary models of theory and practice.

Titles in the Series

Tilling Sacred Grounds: Interiority, Black Women, ad Religious Experience, by Phillis Isabella Sheppard

Christianity, LGBTQ Suicide, and the Souls of Queer Folk, by Cody J. Sanders

Warriors Between Worlds: Moral Injury and Identities in Crisis, by Zachary Moon

Pastoral and Spiritual Care in a Digital Age: The Future Is Now, by Kirk Bingaman

Women Leaving Prison: Justice-Seeking Spiritual Support for Female Returning Citizens, by Jill L. Snodgrass

The Chaplain's Presence and Medical Power: Rethinking Loss in the Hospital System, by Richard Coble

Neuroplasticity, Performativity, and Clergy Wellness: Neighbor Love as Self Care, by William D. Roozeboom

Tilling Sacred Grounds

Interiority, Black Women, and Religious Experience

Phillis Isabella Sheppard

LEXINGTON BOOKS
Lanham • Boulder • New York • London

Published by Lexington Books
An imprint of The Rowman & Littlefield Publishing Group, Inc.
4501 Forbes Boulevard, Suite 200, Lanham, Maryland 20706
www.rowman.com

86-90 Paul Street, London EC2A 4NE

Copyright © 2022 by The Rowman & Littlefield Publishing Group, Inc.

All rights reserved. No part of this book may be reproduced in any form or by any electronic or mechanical means, including information storage and retrieval systems, without written permission from the publisher, except by a reviewer who may quote passages in a review.

British Library Cataloguing in Publication Information Available

Library of Congress Cataloging-in-Publication Data available

ISBN 978-1-7936-3862-5 (cloth)
ISBN 978-1-7936-3864-9 (paperback)
ISBN 978-1-7936-3863-2 (electronic)

Contents

Acknowledgments vii

Introduction ix

1 Audre Lorde 1
2 Visions of Self and Transformation in Black Outsider Art 27
3 Black Women Living Religion in Cyberspace 51
4 "Because I Am a Woman": Vocation and Trauma 87
5 Tilling Sacred Ground: Meditation on Ritual and Resistance 111

Concluding Remarks 131

Bibliography 135

Index 145

About the Author 153

Acknowledgments

I want to give special thanks to my colleagues and friends whose support helped make this book possible. Specifically, I thank my dean Emilie M. Townes for helpful nudges and facilitating faculty writing retreats in 2018 and 2019. These were supportive experiences and generative. I thank Vanderbilt University Divinity School for an important research leave in 2018 that afforded me the time needed to travel for interviews and to complete a bulk of the writing. Jaco Hamman, always steadfast in his support and encouragement, offered helpful suggestions and a listening every step of the way. He is a true friend. Bonnie Miller-McLemore heard about the book long before it actually took shape on the page and I am grateful for her long-standing presence. Herbert Marbury, Amy Steele, and Lisa Thompson were regular conversation partners and interlocutors. Amy Steele in particular read early portions and gave crucial feedback. Lisa Thompson helped me to the finish line with the words of wisdom needed as one nears the end. I am grateful to the women and men in my parish, Upper Room Inclusive Catholic Community, especially Mary Theresa Streck, for their support and prayers for my vocational path.

I am especially appreciative of the Louisville Institute for awarding me a 2018 Faculty Research Grant for "Womanist Ethnography and Black Women's Vocation" project, and I am exceedingly grateful for the women who participated in interviews for the project. I am appreciative of artists Missionary Mary Proctor and David Seehausen for permitting the inclusion of their YouTube videos on her life and art. Zenju Earthlyn Manuel and Monica Roberts, the Transgriot, were generous in allowing me to include their websites in the book. I give thanks to the unnamed activists, musicians, and religious leaders who opened their hearts to the project, reexperienced old wounds, so that their stories could contribute to future readers' flourishing and well-being and scholars' deeper understanding of Black women's experience of religion. Their voices and experiences permeate the book. Without their wisdom and stories, the vision for this book would have been much narrower and less indicative of the complex relationship between religion, society, and Black women's lives. I am also grateful for the womanists who presented at the Womanist Ethnography Conferences I planned and hosted in 2018, 2019, and 2021. They too are present in this work.

I am tremendously grateful to Kirk Bingaman, the emerging Pastoral Theology series editor, for his support for the book, and to Trevor Crowell, editor at Lexington Books, an author's dream editor and collaborator. I conclude this book with deepest gratitude. Any book relies on the kindness of a wide circle of support, and my work has been made enormously easier and more gratifying by the hard work and contributions of my graduate research assistants and I offer deep bows to Kishundra D. King, Aly Benitez, Erica Joy Johnson, and Amina McIntyre. I am grateful for their creativity, intellect, and organizational leadership.

As always, I am thankful for Margaret, who is a source of inspiration and love, and the three children of my heart, Mikayla, Ian, and Evan. And finally, I am grateful to the womanists who came before me, wise demanding elders; to the Black women who, without ever hearing the name womanist, lived it; and to those who have transitioned to the world beyond the now and here to the ever-present, the ancestors. Their bright lights call me into new and deeper questions; I bow in respect.

Phillis Isabella Sheppard
Womanist. All day. Every day.
September 20, 2021

Introduction

Interiority and Public Religion

My interest in Black religious experiences began young and this early memory of discord between my parents is certainly one the earliest catalyst for the position it holds in my research. Standing just on the other side of a sliding wooden door that separated the kitchen from the dining room, I overheard a heated discussion between my parents. There was tension in the air that did not involve me, but I was ten years old and curious. I listened in on the tension-filled conversation. The reason for the conflict was unclear to me, but the discussion took a turn when I heard my mother say to my father, "Your people go to church on Sunday but I know they practice roots." My mother's voice was quiet and angry but, even more so, it was accusatory. She was speaking about some paternal aunts who lived in Florida, whose names and very existence were new to me. In the course of the conversation, I learned these relatives were poor seasonal workers who "worked in the fields" each summer. It was, it seemed, their poorness and secret entwinement with root practices that comprised the accusation. The root practices were the explicit focal point as she kept returning to their practice of roots. This accusation of their spiritual practice somehow put into question the authenticity of Christian religious faith, as well as a cause for shame, and means to shift the power dynamics between my parents. The trace of root practitioners in my father's genealogy afforded my mother the power she needed in this dispute.

In due time, I sought my mother out for more information. No amount of intense interest or feigned disinterest could persuade her to explain what "practicing roots" meant. As an adult, I asked siblings what they knew about these aunts and root practitioners in the family. No one knew anything, but one sister conveyed the familial religious anxiety that the very subject evoked when she responded, "I don't know anything about roots. Daddy's family was Baptist and I don't think they would be involved in that kind of thing." What is glaringly obvious are the strong emotions that such religious practices evoked, first in my parents, but also apparent in my sister's response, and the oppressive silence. "The spiritual practices associated with roots, and it was not clear what practices were being employed," and the silence surrounding them awakened in me a religious curiosity that continues to this day.[1]

The feminist anthropologist Linda E. Thomas captures the way in which culture transfuses our life, shapes our ways of being, and what we know reminds us that

> human beings acquire knowledge through culture. . . . We procure knowledge in the same manner that our lungs receive oxygen. It is a conscious and unconscious process that systematically and deliberately pervades our minds and senses. Amassing knowledge is the process of becoming persons who know.[2]

Thomas's assentation that knowledge acquisition is a "conscious and unconscious process" means that Black women's religious knowledge and experience is also a process fueled by conscious and unconscious forces—both are aspects of interiority, and demands a reading of Black women's religious interiority. Any thoughtful reading of Black women's religious engagement needs to make a move from interior to narrative using Black women's religious lexicons that have shaped their religious experience narrative.

For instance, I take up Audre Lorde who described herself as coming from "the gut of Blackness," and whose religious life moved from a New York Caribbean Roman Catholicism to a diasporic African-based celebration of Black goddesses. Lorde's narrative is important because her poetry, activism, and spirituality inform decades of Black women scholars, activists, poets, and spirituality. We see in her life an example of how religion was the conduit to a religious and cultural past and connected her to her Blackness. She redefines Blackness and religion, and even though she carves out a path that is particular to her life, the way of lived religion is a life force moving from and between the interior, the public, and social. Lived religion was entwined in the process of becoming Black, daughter, woman, lover, spouse, lesbian, mother, and activist as the realities of the social sphere were confronted in a myriad of ways. Lorde stitched together the pieces of a past she discovered in her mother's stories holding her longed-for Caribbean home and in the ritual practices her mother passed on in her cooking, lessons about Caribbean women's ways of being, and in the public practice of Catholicism. A Caribbean spiritual orientation to life was infused throughout the maternal domain of the household.

Lorde's spirituality was a tapestry created from all the parts of her identity... from her Afro-Caribbean Catholicism passed down by her mother in

Caribbean cultural stories, private rituals, and prayers; her embrace of her creativity and her erotic power; she prayed and gave praise to the African Goddesses. But she also struggled mightily against the impingement of racism, sexism, and homophobia into her psyche and life, and a deep sense of cultural dislocation. In her poetry, speeches, and relational life she sought to answer her question, "Does Black mean bad?" A Black African spirituality became a counterforce to psychic and social oppression, and as it permeated her activism and creativity. The religious and spiritual worldview that ultimately shaped her can only be understood if we trace the transformation of interiority made public and social. Lorde was a Black lesbian feminist of a first-generation, West Caribbean immigrant family who answered her question, "does Black mean bad?" only after she found her African diasporic religious self. In order to grasp her lived religion, we must, as she did, reckon with and take up her struggle to reconcile and reintegrate a meaningful sense of being Black and a descent of Black African ancestors. When Lorde nears the end of her life after 14 years of living with cancer, she writes that she is "finishing this piece of my bargain . . . and then I'm going on to something else, the shape of which I have no idea."³ She has taken up a religion that includes death as part of one's spiritual life, a movement to "something else" and yet to be known. In Lorde's short life, we see that the path to a meaningful lived religion is not easy or straightforward for Black women; it certainly is not for any of the women whose religious lives are the subject of this book, and their religious paths take place in the public, relational, and interior realm—often barely noticed.

In this book, I leave the confines of brick and mortar as the site for religious space and enter emergent spaces where religion is *and* becomes. Religion, for instance, is able to emerge in the cyberspace because cables, far below sea level, transmit data above the earth. Roving data, seeking satellite points of connection, become the texts, words, images, and messages we see in virtual spaces because it is in motion in between the depths and above the surface of the earth. Similarly, religion makes its way from the inner life into practice through various forms of expression—into art, spiritual teachings, poetry, and ritual processes. These are generally conceived of as cultural artifacts, and they are, but when considered as dynamic sites, that reside in the interior and the cultural spaces where Black women negotiate the world, I argue they are the underexplored grounds on which Black women live, create, and embody religion.

The reality of the interior life, as a developmental trajectory and, therefore, as an indication of mental health, is generally understood especially in psychoanalysis, spirituality, and practices of care disciplines. This disposition toward the inner experience is in sharp contrast with the fact that, historically, interiority has been obscured in the study of Black women and Black religious experience. Black women, in particular, have been, at best, marginalized in the literature or spoken for by scholars; in the process, their interiority, as an integral aspect of religious experience, has been erased. If we want to understand the complexity of Black women's lives, we need to bring a womanist sensibility where Black women's narratives are the starting point for consideration, a disposition toward deep listening, and an approach where a thick description of lived religion from their perspectives is cultivated. Interiority is at the heart of how and why Black women live religiously, and if we turn to it with a nuanced reading, we can apprehend the aims and effects of living religiously.

SIGNS OF INTERIORITY AND BLACK RELIGION: OCTAVIA BUTLER'S *PARABLE OF THE SOWER*

Religion continues to capture the literary, rhetorical, political, and cultural imagination of Black scholars. Even in spaces where religion is not the focus, the architecture, linguistic, cultural, and rhetorical style of Black religion is an organizing force for many. We see this specifically in Black women's literature and given that Black women's literature is so often a point of departure for finding a door into the nuances of Black women's lives, womanist scholars have made effective use of literature. Here, I turn briefly to the powerful story of Lauren Olamina in Octavia Butler's novel *Parable of the Sower*. Lauren is a young Black woman living and trying to survive in the chaotic and violent-filled world depicted in *Parable of the Sower*, the book reveals the complicated, and sometimes hidden relationship she has to religion. One reading of Octavia Butler's Parable series is that the author makes religion a trope for the interiority of self-selves in fluctuation: firm and fragmented; creative and traumatized; empathic and cruel; hopeful and in despair; relational and isolated; and splits in consciousness and profound awareness. In the world that Butler has created, culture, race, gender, and sexuality permeate religion and all aspects of life.

Parable of the Sower is a tale of admonition and terror, loss and mourning, and, possibly, the seeds of hope. The persistent filament is Lauren's new religion and, therefore, central to the novel is Black religion. From the first teaching of her newly created religion, Earthseed, "All that you touch you Change . . . the only lasting truth is Change. God is Change"[4] to the way she appears to practice the faith of her Black Baptist minister father:

> At least three years ago my father's god stopped being my God. His church stopped being my church. And yet, today, because I am a coward, I let myself be initiated into that Church. I let my father baptize me the three names of that God who isn't mine anymore. My God has another name.[5]

Lauren travels from her interior religion to the public religion of her father. She hides her God and her religion. She also tries to hide her extraordinary empathic sensibilities: Lauren is so inordinately empathically attuned that she is flooded with nearly unbearable pain in the face of others' intense suffering. She tried to hide this "gift" from family and community. Lauren, under the gaze of her father's deep Baptist faith, is viewed as strange, odd, and sometimes a problem—unwanted.

The world outside their barely gated community is a terrifying, horror-filled dystopian space where violence is pursued for entertainment and relief; resources for water, heat, and shelter are limited and the use of a psychotic-inducing drug is spreading. This horror-filled future is encroaching on the enclosed community. The boundary between inner and outer is porous. Lauren perceives the weight of abject terror descending, she feels it in the air, and she sees it encroaching into their daily life. She secretly prepares to leave the gated community. She secretly prepares for survival and, in secret, constructs the religion that will be the guiding faith for her life beyond her family, beyond the Baptist church, and beyond those whose hope rests in the God of three names. Black Religion, in her life, is interior, public, and decidedly complicated. The novel lays bare the interiority of religion and cultural conflict. It is, however, the deep interiority, and the way it makes its way into the public domain, that is embedded throughout the novel. Butler requires the reader to take note of what is often sidestepped in discussion of Black women's lives. Cultural anthropologist Celeste Henery speaks to the missing interiority of Black and brown women with poignancy, calling it a "collective call and landscape"[6] that is often avoided. Instead, Black women's interiority, in a world where a critical reading of the structures of injustice is crucial and necessary, must be animated.

Interiority Matters

Interiority is at the heart of womanist ethicist Emilie M. Townes's *Womanist Ethics and the Cultural Production of Evil* where she makes known the "deep interior material life of evil" and offers "suggestions on how to dismantle it through the intersection of ethical commitment and social location."[7] Townes centers the interior because she must get "into the interior life of evil to unhinge its underpinnings."[8] Townes exposes the imagination—a feature of interiority—made social in public representations, as the linchpin in the cultural, systemic, and relational production and maintenance of evil. But interiority is not limited to seeing and demolishing the methods for the cultural production of evil. For Townes, it is a demand to turn to one's own interior constructions: "We begin with ourselves. Each of us must answer the question: What will we do with the fullness and incompleteness of who we are as we stare down the interior material life of the cultural production of evil?"[9] The interior then is comprised of aspects of our relationship to the broader culture that are apparent and conscious as well as unconscious elements. This requires us to become deeply familiar with our own interiority, face its complexity, and to do the work of interior transformation while resisting the external forces of the hegemonic imagination. If we are to fully grasp Black women's religious experience and social engagement, we must seek out the interior because neither religion nor interiority is spared the intrusion and formation that the wider social forces enact on the psyche. Brenda Sendejo in "The Cultural Production of Spiritual Activisms: Gender, Social Justice, and the Remaking of Religion in the Borderlands" examines

> the intersections of spirituality, issues of social justice, and healing through the theoretical frame and praxis of spiritual activism as put forth by Gloria E. Anzaldúa, who views spiritual activism as an inner call to create outer change in the material world . . . "now let us shift . . . the path of conocimiento . . . [to] inner works, public acts" in the lives of Tejanas.[10]

Sendejo is exploring another aspect of interiority, but like Townes, she recognizes that interiority and the social intersect in powerful and transformative ways lead her to make the claim that "women's activism takes the form of spiritualized activisms, whereby they do the inner spiritual work that gives them the strength to do the outer work of creating social change as spiritual healers, educators, and community activists."[11]

In her seminal essay "Toward the Black Interior," Elizabeth Alexander reckons with Ntozake Shange's claim that "as Black people we exist metaphorically and literally as the underside, the underclass. We are the unconscious of the entire Western world,"[12] by asking "if Black people are the subconscious of the Western mind, where is 'the Black subconscious,' both individually and collectively articulated?"[13] Alexander is tracking how the language, psychodynamic language but not psychotherapeutic, offers a marker for "identifying complex and often unexplored interiority beyond the face of the social self."[14] Even as she describes Black interiority as "dream space," and "hopeful space" a space for creativity, she recognizes that its "race, gender, class, sexuality—our social identities—exist and have been 'always already' constructed in the dream space, even when they are constructed outside of a racist impetus."[15] It is not that the realities, experiences, and even infliction of racism and heterosexism do not show up in the interior dream space, but, rather that dream space is "inner space in which Black artists have found selves that go far, far beyond the limited expectations and definitions of what Black is, isn't, or should be."[16] Alexander argues that in inner space, "the self is made visible in the spaces we occupy, literal "Black interiors" where the interior is made public. As Black women occupy, create, and transform space, there is the potential for such spaces, previously labeled public and secular space, to become religious space because Black women's religious interiority takes form in the public. Just as Townes mines the work of the fantastic hegemonic imagination, made public in the cultural production of evil, this book explores the production of the religious when interiority takes shape in public expression.

Several aspects emerge as interactive and constituent elements of interiority: interiority has subjective, intersubjective, conscious, unconscious, and relational components but develops and is formed in historical, cultural, and social contexts. Taken seriously, interiority can reveal a multiplicity of ways we make our way, and are known, in the world. The artist Torkwase Dyson in "Black Interiority: Notes on Architecture, Infrastructure, Environmental Justice, and Abstract Drawing" convincingly argues that

> the design of our physical world informs the methods in which motion emerges and spatial strategy is organized. For Black people, moving through a given environment comes with questions of belonging and a self-determination of visibility and semi-autonomy. . . . This relationship of interior and exterior—Black mind/body geographic experience—is inextricably tied to lands and waters riddled with architectural and infrastructural histories.[17]

Dyson's description of interiority discusses the kind of complexity that I think is necessary. In this case, environmental racism and architectural constructs are expressions of interiority—of those trafficking in control, dehumanization, and psychological warfare. In creating spaces where Black peoples' sense of self and belonging rise to consciousness and deliberation in response to the appropriation of the landscape for just this purpose tells us interiority is and cannot be closed off to the surround but it can resist its intention by engaging these imposed "questions of belonging and a self-determination of visibility and semi-autonomy." Darlene Clark Hine in her classic "Rape and the Inner Lives of Black Women in the Middle West" argues that interiority is a mechanism employed by Black women as a form of protection against racism and sexism and, more directly, as a means of psychic survival following bodily violation; interiority maintained an element of self-defined integrity.[18] Black women claim interiority as psychic space around which they can, and very often need to, create barriers. Hine calls the installation of these barriers a process of "dissemblance." In the course of dissemblance, Black women present to the world a persona of openness but "sanctity of inner aspects of their lives"[19] in order to "accrue the psychic space and harness the resources needed to hold their own in the often one-sided and mismatched resistance struggle."[20] This aspect of interiority, and its function, has implications for religious experience in the realm of interior space. The work is to make the interior space known space.

When interiority rises to the level of awareness and understood as a feature of religion, religious experience is revealed to be a complex, sometimes beautiful, sometimes tortured, sometimes powerful, encounter. Religious life in Butler's literary imagination is a thorny experience resting in and between the crevices that tether psyche to social, familial, and interior processes. It is mirror and prediction, a social commentary and theological reflection, frightening and, in the person of Lauren, hopeful. Butler's novel, then, reveals Black religion and Black women's experience of religion as deeply interior and public, where these domains overlap and intersect at every turn and expression. As such, what we can note as Black religious experience is always a product of the interchange and, sometimes, conflict. We must move to recover the dynamics of interiority while we also cultivate spaces for its emergence. This kind of work fosters our understanding of the movement from inner to social and public. The convergence of social and inner needs to be integral to our understanding of Black women, religion, and culture.

Lived Religion Is Complicated

Religious experience is a complex matter. This assertion that religious experience is a complex matter, likely, comes as no surprise, especially to those attuned to the psychological as well as rich narratives of religious experience. That said, we often perceive what we have been taught noteworthy of our attention, and what is noteworthy is that which is obvious. Unless trained to listen for the undercurrents in narratives of religious experience or to question, and even interrogate, what we see, we are less likely to be aware of how the interior life shapes, sustains, and transforms religious experience in public domains. Between these two domains, powerful undercurrents are operative. I employ a womanist methodology for three important reasons. The first is that womanist scholars seek to privilege Black women's particularity and, therefore, make their lives the epistemological basis of analysis. The second is that womanist scholars have long valued shining a light on what has previously been missed or ignored in the study of Black life and culture. The third is my commitment to womanist practical theology's attention to praxeological intent aimed at relief from psychological, material, spiritual, and political tyranny. In fleshing out the pervasiveness of the deep interiority in the Black women's private and public experience of religion, I further these efforts. Interior and public religious spaces are crucial to each other, (in) forming the shape of the other, a powerful exchange where neither relinquishes the boundaries of form but are intertwined like tree roots crossing one another below and above the surface, sharing resources, suffering alike the vagaries of weather, poisoned earth, and healing, and new growth over time, again and again.

I am interested in the intersection of cultural experiences and interiority that give rise to religious expressions in different places and ways. Like the ethnographer portraitist Sarah Lawrence-Lightfoot, I strive to be

> witness, . . . storyteller, and mirror . . . probing—the layers and subtexts of human experience; listening for the voices and silences, documenting the good, and honoring the chaos and contradictions, the ironies and ambiguities threaded through our lives.[21]

In approaching Black women and public religion in this way, lived religion includes religious practices that are both "everyday" ways of being religious as well as those in close proximity to institutional and para-institutional contexts. In other words, I am interested in how and where Black women "do" religion as well as those "domains of life where sacred things are being produced, encountered, and shared."[22]

Black religion operates in the lives of practitioners as it does because powerful inner forces are at play. These forces shape how and what we enact, reenact and embody in religious practices, and influence the sites where we seek to satisfy the most powerful of needs. These undercurrents, interior and cultural, are operative in and out of the religious environ; in fact, what might be maintained is that the religious environ is everywhere, seen and unseen, conscious and unconscious. This shift makes for a nuanced view of religious engagement and how it operates. Research that focuses on the positive outcomes of religious engagement, particularly for Black women, in general, is interested in the mental health benefits.[23]

However, in this work, I want to complicate the assumption of straightforward engagement by, for instance, examining how Black women's interiority allows them to live a complex religious life. Lauren from Butler's novel has a new religion that asserts that "all that you touch you Change . . . the only lasting truth is Change. God is Change." What might religion mean in the life of a Black woman who asserts that all you touch you Change? The only lasting truth is Change. And God is Change. And yet Lauren's outward expression of her father's religion continues until she leaves the gated community. The interiority of living into a new religion while practicing the old religion reiterates what we already know from studies of African-derived religions among the enslaved—what you see—what is manifest—may not be what is being experienced and practiced.

Finding meaning in the practices of religion, and the inner processes involved, is no small feat. To do so, one needs to be respectfully curious, capable of great sensitivity, and respect. The womanist ethnographer must have posture receptive to introspection. This book is concerned with the everyday religion in the lives of Black women as well as the nature, meaning, and varieties of religious experience. When I reference "everyday religion," I mean to signify that religion is embedded in life wherever it is occurring, and not limited to buildings or even to specifically defined practices.

INTERIORITY IN PUBLIC SPACES, CULTURE IN INDIVIDUAL PRACTICES: RELIGION AS A SELFOBJECT

As a Black psychoanalyst and womanist practical theologian, I bring to Black religion an ear attuned to and fascinated by the inner life bubbling within religious content. At stake is how we continue to speak of Black women and their humanity in a world where racism and sexism are the means to devalue them, Black culture, and the power of Black religion. It is in the rich ground of interiority that, when moved into the public sphere, Black women's religious life emerges and is even created over and against the practices of occlusion. That is, religion, made public and social, reveals what religion is doing in the inner life as well as in public and social spaces.

The ways in which we, individually and collectively, internalize religion, and the affects and effects religion has on our sense of self, and the group (or group collective identity held in place by shared values, experiences, and ideologies) fall in the psychological category of selfobject experience. In Self Psychology theory, selfobject[24] was originally defined by Heinz Kohut as experiences of one's surround, generally relational, that satisfied the developmental needs of mirroring, twinship, and idealization. As a result of these needs to feel oneself reflected in the care provided, similar to someone, and emotionally held by someone strong and held in awe, the self gradually emerges as cohesive.

His definition, arising out of his psychoanalytic practice, was centered on white, upper middle-class, mostly protestant, and heterosexual psyches. In other words, his theory reflected the patients he saw in his psychoanalytic practice. So, when Kohut included culture as a selfobject, culture meant cultural objects and experiences reported by white, upper-middle-class, mostly protestant, and heterosexual analytic patients. The availability and capacity for culture to meet selfobject needs—mirroring, twinship, kinship, and idealizing—was assumed to occur; minimal consideration was given to one's gender, race, ethnicity, sexuality, or religion. To be sure, the move to theorize cultural experience as interior was a needed and powerful contribution to psychoanalytic perspectives because it opened up space to shift attention to the dynamism between culture and psyche. Kohut's view that "human beings grow within a culture of embeddedness . . . whereby the person enters not only into the cultural system but also into the moral systems of society"[25] widened the scope of the relational sphere to recognize that the self is always situated in a sociocultural field.

As expansive as this theoretical move was, Kohut did not, however, make a full shift from the primary focus on the interior of the individual. Thus, culture is important in one's inner life because of how one relates to it. As a consequence, self-psychological clinical theory and practice ultimately has rendered culture external to the self. Cultural selfobjects were not germane to most of his clinical discussions and this produced a split between theory and practice. Important aspects of lived experience were whitewashed. The systemic realities that shape or disrupt selfobject experiences, and therefore the sense of the self, were ignored. The implication, for Black religious experience, is the denial of its capacity or agency to effect change on individuals, social systems, or culture. Religion, from this standpoint, exists functionally to facilitate the Western idea of the individual cohesive self, and religion's place is to produce a primarily fixed experience of oneself and culture.

I would argue for a cohering sense of self rather than a penultimate cohesive self. A cohering self allows for emergent self-qualities to awaken as context and relational sphere allow or even demand. Second, we need to take account of Black women's experience and cultural expressions, and the fact the "concepts of self and cultural selfobject are cultural productions. And, as cultural productions, the self and cultural selfobjects are unique to the context in which developmental, needs, and care occur."[26] In other words, for instance, we would recognize that Black women do not enter a world prepared to mirror them, positively or toward cohering, as Black, lesbian, women, cis-gendered, trans, bisexual, nonbinary, or heterosexual. We cannot assume that Black women's need for culturally embedded—based on race, class, gender, and sexuality—idealizable figures will be immediately available in social spaces. In this regard, Black women enter comprised selfobject milieus regularly. Religious and racial spaces are not free of the forces that make this so.

This was made clearer to me when I spoke with the "outsider artist" Mary Proctor about her work. Proctor was known as a collector of "junk" that she would occasionally set but, in actuality, just collected in her front and back lawns. The junk was such an eyesore to neighbors, they complained. By the time I spoke with her, she was a self-proclaimed and recognized artist.

> You probably know my story, right? How my art started? My grandmother, aunt and uncle, they raised me, died in a fire. They just burned because they couldn't

> get out the door. It was terrible. I just was depressed. Really depressed for a year. I couldn't do anything. My husband had to do it all.

Mary Proctor's mourning was nearly unbearable for her and so debilitating that every area of life was affected. It was the tie, a thin one at times, to religion that transformed her mourning. And as her mourning was transformed, Proctor became more public with her message. She has several, some self-produced, YouTube videos, and art has been the subject of several scholarly art publications. In each, Proctor reveals her ongoing self-transformation and the place of religion in it.

> And I had asked the Lord, now you took three of my family members, what am I to do? So the first thing that the Lord did—he didn't come right away to tell me what he allowed me to do. He allowed me to go through a time of depression. *And I went through a time of depression for about a year.* And this is one of my first doors. Then God told me, 'Mary paint the door. And that's what I did. I just started painting and I now I am artist. I am Missionary Mary Proctor'.

Mary Proctor's narrative of mourning and transformation is included in this book because in her life we are able to witness, through her mourning *in her art* and her religion, the emergence, from interiority to public a lived religion that moves transformed herself understanding from "junk collector" to an artist to missionary, and now mentor. Her gallery is no longer on her lawn but a gallery she opened in her hometown of Tallahassee, Florida. She speaks with pride of exhibiting up and coming young Black artists and teaching classes to the public because "everybody is an artist." Furthermore, she now sees herself as following the footsteps of Mary McCloud Bethune:

> This is Mary Mcleod Bethune Cookman, one of my favorite women. She's all, you know, just reading about her, talking about how she went out and sold things just to make a college will Bethune Cookman. She did that.

> I feel she's a part of me, that I, I'm doing that same thing today, making things, doing things. So, that I [would have] my own museum . . . one day. I want people to see that Mary has made a museum, and if I can do anything, that you can do it too.[27]

The work occurring in the inner life is not, however, solely integrative and formative of a Black identity unencumbered by society's negative intrusions. Interiority is made up of the collision of culture, gender, sexuality, and religion. And the public expression of religion can reveal the conflicts between Black women's sense of a cohering Black identity and evidence of the residual effects of experiences of racism and sexism. For instance, Alecia Brown, a 72-year-old still pastoring Baptist minister, started the first Black cyberspace church in the mid-1990s. She would go on to form a church in a bus. She is courageous, deeply spiritual, and committed to her call to ministry, but she carries deep anger and pain because of the sexist practices of her religiously conservative community.

> That is the one thing to this day that I've always wanted. To be called to a church. To be able to apply to a vacant church and have the opportunity to go and preach in an interview. But because I am female.

Black sexism is a pervasive theme in her religious narrative, and far more entwined in her sense of self and subjectivity than race or class. At 72 she has had lived well into her vocation but the absence of acceptance and validation from her Black Baptist community has seared her psyche. When she described how a young Black man she had closely mentored for ministry ignored her once he was ordained, the pain was palpable. Her voice shifted from strong and sturdy to one vulnerable and shaky, "that really hurt. I cried like a baby" and I knew that neither her preaching nor the success of her bus ministry would soothe her broken heart or repair her complicated interior experience of gender and race set in motion almost 50 years ago. "It's the Black men preachers who don't want want me in their pulpit but some of the women don't either. They want the pastor for themselves." Alecia Brown pulled herself from the depths of abjection claiming, explaining, that

> somebody has to be small. I have come to accept that. I struggled with that a long time . . . because I didn't see myself as successful. God did not call me to be successful . . . he called me to be faithful.

The Black Buddhist teacher Zenju Earthlyn Manuel, who in some ways presents as "spiritual daughter" of Audre Lorde, by way of Haitian roots, and negotiates race, gender, sexuality, and class with another, non-Christian, model. She grew up in a southern share-cropping Pentecostal family that eventually left Louisiana and made their way to Los Angeles. Manuel's religious trajectory is a pilgrimage from a religious home to another religious home. The past appears in her present religious commitments as memories, practices, and teachings. Today Manuel maintains a website with Buddhist teachings available to the public and has published two books on Buddhism. At the heart of her spiritual teachings and writings is a thirst to find home— an embodied spiritually, culturally authentic, and in community. Finding her way, to home, has not been easy for her.

> Spiritual teachers espouse the thought that home is in the heart. When I ask, "Where do I belong?" they respond, "Look within." But it is difficult to find oneself without acknowledging the social and cultural dimensions of homelessness.

The fact that Zenju Earthlyn Manuel is a well-known Buddhist practitioner and teacher in the California Bay area did not protect her and partner from experiencing homelessness and economic insecurity. They attempted to buy the home they were renting in Oakland but were outbid. Zenju lived in her car for several months. The experience reoriented her and awakened long-submerged feelings:

> I saw that trying to purchase [a] home was an effort to resolve an experience of up rootedness that goes at least as far back as the slave trade.
>
> I was in an altered state, feeling as lost as my ancestors must have felt when they landed in this country. The loss of home . . . uncovered what had been buried beneath each response to rejection my whole life. It marked the beginning of a slow, gradual path toward compassion.[28]

This road to compassion in cyberspace is one where the outside, the social and political, are intertwined with the inside. As she makes her way on the path to enlightenment, Zenju wrestles with her racism, Blackness, sexuality, and religion and renegotiates her relationship to a Black religious past and a hoped-for future.

We would, however, do well to be ever cognizant that the Internet is a linguistic, visual, rhetorical, and communal virtual web of connectivity created out of the same "stuff"—rituals, practices, and mores—that forms, and to our collective and individual detriment, malforms, our religious and social structures, as well as our psyches, in the nonvirtual world. Lisa Nakamura has argued that the "Internet is a place where race happens. In the early days of the Net, technological visionaries imagined the online world as a utopian space where everything—even transcending racism—was possible."[29] Frankly, I did not turn to the Internet to transcend race, its allure for me was the capacity to connect with Black people, the diaspora, and particularly Black lesbians, far and wide. Yes, the Internet is a place where race and racism happen. It is also a place, a space, where gender, sexuality, class, and religion "happen." Two Muslim women bloggers, Jamerican, whose blog "Jamerican's Veranda" reveals the struggle of being a Black woman convert to Islam, and Leah Daily, born into a Black Muslim family, blog about being a large, curvy, fashion conscious, feminist Black Muslim. Their experiences remind us that the effects of racism and sexism go deep and the way up is through the hard work of resisting the negative cultural and religious messages directed at

Black women. The way of undoing the internalization of these messages is distinct but in the public of cyberspace is where they do it.

The very dynamics that make Black culture, Black religion, and Blackness emerge in collectively lived experience also occur in cyberspace. We bring the same hopes and longing for Black life that we hold in the nonvirtual spaces. The cultural tools that make their way into, for instance, storefront spiritual activism, community organizing, religious communities, and political rallies[30] make their way into cyberspace and the depth of Black women's interiority. But because this space, metaphor, or being is dynamic, it is complex.

In her ethnography of Black women's views of faith and church, Daphne Wiggins includes an example of the kind of complex process of which I am writing: in discussing sermon content vis-à-vis racial content, she quotes one woman as saying:

> I welcome hearing how to deal with [racism] at church, but I don't want it to be a constant thing. I don't think everything that happens to me in life in the workspace on the fact that I am Black. I guess I am more or less accepting . . . it's more like, 'Okay, you're Black accept it'. Things are not the same for you, they are not ever going to be the same for you, but then again if they were the same for you, you'd not be a stronger person. We're [Black people] actually more survivors because of the way we've been treated. If we were treated any less, or any other way, I don't think we would be as good as we are . . . I mean I have no problem with going to church with someone white.[31]

Wiggins's interviewee (Gail) was responding to a question about the inclusion of politics and race in sermon content but what I notice is that her interior grappling with the reality of racism, in relationship to religion and self-understanding, is complicated. Wherein the religion and church are places to address the effects of racism, she does not want this to take over her religious experience. She makes demands: accept that I am Black and deal with it, but more strikingly, through an interior process turns the experience of racism upside down and concludes that racism (things not being the same for you) not only makes Black people strong but that without such mistreatment, Black people would not be as strong. The interchange between the social, interior, and public expression of religion is complex. Gail's response begs for a reading specifically in terms of how Black religious experience mediates experiences of race and racism but also in terms of how the inner life develops in a racist context. The idea that exposure to racism builds resilience, strength, or offers psychological enhancement says something about how religious experience and race converge in the inner life to produce explanatory models that guide how one understands experience. Obviously, explanatory models can be flawed, limit one's agency and resistance against racism, or can serve to buffer against the assaults on the psyche. These are not mutually exclusive but require attention and analysis.

Gail's understanding of the place or work of racism in one's spiritual and interior life is remarkably dissimilar to Zenju Earlyn Manuel's spiritual teaching that "if we were to simply walk past the fires of racism, sexism, and so on because illusions of separation exist within them, we may well be walking past one of the widest gateways to enlightenment."[32] Zenju Earthlyn Manuel argues we have to enter into the racism we experience to bring about inner and social change but it is not racism that ignites transformation; it is, rather, the refusal to say that racism, sexism, or homophobia are the last word on interiority. Alecia Brown's reckoning with the sexism she experiences leads her to believe "somebody has to be small. I have come to accept that." Gail values Blackness but her interior is divided between acknowledging the injustice of "things are never going to be the same between Blacks and whites" and the experience of racism has made her more resilient. Church is a powerful force in her life and may in fact be the place where she comes the closest to linking the divide within—if only on a temporary basis.

Religion is a phenomenon of the individual and the public—but they are not separate and require each other to produce meaning in relation to the other. In this book, Black women tell their own stories and define religious experience. In this close reading of interiority and lived religion, we will hear not only how Black women live religiously but also what they intend, and the effects, of living religiously. The meaning they make of their lives will be our guide to a womanist approach to lived religion.

DESCRIPTION AND CHAPTERS

This book turns to the exchange between Black women's interiority and lived religion. Historically, interiority has been obfuscated in the study of Black women and Black religious experience. Black women, in particular, have been, at best, marginalized in the literature or spoken for by scholars; in the process, their interiority, as an integral aspect of religious experience, has been erased.

What do we gain by recovering Black women's interiority? Fundamentally, I argue that in so doing, we assert Black women's humanity as well as their varied ways of being religious, Black, and women. Their lives tell us that religious experience is a complicated experience. I leave the brick and mortar of religious space and turn to Black women whose religious experience is practiced in public spaces—outsider art, cyberspace, poetry, spiritual teachings and womanist preaching, and ritual process. Tracing interiority in our reading of religious life can tell us *how* Black women live religiously but also what they intend of such living—that is, with this nuanced reading, we can apprehend the moral aims of Black women and the effects on the self of living religiously.

The work puts *Black* flesh, bone, culture, and psyche where Black women's religious lives have, with rare exceptions, been whitewashed (study of religion), subjugated (Black religious studies), misrepresented (psychology of religion), and obliterated (feminist psychologies of religion). The womanist ethnographic lens grounding this method privileges a disposition for deep listening and the cultivation of thick descriptions emerging from Black women's perspectives on what is religious in their personal and public living. As such, interiority and sociality are inextricably intertwined threads that must be held, sometimes in tension, together for an understanding of Black women's experience.

From the Gut of Blackness: Audre Lorde

In chapter 1, I turn to Audre Lorde to explore the interiority of cultural and spiritual dislocation and its implications for Black identity. Lorde's sense of dislocation—that sense of being unfettered to one's Black past and present Black cultural situation—created a vacuum that, painful and unrelenting early in her life, became a source for spiritual search.

In her poem "From the Gut of Blackness," Lorde introduces herself and lays out the crucial issues that frame the contours of her reflection: her color, gender, lesbian identity, race, and her Black feminist moral fiber. She wondered if being Black, the darkest in her family, and in society that overvalued whiteness, meant she was bad. Even as she wrestled with what it means to *be* Black, she knew it was not just her "problem." Lorde's question is at once historical and cultural (how are notions of Blackness embedded in the fissures of social relations and cultural practices), psychological (what does Black mean deep within), and, finally, it is a spiritual about the natural of Black humanity. Her pursuit of spirituality begins is innervated by the erotic power and this erotic spirituality forms Lorde's view of the sacred, spiritual, and transformation. Her transformation is interwoven with the sacredness that only an African-inspired diasporic religion could offer.

Lorde is a crucial figure in this work because Black women—feminist and womanist scholars, poets, artists, and those who practice their religion out of the limelight in everyday spaces—have turned to Lorde seeking a way into a Black-centered women's spirituality.

Chapter 2: Visions of Self and Transformation in Black Outsider Art

In chapter 2, outsider art is turned as a rich source for exploring the intersections among Black life, culture and society, and the place of religion. As cultural workers, Black outsider artists are more often situated on the far margins of the museum world and the financial and social privileges associated with it. These artists, rather than experiencing a long period of learning "the" Western canon of art and therefore formed to appreciate works long studied and considered "high" art, find their calling to creativity more spontaneously. The vision and art-making process emerge unexpectedly and, in many narratives, the artist is born of some need to understand a traumatic event. Thus, the artist's identity is conferred not by art school or through exhibit but by an interior calling slowly mirrored in the public sphere. The spiritual dimension to their calling and art is heard in most stories of becoming an artist. Religion, pain, and visionary art are used to describe a powerful communication from God whereby the artist either becomes a conduit for a religious message (a preacher or evangelist) or the art is the message (the canvas holds the sermon and the painting is the sermon).

As visionary artists, they bring a message to their communities and sometimes the world. Their life is part of the vision and so must be shared. Art—displayed in local public galleries, garages, front lawns, or homes—is filled with autobiographical images, religious and spiritual themes, struggle, and historical and political messages, and is in response to their call into the ministry of art. Outsider art-making is a source of communicating, and healing from, internal trauma, loss, and abandonment but also from the trauma of racism, sexism, and poverty inflicted by a capricious society. The interiority and sociality of the religious message are the form or expression of their vocation.

The chapter traces the artist Missionary Mary Proctor's movement from "junk" collector trying to make a way help support her family through a complicated mourning to a religious calling. Hers is the movement from deep interiority to public religious engagement through art-making, and, eventually, a vision for the world. This chapter explores the ways in which Mary Proctor's work reveals her inner life and the process of her experience of being a Black woman who develops a religious vocation after her suffering finds expression in art and in the reengagement with her Black community.

Chapter 3: Black Women Living Religion in Cyberspace

While Black people, Black women in particular, are nearly absent in the rapidly proliferating research literature on cyber-religion, this ethnography of religious experience in cyberspace reveals a growing presence across religious traditions created and maintained by Black women. The Internet is a site for the robust engagement of religion by Black women and Black women are, in fact, creatively teaching, preaching, engaging religious spiritual practices, and forming religious communities in cyberspace. Making the claim for Black women's interiority in cyberspace religion is a claim about the persistence of Black women's experience of religion—more often without the support and affirmation of institutional bodies and a claim about the pervasiveness of religious contexts. However, the pervasiveness of religion notwithstanding, religion in cyberspace though a creative engagement is still subject to the realities that Black women face everywhere: classism, sexism, racism, heterosexism.

I turn to Black women's practice of religion in cyberspace including blogsites, videos, and websites that offer spiritual teachings. In looking at the ways in which religious experience is represented, practiced, and taught by the Black women claiming the Internet as religious space, we can see that cyberspace is an active site of cultural, religious, and interior processes as well as a site for mediating experiences.

This chapter focuses on three women who have sustained presence in cyberspace zenu.org. Zenju Earthlyn Manuel is a Zen Buddhist priest whose teachings focus on sanctuary and the search for a spiritual and cultural home is similar to Lorde's search except that Zenju must integrate physical homelessness into her spiritual path. She does this by way of meditation on her interior state of disorientation and on the African ancestors that she integrates into her form of Buddhism. Convinced that sanctuary comes from facing and undoing the imprint of racism on the psyche and spirit, her spiritual teachings move from the metaphorical to the ritual to material homemaking. The interior is both privileged and interrogated territory.

Jamerican converted to Islam as a teenager and her blogsite Jamerican's Veranda is a site for exposing the difficulty of "conversion" when culture, colorism, family, and community are daily challenges. We hear briefly her from another Black Muslim woman, Leah V. Dailey, whose experiences overlap but who adds "feminist" to her identity and reflections. She uses her blogsite beautyandthemuse.net as a place to challenge sexism and anti-Black and anti-fat messages. She challenges the messages she has internalized of what a good Muslim Black woman should be, say, and do. Both bloggers invite readers into ambivalence and conflict between what they feel, believe, and long for and their convictions about being Black Muslim women. Jamerican reveals her attempts to find a religious space where she can be a Black Muslim convert, a woman, and her love for Islam accepted in spite of the struggles she faces.

Monica Roberts, who died as this book was completed, was a Black womanist transwoman who maintained a blogsite, Transgriot, as a site to advocate for trans-identified people's right to exist and thrive. She was raised in the south, a Texan from Houston, and was baptized young and she remained clear about her religious convictions and sensibilities throughout her life.

Roberts's narrative includes her transition to being a transgender woman with little support from family and friends at time when Black and transgender were seldom spoken of publicly. The messages she internalized from her deep, southern religious context preached of a loving and accepting God but the people, in the church, treated transgender people as "less than human." Her blogsite is the place she negotiated the tension between self, religion, and communities. Whereas her religious home did not accept her as transgender, the mostly white, trans community did not accept her religious sensibilities. Roberts's identity as griot for the Black trans community required her to grapple with her own "internal demons" in order to help other Black trans people to know that they have a right to exist.

Chapter 4: Vocation and Trauma

Chapter 4 is the narrative of Alecia Brown, 72 years of age with some 25-plus years in ministry. She is at a point in life where she is open to reflecting on her time in ministry. She grew up in southeastern Florida in a family of staunch free-standing Baptists with long-standing, intergenerational roots in the tradition. They remain, in her description, "proud Baptists."

Alecia was not interested in a ministry and the experience was "traumatic" and disruptive to her life, professionally, spiritually, and relationally. As she moved closer to "hearing what God was saying," she could not sleep; her dreams frightened her, and she suddenly no longer enjoyed her professional life as a teacher. It was as if she had lost her taste for pleasure. When she tried to discuss it with her mother, her mother replied, "that's between you and God. Don't talk to me." Her pastor was unsupportive.

Eventually, she sold her house and attended seminary and after graduating returned to Florida. Her call to ministry, first realized in a cyberspace church and then in a bus ministry church, remains important to her. Alecia Brown's trauma continues at the interior level. She knows she is able to preach and lead, yet gender and sexism have prevented her from realizing her vision of ministry. She has never had an opportunity to preach a trial sermon, has never been asked to preach from the pulpit of a local church, and has never experienced the pleasure of being recognized as a pastor from the local Black pastors' association. As such, her story reveals a theme of unrelenting mourning coupled with the destabilization of trauma has on the self. In her we see that, though the call to ministry continues to shape her identity, the imprint of sexist rejection regularly disrupts who her sense of self. Sexism is integral to the stories she tells about herself and about others.

Chapter 5: Mediation on Ritual and Resistance

In the final chapter, ritual in the lives of Black women is examined as the site for the public confluence of interiority and sociality of lived religion. Retracing our steps through the previous chapters, and rereading their stories as ritual process, chapter 5 looks at the way in which Black women rely on ritual action (ancestor worship and remembering, libations, purification acts, altars, and petitions) as a means to convey and embody a gateway to a Black religious past and resistance to oppressive structures. Given recent rise in ritual practice in Black women's lives, and theory in womanist scholarship, it is important to understand ritual space as a means to mediate experiences of self, religion, sociality, and interiority.

NOTES

1. Phillis Isabella Sheppard, "Womanist-Lesbian Pastoral Ethics: A Post-Election Perspective," *Journal of Pastoral Theology*, 27, no. 1 (2017). doi: 10.1080/10649867.2017.1315791.

2. Linda E. Thomas, "Womanist Theology, Epistemology, and a New Anthropological Paradigm," *Cross Currents* 48, no. 4 (1998–9).

3. "Twenty-five Years After Her Death, What Audre Lorde Left Behind Most Definitely Has a Life of Its Own," Melville House, 2017, https://www.mhpbooks.com/twenty-five-years-after-her-death-what-audre-lorde-left-behind-most-definitely-has-a-life-of-its-own/. Accessed July 26, 2018.

4. Octavia Butler, *Parable of the Sower Earthseed* (New York, NY: Grand Central Publishing, 2000).

5. Octavia Butler, *Parable of the Sower*, 7.

6. Celeste Henery, "The Tears, Struggles, and Hopes of Black Women," Keisha N. Blain, ed. *Black Perspectives, African American Intellectual Historical Society*, October 26, 2017, https://www.aaihs.org/the-tears-struggles-and-hopes-of-black-women. Accessed December 1, 17.

7. Emilie M. Townes, *Womanist Ethics and the Cultural Production of Evil* (New York, NY: Palgrave MacMillan, 2006), 5.

8. Emilie M. Townes, *Womanist Ethics and the Cultural Production of Evil*, 9.

9. Emilie M. Townes, *Womanist Ethics and the Cultural Production of Evil*, 159.

10. Brenda Sendejo, "The Cultural Production of Spiritual Activisms: Gender, Social Justice, and the Remaking of Religion in the Borderlands," *Chicana/Latina Studies* 12, no. 1 (2013).

11. Brenda Sendejo, "The Cultural Production of Spiritual Activism," 2.

12. Elizabeth Alexander, "Toward the Black Interior," *The Black Interior* (Saint Paul, MN: Graywolf Press).

13. Elizabeth Alexander, "Toward the Black Interior,"

14. Elizabeth Alexander, "Toward the Black Interior," 4–5.

15. Elizabeth Alexander, "Toward the Black Interior," 5.

16. Elizabeth Alexander, "Toward the Black Interior," 5.

17. Torkwase Dyson, "Black Interiority: Notes on Architecture, Infrastructure, Environmental Justice, and Abstract," *Pelican Bomb*, January 9, 2017, http://pelicanbomb.com/art-review/2017/Black-interiority-notes-on-architecture-infrastructure-environmental-justice-and-abstract-drawing.

18. Darlene Clark Hine, "Rape and the Inner Lives of Black Women in the Middle West," *Signs*, 14, no. 4 (Summer, 1989): 912–20.

19. Darlene Clark Hine, "Rape and the Inner lives of Black Women," 912.

20. Darlene Clark Hine, "Rape and the Inner Lives of Black Women," 912.

21. Sarah Lawrence-Lightfoot. http://www.saralawrencelightfoot.com. Accessed December 11, 2019.

22. Nancy Ammermam, "Lived Religion as an Emerging Field: An Assessment of its Contours and Frontiers," *Nordic Journal of Religion and Society* 29, no. 2 (2016): 10.

23. For examples, see Jacqueline J. Mattis, "Religion and Spirituality in the Meaning Making and Coping Experiences of African American Women: A Qualitative Analysis," *Psychology of Women Quarterly*, 26 (2002): 308–20. doi: 10.1111/1471-6402.t01-2-00070; Jacqueline J. Mattis and R. Jagers, "A Relational Framework for the Study of Religiosity and Spirituality in the Lives of African Americans," *Journal of Community Psychology: Special Issue on Spirituality Volume 2*, 29, no. 5 (2001): 519–39. doi: 10.1002/jcop.1034.

24. In the psychoanalytic theory of Self Psychology, these are conceptualized as "selfobject" needs and their satisfaction accounts for the development of the self. I have taken up its utility for Black life in previous work; suffice it to say that selfobject experiences are not universal and must be conceptualized within contexts of particularity, intersectionality, and culture. See Phillis Isabella Sheppard, *Self, Culture, and Others in Womanist Practical Theology* (Palgrave Macmillan, 2011).

25. Phillis Isabella Sheppard, *Self, Culture, and Others in Womanist Practical Theology*, 115.

26. Phillis Isabella Sheppard, *Self, Culture, and Others in Womanist Practical Theology*.

27. Mary Proctor, 2015, Mary Proctor's Folk Art.

28. Zenju Earthlyn Manuel. (2018). "Longing for Home" *Tricycle Magazine*. https://tricycle.org/magazine/the-hunger-for-home/

29. Lisa Nakamura, 2002. *Cybertypes Race, Ethnicity, and Identity in the Internet* (New York: Routledge).

30. Mary Patillo-McCoy, "Church Culture as a Strategy of Action in the Black Community," *American Sociological Review*, 63 (1988).

31. Daphne C. Wiggins, *Righteous Content: Black Women's Perspective of Church and Faith* (New York, NY: New York University Press, 2005), 53–54.

32. Zenju Earthlyn Manuel. http://zenju.org.

Chapter 1

Audre Lorde

"FROM THE GUT OF BLACKNESS"—A BLACK LESBIAN SPIRITUALITY INCANTATION

Now,
You are ancestor sister, survivor.
I call your name and offer three deep bows.
Blue and orange flames flicker, crackle,
and burn sage
holy smoke rising
Inhale, three deep breaths
clear my heart,
purify my intentions,
make sacred this space.
I invite your presence; I pray my vows:
may my speaking be true,
may my heart be just,
may my aim be clear.[1]

INTRODUCTION

I open my meditations with a ritual to remember the ancestors.

First, I light a large bundle of sage held in an alabaster shell to purify the space and then pour a libation to honor, and to summon, the wisdom of my ancestors. I call out Audre Lorde's name as a part of the litany of these saints. For many Black lesbians of my generation, those coming of age in the late 1970s and 1980s, Audre Lorde felt like an elder and ancestor. I did not know her personally—and yet, I know what I had ears to hear in her speeches, poetry, documentaries on her life, and the legacy of her life. Though I only heard her speak in person once, I discerned early in my engagement with her work that she was to be a fierce, determined, vulnerable, flawed, and dedicated spiritual guide. It was in her face, eyes, words as well as in the joys she expressed in laughter and the expressive flow of her arms; it dwelled in the anger released in her poetry and the tightening of her lips when listening to others speak. It was in the pain she lived with, and the fear she neither fully succumbed to nor dismissed. Lorde felt familiar, and like the Black women in my own family, she was a hard truthteller, a Black woman calling a spade a spade, and, like my mother, she died too young from a cancer ravaging her body. I call their names in close proximity, and I claim them both ancestors.

Audre Lorde's work has been the focus of much research on Black feminism, embodiment, sexuality, difference, and the erotic. More recently, scholars have reread her work as contributing to Caribbean literature and postcolonial studies. The Caribbean aspect of her writing was not immediate but very early was making its distinctive character known in her poetry, and, from that vantage point, the postcolonial critique it raised cannot be ignored. Indeed, her writing is now represented in most-edited volumes attending to the Caribbean and postcolonial. I would argue that Lorde is important for her religious-spiritual trajectory and the way in which, over the course of adulthood, she recentered an African-Caribbean spirituality, Black lesbian feminism, and a narrative of reconciling with Black culture and maternal religious symbolism. Lorde's spiritual trajectory was one that reconfigured the meaning and context of Blackness in her psyche, interpersonal relationships, and public life.

Context is everything, we are told, and her context explains the social location of her writing. She was born in 1934 in the middle of the "great depression" in New York City to an immigrant couple, Linda Belmar Lorde and Frederick Byron Lorde, who had left the Caribbean for the possibility for upward mobility. Lorde was so near-sighted at birth that she was legally blind.[2] She was the third born of their three daughters. Her older sisters Phyllis and Helen, according to Lorde, reflected the values and expectations their immigrant parents demanded of their children—compliant, restrained, and respectful. Lorde saw herself as quite different and saw the world differently than the one handed down to her. Her mother expressed surprise that Lorde was a girl because Lorde was so dark, and her mother, born in the colonial context of the Caribbean, placed a high value on light skin. Consequently, she felt herself to be an outsider within her own family. As an adult, she learned that she also had two half-sisters, twins, her father had never mentioned. These sisters remained, abandoned once their father married Lorde's mother, in the Caribbean with their mother. Little is known about them except that they were poor, poorer than the Lorde family in the United States, and suffered greatly. Lorde reported that the one twin willing to meet with her in person embraced her as family and she experienced a familial belonging that was very meaningful and a reparative experience for her.[3]

One is immediately impressed with the sense that Lorde inhabited a liminal space for much of her life—often feeling herself to be an outsider, missing a sense of racial and cultural racial and cultural continuity. More often than not, she felt alienated from her self and from her Black body. She seldom had the feeling of belonging and often described herself as on the way to becoming her full self. Integrating these feelings in useful ways and seeking to recover from their negative psychic and relational imprint was a life quest. These themes are central to her essays, speeches, and poems as points of departure or as aspects of Black lesbian feminist life to be survived and, later in life, to be celebrated in their amelioration.

She took these feelings and associated dynamics with her into almost every milieu. The earliest were with her family, in the surrounding community as Black, first-generation Caribbean immigrant. Though Lorde was born in New York City, her upbringing was thoroughly Black Caribbean. New York outside the front door was foreign and suspect in her parent's eyes and, given Lorde's sense of cultural dislocation, in her eyes as well. In neither of these places did Lorde experience sustained positive reflections of herself or of Black people. Moreover, when coupled with her Black lesbian identity, she was not exposed to the kind of mirroring and appreciation that would facilitate an inner sense of acceptance, cultural rootedness, or a robust healthy self-identity. Lorde's identification as a lesbian was after her eight-year marriage to Ed Rollins, also gay, and two children. It was post-divorce that she named herself lesbian warrior poet mother,[4] and as a result there was always a place or group that could not affirm or acknowledge all parts of her identity. As with other contemporary Black lesbians, such Cheryl Clarke and Pat Parker, Audre Lorde refused to dissect her identities. She was determined to secure a sustained place, a community of women where the combined aspects of who she understood herself to be would be embraced. The absence of affirmation raised existential concerns for her at the deepest level of her being and led her into a search to ferret out the connections between her identity and the sense of a missing spiritual bearing.

This complex search led her to embrace a psycho-cultural spirituality that served as an emotional container for the vicissitudes of her inner life and as a guide in her life and into her death. Over time Lorde adopted the view that Black women have, as part of their cultural inheritance, the wisdom of the ancestors from Africa, before colonization, of the diaspora, and the ear of the Black goddesses. Raised as Roman Catholic, in her adult spirituality Lorde preserved an appreciation for ritual and contemplative practices. Her spiritual life was practiced with a vision and aim of individual and social transformation.

In this "stitched together" spirituality, all the parts of Lorde's identity—from her Afro-Caribbean Catholicism passed down by her mother in stories, private ritual, and prayers; her embrace of the erotic, power, and creativity; her Black lesbian body; and her praise to African goddesses—were combined. Lorde needed her spirituality. She struggled mightily against the psychic impingement of racism, sexism, and homophobia but also cultural dislocation. Spirituality was a counterforce to psychic and social oppression, and as it permeated her poetry and prose, it also fueled her activism. The spirituality that ultimately informed her worldview must be understood in light of her inner life in relation to her experience of her Black lesbian feminist mother and an African diasporic, first-generation, West Caribbean immigrant. In order to grasp her spirituality, we must, as she did, welcome all the parts of her identity as integral to her life.

The spiritual grounding that became the bedrock of her life was still emerging as she faced death at 58. Lorde declared that she emerged from the gut of Blackness and in Blackness she discovered the meaning of her life. Living on the island of St. Croix, Grenada, with her partner Gloria Joseph at her side, and death encroaching upon psyche and body, Lorde came full circle in some ways: while young she changed her name from Audrey to Audre for aesthetic reasons but also because she recognized the power of names and naming to shape one's life. Staring bodily death in the face, among the Afro-Caribbean people, in the place her mother called "home," Lorde entered into a naming ceremony where she took the name Gamba Adisa, "she who makes her meaning clear."[5]

Lorde wrote that she began writing because she "had a need inside . . . to create something that was not there."[6] This "there" of which Lorde spoke is a "there" both inside and outside her. And something she ultimately discerns is a spirituality and religious worldview that can hold all her desires, longings, and Black lesbian feminist mother warrior self. I trace the emergence of Lorde's spiritual life and pursuit of the sacred in this chapter. Drawing on published interviews, the documentaries *At the Edge of Each Other's Battles* and *A Litany for Survival*, selections of her poetry, and her biomythology *Zami: A New Spelling of My Name*, we follow the intertwinement of her experience and theories of Black embodiment, lesbian identity, and the forces of her psyche with the Black spirituality she ultimately claims. This dive into Lorde's experience—from the gut of Blackness—is where, for Lorde, silence unravels, love is expansive, the effects of the master's tools are (being) dismantled, and the interior and the public intertwine to form community "at the edge of each other's battles."[7] Lorde's theorizing is a point of reference for many who identify as Black, feminist, womanist, and queer scholars.

This chapter follows the movements of Audre Lorde's path to a Black feminist lesbian spirituality. I contextualize Lorde in the broader discourse on Black liberation and Black embodiment by positioning her in dialogue with two other intellectual forces addressing similar concerns. I take up Franz Fanon who was a Black Martiniquais psychoanalyst whose work *Black Skin, White Masks* and *The Wretched of the Earth* was taken up by the (Black male) architects of the Black power movement. Fanon was adopted because of his analysis and critique of colonialism noting its effect on Black psychologies and Black relationships. Both he and Lorde turn their focus on the nexus between interiority and racism and social oppression. Next, I turn to her good friend and "sister love," Black lesbian feminist poet Pat Parker. Like Lorde, Parker identified, after two marriages, as Black lesbian feminist radical activist. Both Parker and Lorde were two of the earliest Black lesbians on the feminist literary scene. Lorde seemingly had no connection to Fanon, and yet their concerns are largely parallel in their attention to the interior. Unlike Lorde, Fanon does not consider spirituality or sexuality as sources for Black liberation. In fact, with recent rare exception, they have not been placed in dialogue. Pat Parker, too, did not concern herself too much with religion but she respected its place in the Lorde's life and, like Lorde, was committed to Black liberation that included Black lesbians' liberation. She was an activist poet and her poetry was a Black southern west coast strident voice—quite unlike Lorde's but resonant and even intertextual because of their relationship. More importantly, we see in their relationship how much Lorde changed over time. She was able to love and care for, and be loved by, another Black lesbian feminist poet as a friend. It is apparent how much Lorde longed to be lovingly connected to Black women in meaningful ways. Parker was one such friend.

TO BE BLACK

In her poem "To the Poet Who Happens to Be Black and the Black Poet Who Happens to Be a Woman," she reveals her earliest emotional context of being born Black and female. She recounted that her mother looked at her infant dark body and assumed Lorde was a boy.[8] We do not know the age that Lorde was told the story of her mother's reaction to her, but we can imagine that her mother's affective response was communicated to Audre very early in life. It reveals *something* about her mother's feelings about dark men (and in fact, she married a man darker than herself) and dark women. The words suggest that Lorde should have been male or should have been lighter. It is no surprise that Lorde wrestled with the meaning of being Black. Her mother, Linda Belmar Lorde, placed a heavy burden on her as she problematizes Lorde's gender and color. Lorde did not fit her mother's fantasy about the child she was carrying. At birth Lorde came face to face with the cultural fantasy that to be Black is to not "fit" or belong. In this case, to be Black and female was to be born unmoored to the roots that should hold you in place in a racially hostile world.[9] Audre Lorde's sense of self—comprised of a multiplicity of identities—was profoundly shaped by the responses to her body beginning with her birth.

Lorde wondered if Blackness presumed badness. Lorde's ambivalence is not solely an issue of her inner life because color and gender mattered in 1934 as they matter today. In the year 2018, a health crisis has emerged in Ghana because Ghanaian pregnant women are using bleaching pills to protect their children from the racist attacks they are surely to experience post birth.[10] These are Black mothers doing damage to their children in hopes of sparing them social violence.[11] As an adult and poet, she insinuates a maternal instinct in her mother's concern about her daughter's future. So, Lorde's concern about the negative connotations attributed to dark skin and Blackness must be heard through several vectors. It is psychological because it accentuates the interior deliberations about the Black self and demands an interrogation of psyche and its processes. It requires rigorous introspection by asking what does Black mean, inside me, for my life, and my relationships? It forces us to consider the racial/color experiences of Black bodies as sites of racist projections and the Black body as a site for dismantling the personal and cultural currency of such projections. It is sociocultural and demands that we ask how notions of Blackness are embedded in the interstices of social relations and cultural practices.

In a culture where social constructs such as gender and sexuality shape, and in some places determine, one's life trajectory, it is not surprising that Lorde's imagination concerning gender and social roles were central in her work. Lorde forces us to examine how she came to understand the links between being born Black, female, immigrant, and poor in a Caribbean color-focused and class-conscious family. Lorde realizes that race, color, gender, and sexuality converge not only in her life but in the deepest part of her psyche and shape her spirituality. The intrusion of racism and colorism shaped her relationship with her family and psyche.

We too are compelled to try to reckon with how Audre Lorde came to understand herself as Black, female, and bad. But we must also attempt to understand her keen observation that how she felt was not solely an issue of her interior life: "somewhere I knew it was a lie that nobody else noticed color," or gender. Lorde recalled an incident where she was riding on a subway with her mother at age three. She sat on the seat next to an old white woman. Lorde recalls with vivid images the woman pulling her fur coat away from potential with the young Audre. Lorde is, at first, convinced the woman has seen something despicable but slowly realizes the woman hates being in contact with Blackness,[12] and that this woman is not an anomaly. In fact, from the moment she was born, the battle to be embodied, Black and female was challenged. Her narrative of struggle, both internal and external, is one reported by many, if not most Black and brown women. And this internal and external exchange is part and parcel of Lorde's search for a meaningful spirituality.

LISTENING TO BLACK EMBODIMENT

The Black body is ever-present in Lorde's thinking. She pondered its meaning on her every stage. She was tough in her critiques of those who claimed to pursue liberation while seemingly comfortable with the absence of Black, women, and queer voices. Such critiques also revealed Lorde's personal vulnerabilities. Her accounts of feeling overlooked or silenced also reveal that her reactions were often intense.[13] It is not a stretch to argue that Lorde, like many artists and scholars, wrote from positions of pain, questioning, or anger. This positioning did not invalidate Lorde's critiques but rather put a face to them. She did not write from an abstract theoretical position though she theorized. But Lorde insisted that she remain firmly planted in the real world of Black experience, and she admonished soon to be Oberlin graduates to "learn to use what you feel to move you toward action."[14] And that experience always implicated her Black body. In her essays, she discloses the interlocking and relationship between her inner life and the systemic nature of sexism, racism, heterosexism, and colorism. Yes, all of this sometimes left her feeling demoralized and lonely for a more cohesive community.

The specter of difference loomed large for Lorde; ignored, differences could gurgle beneath her attempts at connection, love, protest only to rise and flood through an outpouring of rage, pain, and distrust. Lorde realized that socially and internally, skin color, gender, sexuality, and class are ever operative, and survival depends on facing them. Lorde's theorizing, whether in poetry, interviews, speeches, or prose, conveys the interior and social struggle to survive the onslaught to psyche and body by reclaiming her Black self.

In her speech delivered at Harvard University in 1982 for their Malcolm X Celebration, Lord reflected on the importance Malcolm X had on her life. It was an influence that took some time to surface. Lorde at first rejected Malcom X and the Nation of Islam. Her affection was a slow brew because of the sexism in the movement and what she saw as a non-activist's philosophy. Even more, she initially internalized and aligned with the public media's negative depiction of him.

> Malcom X is a distinct shape in a very pivotal period of my life.
>
> I stand here now-Black, Lesbian, Feminist—an inheritor of Malcolm and his tradition, doing my work and the ghost of his voice through my mouth asks each one of you here tonight:
>
> Are you doing yours?[15]

What is clear, though not entirely in focus, are two dimensions to Lorde's experience of Malcolm. The first is that Malcolm X is a part of her in some profound way—we hear *him*, she claims, through her mouth, and that the ideas she puts forth on this occasion are not new but him speaking through her. This is important, first because she models change by acknowledging that, initially she could not, hear Malcolm X as a voice of Black liberation. She dismissed him and the Nation of Islam. Long after his death, she claims to have inherited Malcolm's tradition. Second, it is noteworthy because, though she seemed unaware of it, her claim insinuates an evolving interior vis-à-vis her identification with the broader Black power movements. It was the filling in, as it were, of her Black identity. Lorde inserted herself into Malcolm's political lineage—and therefore, asserted her own Black lineage. We can observe a profound psycho-political move here because Lorde not only inserts herself into his lineage, she inserts a gender and sexuality liberation agenda into Malcolm X's tradition.[16]

She extended this process of insertion to the cosmological dimension when she appropriates linguistic imagery of ghost. Lorde's use of ghost is mostly reserved for references to her mother and Black girls and women who did not survive the traumas of their lives.

> A piece of the price we paid for learning survival was our childhood. We were never allowed to be children. . . . Ask the ghosts of the four little Black girls blown up in Birmingham.[17]

In this sense, Lorde reads Malcolm alongside the list of murdered Black girls. They are kindred to him and her. She also revealed the ghost of whiteness and racism that has been internalized by Black people where it lives and works its destruction on our psyche's and between Black people.

> He had . . . begun to discuss those scars of oppression which lead us to war against ourselves in each other rather than against Our enemies. . . . For we must move against not only those forces which dehumanize us from outside, but also against those oppressive values which we have been forced to take into ourselves.[18]

We witness Lorde's interior work that allows her to connect to parts of Black experience she previously rejected. Here we witness the introspection necessary for the change she is making. Introspection always raises ghosts that we have attempted to ward off. Malcolm is a ghost, a stand-in of her father and his lineage:

> I'd read Malcolm's autobiography, and I liked his style, and I thought he looked a lot like my father's people, but I was one of the ones who didn't really hear Malcolm's voice until it was amplified by death.[19]

This picture of her father differs from the one she depicts in her poem, "Father Son and Holy Ghost." The ghost of her father rests in the memory of his judging eyes, his silences, and his power to pull her in death. Lorde's father died when she was 19 and her memories suggest that the loss and the longing for a different father,[20] possibly one like Malcolm X, whose legacy and lineage would sustain and inspire her, was still a powerful force for her at age 29. Though she never saw her father's grave site, he remains as a part of her interior life and she on hearing Malcolm X's voice, her father's ghost is summoned in her memory.[21] So powerful was his presence, Lorde avoided writing about her father until after he had died because she feared the power of his presence in her psyche.[22]

These ghosts are imagoes—the internal vestiges of relational dynamics with important early figures in one's life and the affects integral to them. Part of the complexity of Lorde's writing is that these ghosts are of the past, and of the ancient Spirit forces who are guiding her home. The Spirits are the female goddesses to whom she prays, offers praise and verbal libation in her poems. In her poem "Call" she brings Mother ghost—Aido Hwedo—and spiritual force together and introduces the themes of recovery, and the decolonizing of self and of Black religious culture. She recovered the names and cosmologies she needed. Poetry is a spiritual practice of praise, prayer, and libation. In *Postcolonializing God: An African Practical Theology*, Emmanuel Yartekwei Amugi Lartey writes that the "art and practice of libation embodies cultural, religious, and ethical beliefs"[23] held by the practitioners. It is not an individual practice but invokes the community's "self," and thus is for the edification of the community. The Holy Ghost Mother turns her attention to the concerns of Black women in the here and now. In this poem, Lorde reckons with the internalized past and the struggles for liberation. Her naming and calling upon the Holy Ghost Mother is initiation and renaming; part of a ritual process of becoming a Black woman because it is not only Holy Ghost mother who has been called out of Her name—all Black women have. To get here, Lorde has embarked on a path of cultural recovery, and beginning in the 1970s, she began visiting various countries in Africa and the Caribbean. It was through this process that she began to acquire a sense of herself as part of a Black diaspora community that included relationships and political connections she was cultivating with Afro-German women and South African women. Lorde recognized that the struggle for Black liberation linked Black people everywhere and she began to express a Pan-African spirituality, a bricolage[24] of African goddesses and religious practices.[25] She recovered names and peoples and called forth the memories and spiritual work of recognizable Black women warriors: Fannie Lou Hammer, Assata Shakur, Winnie Mandela, and Yaa Asantewa in a litany of saints where directs her supplications to Mother Goddess and the response is "Aido Hwedo is coming."[26]

Ghost, Holy Ghosts, and Black lesbian experience are intertwined in Lorde's understanding of the cosmological. For Lorde, a full life involves having an awareness of the indwelling of Holy Ghost, communion with the ancestors, new life in the revivification of the Black body, and life continuous. A life where even as she faced death, she could recognize and proclaim the unending nature of being by declaring that her earthly existence is ending but there remains an unknown future.[27] Lorde seems to know she will become, in this new shape, an ancestor, ghost, and muse. Lorde positions the divine within her interior and the experiences of her Black body. Interiority and embodiment must be stitched together.

READING BLACK BODIES AND BLACK PSYCHES: SITES OF BLACK EPISTEMOLOGIES

Audre Lorde's Black lesbian body living with cancer, and living with a scar left by a mastectomy, grounds her work epistemologically. She situates her analyses of her living experiences, including her feelings and thoughts about her body, in the social-cultural contexts where bodies are socialized and inscribed with meaning. Such inscriptions shape responses. Theorizing Black bodies is not only phenomenological but psychological too. Among many Black scholars, particularly those of the Black power movement of 1960s, the relationship between interiority and the body (*body and bodies*) was largely influenced by the psychoanalytic perspectives, it is Franz Fanon. There is significant overlap between Lorde and Fanon's attention on Black embodiment. Lorde likely would have encountered his work, directly or indirectly, because of his significance for Black power figures. More importantly, Lorde and Fanon were both Afro-Caribbean and wrote from their diasporic location as a resistance to the continuing legacy of colonialization and racism.

Lorde and Fanon's Caribbean immigrant roots also connect them by proximity; the distance between the Islands Carriacou and Martinique is 152 miles. As with the whole of the Caribbean, these islands were colonized by the French and British. Lorde's parents immigrated to the United States from Grenada, and Fanon migrated to France. Lorde's mother was from

Carriacou—an island of Grenada that had nearly been disappeared through the cartography of colonization. Carriacou was first colonized by France (1743) and 20 years later turned over to Britain as spoils of the war of 1763. In the colonizing process.[28] Carriacou disappeared from many maps. Lorde's mother spoke frequently and longingly of Carriacou and was, in Lorde's memory, the carrier of the culture and spirituality of the Caribbean. However, because it was no longer on a map, Lorde eventually wondered if her mother's memories and spiritual teachings were her fantasies.

As a part of her cultural and spiritual search, Lorde wanted to learn more about this mother island, and she may have needed the proof that she came from a deeply spiritual and special place. The evidence, of course, was already there in some of her mother's stories of home, and religious practices, but in her early development, Lorde could not internalize these as a child or adolescent because of the strain in their relationship. However, by 1977 she could recount the story of her mother's mortar and proudly declare that she had learned from her mother that every West Indian woman has one from the island. Lorde's mother prized mortar was special because it was from home—Carriacou, West Indies, the cultural world that could not be replicated in the foreignness of New York.[29]

Lorde finally found this home island of Carriacou on a map, when she was 26 years old, in an old Encyclopedia Britannica.[30] Only then was she sure the island truly existed. The colonial strategy of cartography, making places such as Carriacou disappear, meant that the gifts of culture and spirituality handed down through Lode's mother could only be internalized with ambivalence and question. This is a colonial strategy and an effect of colonization. Failing to destroy the culture, the strategy is to make memories and inheritance, is questionable. In so doing, the link that creates the continuity of the self with the past and cultural community is compromised or, in some cases, destroyed. In Lorde's case, she was involved in a long journey to restore this link. Her work then is an attempt to mediate, if not heal, a transgenerational trauma. It is transgenerational because Lorde's mother missed home, conjured and remembered home, but was never able to return home. She, therefore, passed onto Audre, the significance of Carriacou but also the longing to return.

We do not hear such longing in Franz Fanon's life. In fact, we hear just the opposite. Fanon was born in 1925 on the Caribbean island of Martinique under French rule. Martiniquais are French citizens who were required, under French colonial rule, to speak French. He was educated in a prestigious school where Aime Cesaire, the post-colonialist poet, playwright, and politician who advocated for Black diasporic solidarity, was his teacher. Fanon left Martinique to fight with the French resistance to Nazism where he learned firsthand the depth of French racism. It became clear that though many of the Black Martiniquens spoke French, identified with French culture, and were French citizens, they were not viewed as such by France. The racism that permeated colonialism was laid bare when the French military took over Martinique, abused the people, and denied them French in due process.[31] Fanon escaped by immigrating to France to pursue his medical education. In France, he did not escape the racism but was brutally confronted with the meaning of his Black skin in France. In France he was forced into a psychological confrontation with his Blackness and the gaze of white Parisians. He was woefully unprepared to be seen himself as reflected in the white gaze of colleagues and patients. In *Black Skin, White Masks* he unveiled the psyches of the colonized and colonizers and the ways in which they are tethered.[32] Like Lorde, he too had parents who raised him to avoid *being* Black in speech, behavior, associations, and cultural identifications. This psychic and social formation of racial dis-identification informed Lorde and Fanon's theories of the body and Black liberation but with different outcomes.

Lorde's immigrant status, her gender and sexual identity, and her role as a mother and warrior, however, often separated her from the Black Power Movement that appropriated Fanon. They both came from still colonized contexts that overvalued whiteness and white skin. In 1990, Lorde argued Grenada was still colonized by the United States and that this status and associated policies undermined Black people's freedom and sense of self.[33]

Both Fanon and Lorde understood that in order to disassemble the structures of oppression, Black people would need to relinquish their ties and identifications with those who oppress. Both make a case for interrogating the interior. This means not only do we interrogate the bodies of knowledge we have learned; we must interrogate their effects in Black peoples' lives. Lorde argued that Black women must define themselves on their own terms. In a Black hating world, a spirituality bubbling up from the depth of Black loving Blackness is imperative. Both Fanon and Lorde recognized that to love Black bodies requires an active conscious resistance to, and conversion from, the cultural love of white bodies. For Lorde, this was not just political liberation; Black love required a spiritual liberation wherein one recovered ties to African spiritual forces and their power to hold her in community. With resistance comes a conversion process, and this conversion is nothing short of a disruption. It requires a turning away from the lessons of self-hatred toward a love of one's Blackness. In this sense *being Black* is to begin a process of becoming Black. We hear this throughout Fanon's *Black Skin, White Masks* and in Lorde's collection *The Black Unicorn* and in her essays and speeches. Both recognized that becoming Black necessitated the convergence of Black embodiment, sexuality, and gender. Fanon, however, retained the colonialized structure of sexuality and gender, thus privileging maleness, even as he sought to undo the effect of colonialization on Black psyches. Lorde and Fanon are akin in their commitment to interrogate the content of Black interiority as a necessary feature of Black liberation. The connective tissue between them is that both direct their attention to the colonized Black psyche, the psychic alienation colonization levies on Black people, and how this alienates Black people from Black bodies and Black ways of being. Lorde, like Fanon, found the psychological point of view essential to recovery from colonial trauma. Lorde worked to heal from her own trauma through the practice of writing about her psychotherapy.

Lorde recognized the deep incision that racism, colorism, sexism, and homophobia make on the psyche. She spent many, if not most, years of her adult life in therapy. Her close associates were in therapy. Her partner of 17 years, Frances Clayton, a white woman and a psychotherapist, was treated by the same therapist. This therapist also treated them in couple therapy, and she treated Lorde's former lover and many of her friends. There's was a therapeutic community of sorts. By all accounts, Lorde and Frances had a deep but, frequently, difficult and volatile relationship, in part because Lorde had numerous extra-partner sexual relationships with other women while they were still a couple and because Lorde was still discovering the meaning of Blackness for her life.[34] Their foray into the world of psychoanalysis in 1970s New York was not unusual as it was part of the cultural air for the educated, mostly white, privileged circles. Lorde's first therapist was white, and Lorde felt this limited the depth of her introspection. When she began working with a Black therapist, a woman, she was brought face to face with her own fears and hopes about relating deeply to Black women. This practice of turning to the interior for reflection on the past and present made its way into her writing and spirituality.

Lorde differed from Fanon in her antidote to oppression when she began to foreground the necessity of connecting a Black spiritual lens to her theorizing and poetry to the political activism. Lorde's poetry, in particular, revealed the centrality of spirituality in the struggle toward freedom. The spiritual was not solely in terms of spiritual practice, though she saw this as essential. Lorde advocated for the retrieval of an African spiritual heritage and cosmological worldview that predated colonization and that continued into the diasporic future. Her collection *The Black Unicorn* embodies this and her poems are filled with places, symbols, goddesses she encountered during her visits to West African countries. At the end of the collection, she includes a glossary. She recovers places and deities: Abomey, Akai, Amazons, Dahomey, Dan, Elegba, Eshu, Orisha, Mawulisa, Orisha, and Yemanja. And she includes a very brief bibliography on Yoruba, and on religions of Africa. Also noteworthy is that *The Black Unicorn* was dedicated to her parents, signaling an internal shift in relation to them. Lorde was also signaling that she intended more than the cultural and religious appropriation of religion for poetic purposes. She was seeking a total transformation by immersing herself in the worldview and spirituality. This turn to Africa was a turn toward her parents' generation. The work of religion in her life did not undo the complex relationship with her parents, but it allowed her to claim her family and ancestral roots in a way that affirms her personhood and their contribution to it.[35]

The shift in her interior demonstrates how the relationship between culture and self is tethered. Ambivalence in one area affects one's relationship to the other. Religious practice can provide a means to expand one's life narrative. Her view is quite different from Fanon's who neither claims the colonized Catholicism he inherited nor African spiritualities seemingly lost to his Martiniquen family.[36] As far as Fanon is concerned, religion is utilitarian in the service of the revolution but not as a force in the life of the practitioner. As such, Algerian Muslim women could use their modest, non-Western, clothing to hide weapons actors in the resistance to French rule but its use beyond that was negligible.[37]

Lorde and Fanon both grasped stakes for Black post-colonized and diasporic people, and this made them partially aligned. They both knew, firsthand, that the racism often made its way into the Black psyche in a myriad of destructive ways; they grasped the depth of rage and anger that are the results of having been of a colonized and silenced people. Both wrestle with the place of anger in the work of liberation. Fanon argues that a violent revolution is inevitable.[38] And while he is mistakenly read as advocating violence, he did not fear organized political violence. But unlike Lorde, he did not reflect on his desire to do violence; his was a reflection on its utilitarian function, and it is inescapable facet of the pursuit of Black liberation. Fanon argues that the dynamics, social and political, of oppression make their way into the intrapsychic and it is only through wrenching psychic expulsion coupled with a violent overthrowing of colonial structures will liberation be achieved.

Lorde argues against a path of violence but acknowledges that she is not a stranger to violence. As a Black mother, like Black mothers today, she fears the violence to which Black children will be subjected—driving while Black, jogging while Black, sleeping while Black. The fatal incision of police violence is what she fears,[39] but Lorde's relationship to violence is more complex than the force of the outer world directed against her. Violence misshapes the inner life. She also recognizes that violence insidiously circulated her world through her writing and in intimate relationships.[40] Her own tendency toward violent outbursts, in one form or another, rendered her children and those she loved vulnerable to her abuse of her power. She noted this problem in her relationship with her children when she caught herself displacing her anger from a "racist bust driver" into "screaming at my daughter's childish banter making her (daughter) its innocent victim."[41] And in her poem "Power," Lorde describes the murder of a 10-year-old Black boy by a white policeman, who watched and urged him to die.[42] As if a premonition of the police violence claiming Black bodies today, at his trial, the officer argued that it was the boy's color that determined his reaction. The jury comprised of 11 white men and one Black woman who said that the 11 men convinced her to join them in the acquittal. With Lorde, we can only imagine the harassment and veiled threat to which she was exposed.[43] Lorde's rage at the officer, the jury, and the Black woman permeates the remainder of the poem but the final stanza is a cautionary message that rage can destroy the good we seek.[44] In so doing, she forces us to see the interior as creative and destructive space.

Lorde needed her writing to hold her anger. It was not always an adequate ampoule. In her powerful biography of Lorde, Alexis De Veaux recounts numerous instances where Lorde's anger erupted into violence and exposed the split between Lorde's theorizing and her actions in intimate relations. On one occasion she hit her husband because he ate her favorite piece of turkey.[45] On another occasion, Lorde reported that after the court case where her divorce with Rollins was finalized, she picked up a "girl" at a bar and almost battered her.[46] Picking up the white woman at the bar combined with the temptation to do violence to her was an indication of Lorde's struggle to contain her rage and to resist projecting onto this white woman rather than Lorde's white husband. Even so, Lorde sexualized her desire to commit violence. She did not gratify her wish to strike the woman but her fantasy about inflicting violence remained intact. The encounter was indicative, of course, of Lorde's projection of her anger toward her white husband unto this white woman, but it was also indicative of Lorde's need to feel powerful and to feel her power in relation to another person. The relief Lorde hoped the woman could provide could only be achieved through the woman's objectification and only partially; the encounter was barely sexual, not sensual, and certainly not spiritual. It was a substitute for a genuine source and exercise of power.

Her rage was not only turned outward but was somatized and, for instance, Lorde would endure excruciating migraines after silently enduring racism from white feminists.[47] The migraine split her anger from the source. Lorde's potential for violence was most often realized when she felt diminished. There are three documentaries[48] and numerous YouTube videos of Lorde in various speaking and social contexts. These are poignant and invite a visual ethnography of the relationship between self and context. In each, Lorde seems to relish being respected, listened to, and even adored by her audiences. It may be that being viewed in a powerful and positive light helped to modulate the intensity of feelings of anger and invisibility she could experience. In her poems, she warns readers of the reality of violence and calls us to look inside ourselves too. She resisted the violence circulating within, though does not ever eradicate it. She calls readers to the same resistance.

A PULSATING INTERIORITY: SPIRITUALITY AND THE EROTIC

Recovering the erotic within was a way to resist the pull of violence within. Lorde understood the erotic as part of the deep reservoir of the female interior.[49] When we access it fully, it is an all-encompassing dimension to life.[50] As an electrifying element pulsating throughout our being, the erotic shapes us, makes demands of us, and calls us into integrated being. The erotic is a catalyst for ethnical living and integrity.[51] Violence is then a counter-response that does not lead us to integrity. However, the erotic is the resource against violence and the heart of her understanding of spirituality. The erotic is what makes the spiritual transverses between the individual and the communal. The erotic push is the life force that initiates our human beingness; as such it is the force that moves us toward life, survival, and thriving.

The work of the erotic, as a source of women's power and a constituent of the spiritual dimension, is constantly under attack by the tactics of sexism, heterosexism, and racism in order to undermine Black women's liberation work. Lorde argued that women have been taught to fear the erotic in themselves and to see it as a proof of their weakness. She wanted women to find and embrace the erotic because it is a distinctive female source of women's power. Black women's ability to feel, love, and touch and be touched, physically and emotionally, is due to the dynamism erotic. The erotic fuels Black women's spiritual life and social activism as well as their sexual and affectional desires. The body is implicated in this, obviously, but the erotic is not restricted to the body. Whether one is engaged in lovemaking or in protest, the erotic is the catalyst of impetus and commitment. Our perception of the erotic often originates in bodily and sensual experiences though not necessarily sexual. Poetry, music, and love arise out of the embodied knowledge of the erotic. So too spirituality and prayer. The erotic is a source of knowledge about life and the divine and Lorde saw it operative in all women.[52] Lorde's spirituality exists in and emerges from her Black lesbian erotic source, formed first in the particularity of her Black family life.

Where the erotic is contravened, ignored, or denied expression, violence and aggression gain traction. This traction then creates social and intimate space whereby the more powerful spew negative projections onto those marginalized. Racism is one such form of projection whereby a mythical norm based on whiteness is represented as the status quo and norm.[53] When the norm is internalized by those marginalized, it enforces bodily self-alienation.

When Lorde wrote of this *mythical norm*, she was writing of her experience as a Black, woman, lesbian, feminist living with cancer. Lorde brought her body and her bodily experiences into the center of writing and life. She revealed a woman compelled by her body to reveal, dis-veil, expose, and satisfy her body as part and parcel of her writing, love, resistance, and speaking. Her body was part of the work of dismantling oppressive systems and structures and the psychic space.

Relying as he does on a psychoanalytic lens in *Black Skin, White Masks*, Fanon offers an analysis of the Black male experience of embodiment that he can only see through and in the relationships between Blacks and whites. He posits a dual symbiotic, if you will, narcissism. Fanon thus establishes the primary source for his examination—the Black man in relation to the white man. By so grounding his essay, Fanon's is a psychoanalytic examination of the Black man's psychic alienation and it begins with an asymmetrical analysis: the Black man, in Fanon's view, only experiences psychic alienation. Fanon concludes that whiteness is the Black man's destiny.[54] Lorde, who begins much of her journey in relation to, or opposition from, white women, ends her life with a distinctively different vision—and it is not white. It is Black; it is African; it is spiritual.

Situated in the broader context of the Black power movement, Lorde refigures Blackness, gender, sexuality, and activism as the spiritual path into the interior and back into the world for the work of liberation. Lorde's interior positioning in relation to her Blackness and lesbian self leads her home to an Afro-Caribbean in contrast to Fanon. As Fanon psychoanalyzes, he cements his distance from his home, Martinique, and the Afro-Caribbean self. Lorde, returns, psychologically, spiritually, and culturally to the psycho-spiritual geography of her parents. She returns home. He leaves. Like Fanon, she learned early the overvaluation of whiteness, upward mobility, and language acquisition of the colonizers—for him, perfect French; for her, perfect English. The colonizers' languages, however, directed attention to how colonialism reads Black bodies and Black culture and forces Black people to read their Blackness through the lens of whiteness.

In linking Lorde and Fanon in this dialogue, we see Lorde's trajectory to her spiritual home is linked to Black embodiment and the psychological but is quite distinct from Fanon. Lorde sought to decolonize her psyche *and* her spirituality. She begins this as she faces her fears of Black embodiment and death and embraces the erotic as a source for being fully present. She accepts her need for Black feminist community and exposes herself to the love and challenge of sister loves. This was only possible as she discovered the needed Black spirituality.

FACING THE FEARS IN THE MIRROR

Fear is a teacher if we face it. Audre Lorde lived with or confronted fear for much of her life. Growing up with parents who had little patience with emotionality or "foolishness" associated with longings, disappointments, or the pain of racism and injustice, Lorde feared her mother's responses and her own ability to manage intense feelings. And she feared her own Blackness. She longed to be seen, desired, and recognized but feared being seen. But being seen is not under the control of Lorde or any of us. For all the layers of concealment designed to keep secret her deepest pain, her body exposed her vulnerability against her own will. Shortly after having had an abortion, Lorde was determined to get back to work, mostly because she needed the money. Hiding in the bathroom doubled over, a "wise woman" who worked with her came in and like an elder sage tried to convince her to go home. Lorde lied and said she was just having cramps. But Ms. Lewis was not fooled and admonishes her to go home to bed and to her mother's care. Lorde cannot, of course, confide in her mother about her trouble. Ms. Lewis reaches into her purse and gives Lorde money to take a taxi home.[55] Ms. Lewis saw in Lorde's reflection the need for a "mama" who would have been able to offer the care and rest needed in this moment; in the absence of such a maternal figure, Ms. Lewis offered what she could, wisdom and money for a taxi.

Ms. Lewis's as a spiritual voice directs our attention to a site for mirroring and fear when she tells Lorde "the way your eyes looking." The eyes are significant for Lorde. She is often afraid to look into someone's eyes and sometimes determined to see with eyes wide open. In the bar scene of the 1950s and 1960s, fraught with emotional desire and demand, Lorde searched for Black lesbian women who would mirror each other's existence. But such searching was permeated with fear. The emphasis on gender roles frightened her as did the reflection of her own Blackness.[56] These women knew each other but were afraid to fully acknowledge each other because they spent much of their energy hiding the inner life of being a Black lesbian. Looking deep into each other's eyes was a radical form of transparency and self-exposure.[57] And yet, Lorde could also experience excitement when the mirror of a Black woman's eyes matched her desire.[58] Such mirroring was complicated and revealed a sexual embodied spirituality.[59] There is not sacred verses profane, in Lorde's spiritual world. In this world, in these moments of confronting herself, Lorde can face herself past and present. She can face the Black ambivalent girl she used to be.[60]

Her memoirs *The Cancer Journal*,[61] beginning with the first diagnosis, and *Burst of Light*[62] focused on the last diagnosis, journal her refusal to hide her sick body, her embracement of her Black body, her fight against the invading cancer, and ongoing struggle to continue to hope. Lorde refused to sentimentalize cancer and in her public, one breasted amazon warrior way, called other women living with cancer to share their stories to resist the social silencing.[63]

It would be easy to focus on Lorde's courage as if it was void of fear, depression, and even despair. Lorde's vision was hard won. She could divulge that the fear of the finality of death could be debilitating.[64] Lorde's transparency around her feelings always revealed her desire for truth-telling, as much as she could, about herself. Maria Popova captures well the interior-social dynamic of fear: "In our interior experience as individuals, as in the public forum of our shared experience as a culture, our courage lives in the same room as our fear."[65] And, we find out who stands with us in solidarity. Deep solidarity with someone, according to Lorde, always includes access to deep interiority. For as much as Lorde spoke of her inner life, she did not allow many to access to this deep level of her experience. An exception was her friendship with the poet Pat Parker.

SISTER LOVE

The poet Pat Parker[66] was a Black lesbian radical and her partner, Mary Dunham, was a white lesbian with whom she raised Anastasia, their daughter. Parker died young, at the age of 45 years, from breast cancer. Like Lorde and because of Lorde's influence, she refused to wear a prosthesis after her mastectomy. Both poets made class, race, gender, sexuality, and Black embodiment themes in their poetry and essays. Pat Parker's early life began in Houston, Texas, and her family lived in near abject poverty. She grew up around roughness and brought that quality into her poetry. Along the way, she married twice. She married her first husband, Ed Bullins, at 18. He was a playwright and, as was she, a member of the Black Panther Party. He was BPP's Minister of Culture. They were married for three years. The relationship was turbulent and violent—so much so that Parker said, "she feared for her life."[67] She left him after he caused her to miscarry by pushing her down the stairs. Her second husband, Robert F. Parker, was also a writer. After it was clear that the marriage was not working, she divorced him and claimed her previously rejected Black lesbian identity.

Lorde was Parker's mentor and taught her how to survive as a Black lesbian radical poet. She sent her basic supplies, money, stamps, and advice. Together, they moved from typewriter to word processor, from pro bono to speaker fees. Life was not easy for either though Lorde was more established and had more resources. She shared generously, and they shared their hopes and aspirations for their own lives and the lives of Black women. Love was freely expressed between them *Sister Love: The Letters of Audre Lorde and Pat Parker 1974-1989* edited by Julie R. Enzer. Mecca Jamilah Sullivan, in her introduction to *Sister Love*, argues that the letters reveal a lovely intimacy lived in the midst of struggles as they both lived with cancer and knew that their lives would be cut short.[68]

These two Black lesbian women were vulnerable with each other in a way not often portrayed in the writing on either of them. Their advice to each other is part of their legacy to those still benefiting from their work. For those of us who push to put words to paper, Lorde's advice to Parker in 1985 to not succumb to the internal and external pressures to produce is relevant today. Lorde maintains an explicit awareness that the interior terrors are fueled, if not produced, by the social milieu.[69]

Intimacy is the pulse that runs through their relationship. Parker is vulnerable enough to express affection, deep love, and anger at the miles that separate them while Lorde is in pain,[70] and Lorde brings a wisdom that comes with knowing the inner working of fear of failure and fear of anger. Parker wants to be inside Lorde's pain; she wants to protect her from the isolation of pain and the assault on the psyche that bodily trauma, such as cancer, can inflict. Theirs is an erotic feature that has been formed, maybe transformed, in the service of genuine and honest sister love. Parker is able to express her love for Lorde and her frustration at how Lorde sometimes, with blunt force, presented herself as teacher, boss, and mentor. When Parker sent Lorde the poem "For Audre," she hoped Lorde would not be embarrassed because it was sent with love but explains that they are tied, inextricable by the similarities of being Black lesbians.[71]

Parker's poem is intertextual—she is in dialogue with Lorde and begins each section with a quotation from various poems and prose Lorde has published. She vividly describes how Lorde thrust herself in Parker's life. Parker, for all her complaints about this woman making demands on her also knew that that they are tied to each other in their Blackness, creativity, and queerness—they have been brought together for a purpose beyond themselves. Parker is faithful, on her terms, not willing to succumb fully to Lorde's demands. Instead, Parker promises love and sisterhood.[72]

Parker's promise is one that both she and Lorde try to live into even as they are with cancer while trying to change the world. Parker is, in small deliberate ways, a conduit to the spiritual path that is Lorde's. Pat's way with Lorde is love and empathy without capitulation to Lorde's demands.

When Lorde failed to respond to a letter, Parker wrote that she was anxious and hurt by the silence and needed Lorde to just send a message.[73] Pat's approach with Lorde is anxious concern, rebuke, love. This is a shared approach as Lorde more than a few times rebuked Pat for not writing, following through on advice or directives but included an expression of intimacy, care, and awareness of their deep connection.[74] At every point, they remind each other that love anchors their relationship.

In a letter in 1988, Lorde tells Pat their relationship held mostly in their letters was a part of how they each were working to transform the world.[75] Pat Parker embodied a Black lesbian ethic of social responsibility and care that was inseparable from her relational life. Parker was working class and she challenged Lorde to see the privileges, by comparison, that afforded

Lorde a modicum of protection from the dire straits of which Parker was all too familiar. Parker, though she was widely known on the west coast, her feminist lesbian poetry scene did not, and could not, sacrifice her poor and working-class roots. They informed her poetry, speeches, and life. Lorde saw this unpretentious Black lesbian as mentee, sister, and an example. An abiding link was their refusal to represent a splintered experience. Parker wrote a poem, "Movement in Black" where she described a revolution as a time when she could bring her whole—Black, lesbian, educated—self to all her communities.[76]

It is this dynamic of radical social activism realized in love and action that Pat embodied that made her a quiet spiritual figure for Lorde. The demands of the relationship, especially after both were living with cancer, made self-disclosure, confession, honesty as well as anger, grief, and mourning the conduits for self-transformation. And Lorde, for all her gifts and commitment to the struggle for liberation, needed transformation. It is often forgotten or not known that when Parker and Lorde first were developing their friendship, Lorde was not yet out and Parker encouraged and confronted this dissonance between the integrity Lorde valued and the semi-secrecy around her sexuality. Parker died in 1989 at the age of 45 and just 3 years before Lorde's death at 58. Their letters and relationship help remember that Lorde gradually grew into the radical feminist lesbian warrior over a lifetime and she brought her gifts and faults along for the journey.

Johnetta Cole, Lorde's friend and colleague, recalled Lorde's courage, her determination, her brilliance as a poet, essayist, and activist, and her solidarity as a friend. She also recalled that Lorde was flawed and that her flaws were lifelong even if not as intense when she was younger. Success did not eradicate the painful and debilitating ghosts of the past and Lorde could fall prey to them in ways that challenged her relationships. Cole rightly reminds us that Lorde was not protected from her own insecurities about colorism and class status or her fear she would not be accepted by Black women. Lorde suffered from her insecurities but she struggled with them as well.[77] It is this highly successful and well-known but also quite flawed Lorde that Pat Parker embraced and called sister love. What is also clear in these letters between Parker and Lorde is that Parker loved Lorde with fierceness, and this was reciprocated, and that Parker's love was vital to Lorde's development as a person and, I argue, of her spiritual life. Lorde did not overcome her flaws, but she grew to know herself as vulnerable to their pull because friends and communities of women, like Parker, loved her. And she matured. This is evident over the course of her oeuvre, especially as she moved closer toward death and to the realm of the waiting ancestors. Lorde's longing to fill in missing parts of her interiority and to have a sense of inner continuity, culturally and spiritually, were mitigated.

HOMEWARD BOUND

Shortly before her death, Lorde was asked about the relationship between spirituality and cancer, and which should be prioritized for an article. On reflection, Lorde recognized the futility of the question. She was being asked to first separate her body and the cancer from her spirituality and, second, to privilege one over the other. This was the kind of dualism that Lorde long resisted. Furthermore, it was a question not unlike earlier demands for her to show up Black or lesbian but not both. Such splitting was neither helpful nor quite possible at this point. Again, her drive toward a continuity of being pressed forward and she resisted the demand inherent in the question to misrepresent her understanding of herself for the benefit of someone else's agenda. She resisted a psycho-spiritual split.

The futility of splitting psyche, body, and spirituality is captured in Lorde's response to the deficit model of "why" someone gets a diagnosis of cancer. The deficit model argues that cancer is the result of an individual's lack of willpower, faith in the power of healing, or ego capacities. In other words, the problem is an interior one that has manifested in somatic symptoms. The social dimension is disregarded in favor of moralizing. In a medical model, healing is the eradication of the disease, and in a psychological model, it is the eradication of psychic distress. But as Lorde neared the end of her battle with cancer, connecting death with continuity was the final leg of life's journey, she was able to admit that, though something loomed ahead beyond death, she did not know what life beyond death meant.[78] Her spirituality and religious engagement afforded her the capacity to trust in an unknown future to live into the next stage of life and to value her work without the constant desire to direct the hereafter.

Throughout her life, Lorde was on a search for a home that could hold all the pieces of who she was. She found it most fully in the last year of her life in an African-Caribbean-based religion and spirituality: on the island of Grenada, in the loving relationship with her partner from Grenada, Gloria Joseph, her children Elizabeth and Jonathan, and Black women she met from around the world. She also found it in her own writing and speaking.

Transformation did not come quickly or easily. She stitched together a Black lesbian spirituality that reestablished her tie to her religious, spiritual, woman-centered cultural roots. She achieved what Catherine John refers to as a "spirit consciousness and collective consciousness" that allowed her to move from "individualism and spiritual numbness."[79] The recovery of these roots helped Lorde to stabilize her sense of her Black lesbian self. This was a reparative process, not completed but in process, of the individual and intergenerational psychic wounding she suffered. As Lorde claimed her version of African-Caribbean lesbian spirituality, she could also reimagine her tie to, and need of, her mother. In her poem "From the House of Yemenja," she could pray that she needed Mother Blackness to survive.[80] Ultimately, Lorde's life was always about her Black lesbian spirituality.

NOTES

1. Phillis Isabella Sheppard, "Incantation." 2018.
2. Alexis De Veaux, *Warrior Poet: A Biography of Audre Lorde* (New York, NY: W. W. Norton and Company, 2004).
3. Alexis De Veaux, *Warrior Poet: A Biography of Audre Lorde.*
4. Alexis DeVeaux, *Warrior Poet: A Biography of Audre Lorde.*
5. Alexis DeVeaux, *Warrior Poet: A Biography of Audre Lorde,* 365.
6. Audre Lorde, *Litany for Survival: The Life and Work of Audre Lorde,* Directed by Ada Gay and Michelle Parkerson Griffin (New York, NY: Third World Newsreel, 1996).
7. Audre Lorde, *Litany for Survival: The Life and Work of Audre Lorde.*
8. Audre Lorde, *Our Dead Behind Us: Poems* (New York, NY: W. W. Norton and Company, 1986); "To the Poet Who Happens to Be Black and the Black Poet Who Happens to Be a Woman," in Our Dead Behind Us (New York, NY: W. W. Norton, 1986).
9. Audre Lorde, "Age, Race, Class, and Sex," in *Sister Outsider: Essays and Speeches, Feminist Series* (New York, NY: The Crossing Press, 1984).
10. Kimberley Richards. "Pregnant Women in Ghana are Taking Skin Bleaching Pills for Their unborn Babies" *The Atlanta Voice*, https://www.theatlantavoice.com/articles/pregnant-women-in-ghana-are-taking-skin-bleaching-pills-for-their-unborn-babies/
11. Emmanuel Lartey reporting at the Society for Pastoral Theology Annual Meeting, Post-Colonial Study Group, June 14–17, 2018, Atlanta, Ga.
12. Audre Lorde, "Eye to Eye: Black Women, Hatred, and Anger," *Sister Outsider: Essays and Speeches* (Trumansburg, NY: Crossing Press, 1984).
13. See Alexis De Veaux, *Warrior Poet: A Biography of Audre Lorde* (New York, NY: W. W. Norton and Company, 2004); also see Johnetta B. Cole, "Audre Lorde: My Shero, My Teacher, My Sister Friend," in *I Am Your Sister Collected and Unpublished Writing of Audre Lorde*, edited by Rudolph P. Byrd, Johnetta B. Cole, and Beverly Guy-Sheftall (New York, NY: Oxford University Press, 2009).
14. Audre Lorde, "Commencement Address Oberlin College, May 29, 1989," in *I Am Your Sister: Collected and Unpublished Writings of Audre Lorde*, edited by Rudolph P. Byrd, Johnetta B. Cole, and Beverly Guy-Sheftall (New York, NY: Oxford University Press, 2009).
15. Audre Lorde, "Learning from the 60s," in *Sister Outsider: Essays and Speeches* (Berkeley, CA: The Crossing Press, 1984).
16. Audre Lorde, "Learning from the 60s."
17. Audre Lorde, "Eye to Eye: Black Women, Hatred, and Anger," 171.
18. Audre Lorde, "Eye to Eye: Black Women, Hatred, and Anger," 171.

19. Audre Lorde, "Eye to Eye: Black Women, Hatred, and Anger," 171.
20. Audre Lorde, "Father, Son and Holy Ghost," in *The Marvelous Arithmetics of Distance* (New York, NY: W. W. Norton and Company, 1993).
21. Audre Lorde, *Zami a New Spelling of My Name* (New York, NY: Crossing Press, 1982).
22. Ellen Shapiro, "Audre Lorde," in *Conversations with Audre Lorde*, edited by Joan Wylie Hall (Jackson, MS: University Press of Mississippi, 2004).
23. Emmanuel Yartekwei Amugi Lartey, *Postcolonizing God an African Practical Theology* (London, UK: SCM Press, 2013).
24. For the conceptualization of bricolage see Melissa M. Wilcox, *Queer Women and Religious Individualism* (Bloomington, IN: Indiana University Press, 2009).
25. Alexis De Veaux, *Warrior Poet: A Biography of Audre Lorde*.
26. Audre Lorde, "Call," in *Our Dead Behind Us: Poems* (New York, NY: W. W. Norton & Company, 1986).
27. Ada G. Griffin and Michelle Parkerson, *A Litany for Survival: The Life and Work of Audre Lorde* (New York, NY: Third World Newsreel, 1996).
28. John Angus Martin, Joseph Opala, and Cynthia Schmidt, *The Temne Nation of Carriacou: Sierra Leone's Lost Family in the Caribbean: Sierra Leone's Lost Family in the Caribbean* (Chattanooga, TN: Polyphemus Press, 2016).
29. Audre Lorde, "My Mother's Mortar," in *I Am Your Sister: Collected and Unpublished Writings of Audre Lorde*, edited by Rudolph Byrd, Johnetta B. Cole, and Guy-Sheftall (New York, NY: Oxford University Press, 2009).
30. Audre Lorde, *Zami a New Spelling of My Name*, 14.
31. William Strickland, "Frantz Fanon: His Life and His Work Frantz Fanon: His Life and Work (1979). International Tribute to Frantz Fanon. 8. Retrieved from Https://Scholarworks.Umass.Edu/Afroam_Faculty_Pubs/8," Scholar Works University of Massachusetts (1979).
32. Frantz Fanon, *Black Skin, White Masks* (New York, NY: Grove Press, 1967).
33. Charles H. Rowell, "Above the Wind: An Interview with Audre Lorde," in *Conversations with Audre Lorde*, edited by Joan Wylie Hall (Jackson, MS: University of Mississippi Press, 1990).
34. Alexis De Veaux, *Warrior Poet: A Biography of Audre Lorde* (New York, NY: W. W. Norton and Company, 2004).
35. Audre Lorde, "Winds of Orisha Unicorn," in *The Black Unicorn* (New York, NY: W. W. Norton, 1978).
36. Frantz Fanon, *The Wretched of the Earth* (New York, NY: Grove Press, 1963).
37. Frantz Fanon, *The Wretched of the Earth*.
38. Frantz Fanon, *The Wretched of the Earth*.
39. Audre Lorde, "Age, Race, Class, and Sex."
40. Alexis De Veaux, *Warrior Poet: A Bibliography of Audre Lorde*.
41. Audre Lorde, "Turning the Beat Around: Lesbian Parenting," in *A Burst of Light and Other Essays* (Ithaca, NY: Firebrand Books, 1988).
42. Audre Lorde, "Power," in *The Collected Poems of Audre Lorde* (New York, NY: W. W. Norton & Company).
43. Audre Lorde, "Power."

44. Audre Lorde, "Power."
45. Alexis De Veaux, *Warrior Poet: A Bibliography of Audre Lorde.*
46. Alexis De Veaux, *Warrior Poet: A Bibliography of Audre Lorde.*
47. Audre Lorde, "Turning the Beat Around: Lesbian Parenting."
48. Ada G. Griffin and Michelle Parkerson. *A Litany for Survival: The Life and Work of Audre Lorde* (New York, NY: Third World Newsreel, 1996).

Dagmar Schultz, Michael Seidel, Ika Hügel-Marshall, Ria Cheatom, Aletta Vietinghoff, Corasón, Audrey Motaung, and Christian Wilmes. *Audre Lorde: The Berlin Years, 1984 to 1992,* 2012.

49. Audre Lorde, "Uses of the Erotic: The Erotic as Power," in *Sister Outsider: Essays and Speeches* (Freedom, CA: Crossing Press, 1984).
50. Susan Leigh Star, "Sadomasochism: Not About Condemnation: An Interview with Audre Lorde," in *A Burst of Light and Other Essays by Audre Lorde* (Ithaca, NY: Firebrand Books, 1988).
51. Susan Leigh Star, "Sadomasochism."
52. Audre Lorde, "Uses of the Erotic: The Erotic as Power," 53.
53. Audre Lorde, *Sister Outsider: Essays and Speeches* (New York, NY: W. W. Norton, 1984): 48.
54. Franz Fanon, *Black Skin, White Masks* (New York, NY: Grove Press, 1967).
55. Audre Lorde, *Zami: A New Spelling of My Name, 114.*
56. Audre Lorde, *Zami: A New Spelling of My Name.*
57. Audre Lorde, *Zami: A New Spelling of My Name.*
58. Audre Lorde, *Zami: A New Spelling of My Name.*
59. Audre Lorde, *Zami: A New Spelling of My Name.*
60. Audre Lorde, "Eye to Eye: Black Women, Hatred, and Anger," 167.
61. Audre Lorde, *The Cancer Journals* (San Francisco, CA: Spinsters Ink, 1980).
62. Audre Lorde, *A Burst of Light and Other Essays* (Mineola, NY: Ixia Press, 2017).
63. Audre Lorde, *A Burst of Light and Other Essays,* 118.
64. Audre Lorde, *A Burst of Light and Other Essays.*
65. Maria Popova, "Audre Lorde on Poetry as an Instrument of Change and the Courage to Feel as an Antidote to Fear, a Portal to Power and Possibility, and a Fulcrum of Action," *Brain Pickings,* May 6, 2018. https://www.brainpickings.org/2020/10/18/poetry-is-not-a-luxury-audre-lorde. Accessed May 6, 2018.
66. Pat Parker published five volumes of poetry: *Jonestown and Other Madness* (Firebrand Books, 1985); *Woman Slaughter* (Diana Press, 1978); *Movement in Black* (Diana Press, 1978); *Pit Stop* (Women's Press Collective, 1975); and *Child of Myself* (Women's Press Collective, 1972).
67. Anita Cornwell. (1975). "Pat Parker—Black Lesbian Poet Radical Pioneer readings/ appearances of *Movement in Black* interviewed by Anita Cornwell." http://www.amusejanetmason.com/Pat_Parker2.htm. Accessed January 20, 2020.
68. Audre Lorde and Pat Parker, *Sister Love: The Letters of Audre Lorde and Pat Parker1974-1989* (New York, NY: A Midsummer Night's Press, 2018).
69. Audre Lorde and Pat Parker, *Sister Love.*
70. Audre Lorde and Pat Parker, *Sister Love.*

71. Audre Lorde and Pat Parker, *Sister Love.*
72. Pat Parker, "Movement in Black," in *Movement in Press* (New York, NY: Diana Press, 1978).
73. Audre Lorde and Pat Parker, *Sister Love.*
74. Audre Lorde and Pat Parker, *Sister Love.*
75. Audre Lorde and Pat Parker, *Sister Love.*
76. Pat Parker, "Movement in Black."
77. Johnetta Cole, "Audre Lorde: My Shero, My Teacher, My Sister Friend."
78. Melville House, "Twenty-Five Years after Her Death, What Audre Lorde Left Behind Most Definitely Has a Life of Its Own.," Melville House, https://www.mhpbooks.com/twenty-five-years-after-her-death-what-audre-lorde-left-behind-most-definitely-has-a-life-of-its-own/.
79. Catherine A. John, *Clear Word and Third Sight Folk Groundings and Diasporic Consciousness in African Caribbean Writing* (Durham, NC: Duke University Press, 2003).
80. Audre Lorde, "From the House of Yemenja," in *The Black Unicorn* (New York, NY: W. W. Norton and Company, 1978).

Chapter 2

Visions of Self and Transformation in Black Outsider Art

ART AND CULTURAL MIRRORING

There are a number of ways to think about interiority and religion (such as we do in anthropology, religious studies, or psychoanalysis); however, one informed by womanist approaches, regardless of discipline, takes Black women's experience, cultural landscapes, and social locations as the epistemological point of departure. An important dimension to womanist approaches is locating the particularity of Black life within cultural life and the way in which Black women are formers and shapers of Black cultural life. Outsider artists are cultural workers.

In her introduction to *Black Women As Cultural Readers*, Jacqueline Bobo writes that even though the novel *Waiting to Exhale* made the *New York Times'* bestsellers list, was enthusiastically engaged by Black women and eventually transformed into a movie, it was dismissed by literary critics. The book's four main characters were seen as male bashers, and because they were middle-class Black women engaged in activities associated with middle-class boredom, they were dismissed. Bobo argues that as many of the critics did not understand Black women's experiences, they did not recognize the important cultural work of the characters *on behalf of Black women*. Black women who are outsider artists are too often dismissed by those with access to make their critical reviews central to a section of those engaged in public discourse. Black women's cultural work is often undervalued, on the rare occasions their work is the subject of scholarly discourse. However, as Bobo has argued, Black women read Black women's work as cultural work because Black women bring a different set of criteria to the table—the least of which is the expectation of seeing something about their life, worldview, spirituality, and/or social condition represented in the Black art.

Thus, Black women's need of, for example, cultural mirroring is met by a different set of reflections than that of the literary critics who dismiss the Black cultural production of Black life. Here, the concept of cultural selfobjects, as construed by psychoanalyst Heniz Kohut and critiqued, revised, and then appropriated by womanists, is useful.[1] The idea of cultural selfobject's needs and experiences gave rise to the notion that there are persons in the arts, religion, sciences, and so on, whose creative output conveys the aspirations, hopes, troubles, and worldview of a people group. This is what Kohut called the group "self": those who galvanize the values, idealized narratives, as well as unfulfilled or latent needs of the group.[2] These selfobject experiences include the need to have our mirroring, idealization, twinship, and kinship gratified.

As such, we benefit from directing our attention to Black women's cultural productions, in this case their art, because they capture and carry the many streams that run through their communities and cultural lives. They give shape and form to nuances communicated across generations and to voices emerging in the contemporary contexts. From their positionality, they convey what is operative, forceful, animating, and sometimes unconscious in our surround. Thus artists, and other persons who are experienced as cultural selfobjects, identify and grasp the import of the connective tissue or "glue" that permeates and links individual and group experience. These figures may also envision and point the way toward vital change. Creative cultural "workers give expression to aspects of the cultural milieu important to the group's sense of self or us-ness."[3] They support, celebrate, resist and grieve assaults to the group self. As such, they give shape and form to society's manifest and latent illnesses. Thus, these figures announce the good emerging and what troubles and assails the community; they are sometimes Truth Sayers, shaman figures, and holders of dreams and nightmares for their communities. They are also artists.

As cultural workers, Black outsider artists are, more often than not, situated on the margins of the art world as well as the financial and social privileges associated with it. Rather than the long period of gestation learning the canon and history of art, and therefore being formed to appreciate works already determined to be valuable art, outsider artists find their calling more spontaneously. Often it emerges unexpectedly in a sudden focused act of artmaking by a person trained by a vision rather than by the catechism of an art school. This spontaneous outpouring of art is announced with little fanfare, social recognition, or financial support. These artists do have the safety net provided by some well-off patron. In most cases, the artist has not previously identified, in vocational terms, as an "artist," and when her art-making begins to spring forth, she continues without expectation or clear aspiration for recognition in the "formal" art world. Instead, outsider artists are often motivated to create by a sudden experience of a compelling inner vision or message.

A number of artists describe these visions as including a powerful communication from God whereby the artist either becomes a conduit for a religious message (a preacher or evangelist) or the art is the message (the canvas holds the sermon and the painting is the sermon). Their art—displayed in local public galleries, garages, front lawns, or homes—is filled with autobiographical images, religious and spiritual themes, struggle, historical, and political messages, and it interweaves their call into the ministry of art. Each artist eventually begins to understand her life of art-making as a conduit of healing and recovery from trauma, loss, and abandonment for themselves. As a religious message, this gift, teaching is an expression of their vocation to their communities.

OUTSIDER TO INSIDER: CALLED TO CREATE

Black women's art, as the subject of exhibits and research, is a reality still pressing against the doors of exclusion. Ashton Cooper sheds a bright light on one of the myriad of ways that patriarchal exclusionary practices work, and render invisible, the cultural productions of those who live close to the margins of those marginalized.

> When it comes to the everyday written materials we consume about artists, again and again the social and political forces that marginalize women artists are ignored. What if we tried to also understand the material realities of these women's lives? . . . '. . . the best artists do not simply rise to the top based on the high quality of their work—without any consideration, say, of their genitalia."[4]

Even with Cooper's emphasis on the marginalized status of women artists and the social forces supporting such, none of the artists he cites in the article is identified in terms of her race, ethnicity, religion, or sexuality. Should we just know? Cooper is, of course, correct but neglects to recognize that genitalia is gendered and racialized. To ignore this reality is to argue, implicitly, that for "women," social and political forces are perpetrated against women universally. This enforces the same patterns of exclusion and invisibility that Ashton hopes to disrupt. Some women are then further marginalized. Haley Coopersmith countervotes this expression of privilege when she states,

> Specifically, I am interested in how Black female artists subvert the canon by producing innovative performances and how these artists write about their

personal experiences themselves rather than waiting for another article that dismisses their work in favor of their biographies.[5]

Outsider art and artists have historically had their personal experiences and their art analyzed in ways that sometimes conceal their subjectivity and personal and social agency.

In her essay "In Search of Our Mother's Gardens: The Creativity of Black Women in the South," Alice Walker reflects on the link between spirituality and creativity in the lives of Black women and the unconscious forces that infused their unacknowledged art. Pressing against these creative forces were also social forces aimed at denying their personhood.

> When the poet Jean Toomer walked through the South in the early twenties, he discovered a curious thing: Black women whose spirituality was so intense, so deep, so unconscious, that they were themselves unaware of the richness they held. For these grandmothers and mothers of ours were not Saints, but Artists. . . . They were Creators.[6]

In this well-known essay, Walker is driving home the point that Black women, particularly those of Jean Toomer's generation, were denied the space to claim their creativity and because their subjectivity was a threat to the social order where Black bodies were appropriated for exploitation and denied the psychic freedom to create.[7]

Black women instead put their artistic yearnings in everyday expressions needed in the home where quilting, gardening, cooking gave witness to a future not yet imagined. Walker could recall her mother's garden and its enlivening effect on her. As an adult, Walker could see that this was the work her mother's soul demanded.[8] Her mother's generation were women whose art would only be recognized as such in the future, much like quilt in the Smithsonian attributed to "anonymous."[9] But anonymous did the work her soul required.

The work their souls must have. I read Black outsider artists' lives and art, with Walker in my heart and alongside the critical points made by Eugene W. Metcalf's in his article "Black Art, Folk Art, and Social Control." Metcalf's analysis of the marginalization of Black art and Black artists as a form of social control to thwart Black art and artists' emergence as a (potential) threat to the social order is critical. He argues that when Black artists depict the value and humanity of Black life, it interrogates negative misrepresentations and makes visible the interior aspects of Black life that have been rendered invisible. Thus, naming Black art as a category and as a function of social-political relations is a strategy that is political, aesthetic, economic, and spiritual.

Furthermore, recognizing Black outsider art as cultural production can function as subversive strategy that undermines spaces of privilege and exclusion. In his discussion of art collecting, specifically American Folk Art, Metcalf argues that museums turn a selfish act—collecting for individual pleasure or to satisfy acquisitiveness—into a sanctioned activity for "community service" because museums are thought to provide a space for the "presentation of the universe." Therefore, the museum has been complicit in undermining some art's meaning or artists' worldview of the universe by ignoring it, critiquing based on European perspectives, and attacking artists' interiority labeling the artist incoherent, incomprehensible, and lacking artistic complexity. This undermines Black outsider art's social value and social currency as art. Whereas, some art might frighten us or "cause us to critically reexamine accepted social dogma, the museum" presents these works in a benign settling and effectively diminishes their demands to rethink what we know about the world and our surrounds.[10] Museums *can* defang art by removing it from the sociopolitical contexts in which the artist's interior-social reflections were formed while also legitimizing it by displaying it. Art labels such as "Outsider," "Visionary" "Self-taught," and Black folks, in general, have been designated as "outside" the realm of high society art—and sometimes society in general. All too often, if their art is noticed and positively appraised, it is described as a surprise, fluke or an exception in the artist's world and in the artistic world. Moreover, outsider artists' creative expression is often surmised as a product of their intrapsychic struggles and not an expression of or an engagement with the broader social contexts and its communities. Daniel Wojcik has argued that the idea that these artists somehow produce work "completely free from social influences, is inaccurate, elitist, and dehumanizing, emphasizing stereotypical notions of the insane or primitive"[11] is misguided. I would add that it is strategic as it reifies some art and artists while rendering invisible artists as standing outside the mainstream and offering a social critique of it. Christine Smallwood reminds us that "according to one theory of language, a word means something only because of its opposite. Inevitably, each word-pair summons a hierarchy, a story of power,"[12] where "outsider artist" is asymmetrically situated on the underside of the power arrangement. As such, outsider artists are depicted as incidental to the social order; they neither accept it nor challenge it through their art-making. Metcalf has argued that the "aesthetic and social issues in the history of Black American art have often been difficulty to disentangle from one another."[13] This is due, in part, to the place art has in society as a mirror of what is considered of value; indeed, "the ability to create and appreciate art implies heightened human sensibility and confers social status and prestige."[14] This infers that art confirms (Western) society's self-image, constructed over and against—in opposition to—non-Western images. The refusal to recognize a group of artists' creations as art serves to deny, or at the very least, the question of their humanity. Metcalf convincingly argues that although folk art is an important dimension of Black cultural, the dearth of research would suggest otherwise, and where it is included in research, it is valued for its proximity to "aesthetics standards . . . high culture."[15]

There is a calculated dimension to this absence of a sustained discussion of Black artists' contributions in the discourse on folk art and culture. Black artists are treated as "other" and only acquire social currency or status as artists when it is decided, based on their approximation to Western European "high" culture, and I would suggest that Smallwood's claim that "meanwhile, in the art world, one of the most profound shifts has been that of so-called outsider art, which has finally come all the way inside," because race, gender, and class dictates how the artists are recompensed for her art—it is not enough just to have one's art acquired by a museum for special occasions on marginalized figures and their works. In order to approximate this vision of "high" culture, their work has to be recognized, be the subject of exhibits, worthy of scholarly engagement, and for the artist to be remunerated justly. This is not the experience of most Black outsider artists.

SUSPECTING ARTISTS' INTERIORITY: DEEPING A STRATEGY OF SOCIAL CONTROL

Much of what has been written about Outsider Art as a category begins with Jean Dubuffet's term "art brut." Dubuffet categorized art brut as art "produced by persons unscathed by artistic culture, where mimicry plays little or no part." Later, Roger Cardinal in his 1972 work *Outsider Art* used the term "outsider art" because his publisher thought art brut would not engage readers. Art brut was also used to describe psychiatric patients' artistic productions and this designation influenced the assessment and scholarship related to later outsider art. The art of these patients, and eventually including artists in non-psychiatric contexts, lacked formal training and were rarely discussed as real art. Instead, the art was treated as a diagnostic confirmation and psychiatric exhibit. The art produced in the context of asylum-based psychiatric treatment was popularized and emerging outside established conduits of formal art training[16] and was strange—maybe even stranger than an artist who would cut off his own ear and still achieve long-lasting acclaim. Producers of art brut were characterized as pathological and beyond the laws that govern successful artists' choices. These creative persons were viewed neither as artists nor noteworthy; they lived on the margins, and their art offered a lens into their psychology, solitary interiority, and their life of lonely existence. They are, as the narrative generally posits, limited in social engagement; indeed, they are outsider artists in multiple dimensions of life. An example of such a social imaginary shaping expectations is depicted by Roger Manley in his recounting of his taking an international group of scholars who were in the states to a symposium on the artist Annie Hooper. He led the group on a tour to meet a local outsider artist, Clyde Jones. Upon arriving at the destination, with Clyde arriving shortly thereafter, the scholars of outsider artist were "confused. Accustomed to dealing with psychotic artists in institutional settings, they found Clyde Jones' behavior to be too 'normal' to be genuinely 'outsider.' Neighbors stopped by to chat with him . . . and he didn't behave in any way that would indicate"[17] that he was psychotic or abnormal. For these scholars, outsider artists' psychological makeup, their inner life, is outsider interiority—complex and suspect. "The friendly everyday atmosphere clearly disturbed these curators and professors, who had grown used to finding outsider art in isolation . . . or with abnormal social interactions."[18]

The strategy of pathologizing the bearers of cultural narrative that counter dominant cultural religious, political, and social commentary should not surprise us; strategies of pathologizing serve to maintain hierarchical social order. Here, the "experts" represent the educated class. Even though various attempts to contest narratives of pathology have emerged in recent years, depictions of outsider artists as socially isolated and mentally ill continue to overwhelmingly influence the discourse. An example is represented in Roger Cardinal's article "Outsider Art and the Autistic Creator." Cardinal first provides a definition of Outsider Art

> as a mode of original artistic expression which thrives on it independence, shunning the public sphere and the art market. Such art can be highly idiosyncratic and secretive, and reflects the individual creator's attempt to construct a coherent, albeit strange, private world.[19]

And later, "I insist that Outsider Art earns its name not because of an association with a lurid case history or a sensational biography, but because it offers its audience a thrilling visual experience."[20] By combining "strange private world" and thrilling visual experience, Cardinal undermines his attempt to have us resist linking outsider art with mental illness by, instead, directing our attention to the content of Outsider Art. This strategy is less than successful because even though he ultimately suggests that it is the content of the art that is strange—but the content emerges from the interiority of the artists. Thus, the outsider artist's interiority is other than that which takes up non-outsider artists' interiority. Our interior world, he suggests, does not contain vivid thrilling strange experiences. Instead, he projects what he *experiences* as bizarre and *strange* into the outsider artist:

Outsider Art is an art expression with unexpected and often bewildering distinctiveness, and its outstanding exemplars tend to conjure up imagined private worlds, completely satisfying to their creator yet so remote from our normal experience as to appear alien and rebarbative.[21]

He makes what he is conscious of in his private world, and those he imagines to be like him, the model for normality. He makes the claim that the outsider artist is different and distinct not only from the rest of the world in terms of psychological makeup but also in relation to the cultural domain. "A central element in the definition of Outsider Art, . . . is that it diverges radically from our shared cultural expectation as to what art ought to look like."[22] Cardinal's work, others' outsider art, its producers, and his rendering falls in line with many other critics of the work. In this othering of their interiority and art, and the asymmetrical ordering of art, the artists not steeped in the privileged world of art society are ignored as artists, and their views on the world that shape their lives and work are ignored. They are, instead, discussed, but seldom treated as if they have agency, a vision of life, or connection to culture, or broader community. Unlike artists who are represented as highly esteemed figures who capture the undercurrents of the social milieu and give them form (thereby making them essential), outsider artists are often rendered autistic—communicating more within their own individually constructed world wherein few have access to their lexicon. These artists, in addition to receiving social recognition, have their art evaluated as a social good because it serves a social function. Outsider Art is approached with presumptive questions related to the artists' mental health status. Thus, outsider artists' interior sources of creation are depicted as unreliable, suspect, and of dubious value.

During the Q & A session following a paper I delivered on the artist Missionary Mary Proctor, a member of the audience, a white male in his thirties upon learning that the artist had experienced deep despair following the loss of family members in a fire, stated, "but she's mentally ill, right?" Proctor had experienced a prolonged and complicated grief following the tragic death of close family members. This person thought that this deep grief, her accompanying withdrawal, and her now prolific artistic output indicated that Proctor had been, and likely remained, mentally ill. Even though she emerged from this grief with a clear artist vocation, a committed religious worldview, and a clear sense of herself as connected to Black social and cultural expressions, her agency was lost in this othering process. But it was not just her trauma and grief that rendered her incomprehensible; the convergence of her social location, interiority, and religious life displayed in the public space (a rich gallery of her art filled almost every space of her lawn and garage) that was viewed as suspect. Proctor was filmed, without the benefit of deceptive editing or refinement, and posted on YouTube as its own exhibit. Thus, it was not Proctor's grief and art that signaled "irrational" but her place on the margins, and in a subtle sleight of hand, she is rendered pathological and mentally ill. Social outsider status, to the viewer's perception of meaningful life, was read as impotent and without purpose beyond the personal and psychological. This rhetoric of mental illness has political currency and economic power to silence alternative worldviews and alternative visions to the ways of the world; outsider artists represent such an alternative worldview.

These forms of subjugation and silencing, and instantiating hierarchies of status are all too familiar to those who must resist their debilitating effects daily. Pollock and Battleground note that "a marginalized or alienated art community often mirrors the similarly marginalized groups of society that have been divided by lines of gender, race, sexuality, class or age."[23] When their art is "discovered" as art or potentially art, it is a surprise, a fluke, or an exception in the artist's world and the artistic world. I argue that a portraiture of Black outsider artists, contrary to this trope of distorted interiority, reveals a rich source for exploring the convergence of religion, interiority, and culture. As Elizabeth Alexander so poignantly states, "Art is where and how we speak to each other in tongues audible when 'official language' fails. It is not where we escape the world's ills but rather one place where we go to make sense of them."[24] Furthermore, the outsider artist is, in her material production and its effect, a container for their aspects of their communities' experiences, hopes, disappointments, histories, moral interests, struggles, and religious perspectives. Thus, the dynamism between artist and surround is complex.

This complex engagement can be seen in the way in which religion and religious themes are integral and are woven throughout the trajectory of their work. Also embedded, and sometimes central, are epistemologies of race, gender, sexuality, and cartographies of relationality and love, longing, and loss. Outsider artists speak to us through their lives and art—thus sharing their interiority in their public unveilings. Along with these concerns, race, gender, and sexuality are intertwined aspects of self-understanding in this discussion.

The chapter traces Mary Proctor's movement to and from deep interiority to religious engagement, art-making, public reengagement through art, and her rendering of a vision for the world. There are a number of ways to think about interiority, particularly a womanist-informed psychological perspectives that take Black women's experience and their social location as the epistemological point of departure. Here I emphasize the link culture, religion, and interiority and explore the ways in which the artist reflects personal and social experience, and art intersects with forces of religion and society.

The remainder of the chapter leads the outsider artist Missionary Mary Proctor to consider "What dynamics of interiority are integral art-making?" "What does art reveal about interiority?" "What does it reveal about religious experience?" "How do gender, race, religion and culture shape the self-understanding of outsider artists?"

My introduction of her in the way begins with how I learned about her—via two brief YouTube documentaries. In the first one, filmed in 2007 and posted to YouTube in 2011, Proctor is interviewed at her home gallery by the videographer/researcher David Seehausen,[25] and the second one, filmed and posted in 2015, is Mary Proctor giving a tour of her new gallery. In both, Proctor's voice and narrative claim our attention and her perspective directly into the camera. Very quickly, we forget that someone else is recording her; she has a story she wants us to hear.

The opening of the Seehausen video shows a painting on wood, approximately three feet tall, with a bright white background with Black lettering: "The Church of Art by Missionary Mary Proctor Since 1995." The painting serves as the narthex to her Church of Art. Leading into the sanctuary is a wall of signs hanging on a fence: "Psalm 23 I shall not want," "He maketh me lie down," "We all hurt for the Families of 9/11," "Fear not for I am with you," and "Mercy, Never Give Up, We Never Give Up."

MISSIONARY MARY PROCTOR
"THIS IS MY CALLING"

Mary Proctor was born in Lloyd, Florida, in 1960. It was a small community with a population of 215 of which 112 were Black people. Then, as now, it was a rural area with no sidewalks, an area where racial relationships were managed through segregation, education, and economics. It was a southern town steeped in religion and religious behaviors, a town where various spiritualties lived side by side. As child, she was told that she was born with a caul on her face.

> When I was born, they removed a caul. That made me a special child, and my grandmother always said I would be called to do something. I was said to be a caul baby. They relied on what I say, know I had a special gift about me, insight.[26]
>
> Verbatim 1: Mary's American Folk Art Museum

As the camera leads us further into Mary Proctor's church in her yard, her paintings and art are icons inviting the viewer into her spiritual worldview.[27] Music plays in the background and she appears and welcomes the viewers.

Surrounded by art, she invites us in. Listening to Mary's voice, one of the first things of which I am aware is the pleasure of having someone introducing herself and her art to the world. That she does so while wearing dark sunglasses conveys a sense of exposure and vulnerability along with her excitement: she will show us her art, and her heart, and tell her story—but she will keep her eyes covered throughout the brief introduction.

> Hi welcome to my wonderful folk art, American Folk Art Museum and Gallery. I'm Mary Proctor and I'm very glad to . . . invite you here. And I'd like you to come along and to walk along and see my art and tell you a little bit of my story. Come along with me. First of all, Peace Be Still Today.

Mary started the guided tour of her gallery by letting us know that she is spiritually directed—"First of all, Peace Be Still." And "Lead us beside still waters." "Come along to see the wonderful messages—Rejoice!" But she also conveys her longing for an inner peace and stillness, and a life not ruled by emotional upheaval. Some of those who come ostensibly to view, collect, or study Mary's art reveal that they too are on a spiritual search. One of these attendees was Katherine Webb-Hehn, a white journalist who had stopped writing in search of something. She wrote:

> I thought I'd drive to Tallahassee to visit Mary Proctor as if I were on some spiritual journey, where I'd be graced by her magnetic presence and mystical wisdom, then return home, my infant son glowing on my newly enlightened hip . . . I was on my way to interview an artist . . . who upholds long-held cultural traditions, while using her art to heal, to connect and to communicate the philosophical and religious principles of a purposefully simple life. That life, she says, "is all about raising a family, honoring God and preserving the dead."[28]

Some years earlier, Webb-Hahn had visited Mary and recognized a kind of spiritual wisdom in her when Mary said, "Tell me why ya ain't content."[29] Mary discerned that Webb-Hehn was on a spiritual journey. Webb-Hehn used her interview to experience this wisdom but she also was not sure if Mary actually uses this spiritual power. Webb-Hahn believed and disbelieved simultaneously. Mary's deep spirituality is the kind that is hard-earned and the spiritual gifts that come with it are part and parcel. Like the biblical Hagar, she has questioned God directly from a place of despair and has come back transformed.

"NOW WHAT GOD?" LOSS, MELANCHOLIA, MOURNING, AND CREATIVITY

Mary retells her story of origin as an artist and reminds the viewer of the trauma of losing her family and God directing her to paint a door. This telling marks her journey of transformation. Prior to the fire, she maintained a flea market, "a little junk here and there." After the fire she became depressed and,

> asked the Lord, now you took three of my family members, what am I to do? ... So, the first thing that the Lord did, He allowed me to go through a time of depression for about a year.

And this is one of my first doors, it says,

> Welcome. I'm Mary L Proctor, born June 11, 1960, married three boys and adopted an eight-year-old girl, inspired by the Lord Jesus Christ to carry his message on a door because Jesus said ... I am the door. ... My mission and vision of painting doors came, it says on the painted door, began in February 1995.

The movement from immobilizing grief to mourning and then to painting the door can be viewed as a mourning ritual involving loss, withdrawal, reengagement, and generative creativity. While this is the most profound loss and mourning Proctor describes, mourning is a reoccurring theme in life. The loss of her family in fire was made more difficult and traumatic because earlier during the night the fire occurred, Mary awakened from a vision dream in which she "saw light going all the way up into heaven [and said] there's something going on." Mary's husband tried to calm her. She later learned that she awakened the same hour her family died in the fire. Once alerted about the fire, Mary and her husband drove to the home and saw the police and ambulance personnel "taking shovels and throwing out legs and heads and bodies, I was screaming and hollering, and looking at all that. And I shouldn't have been looking."[30] It is important to note the process of trauma and interiorization that Mary underwent.

She says she should not have looked and thereby internalized responsibility for what she saw and how it affected her. But what did she see? She not only saw her family members' dead body parts but she saw how they were treated by those entrusted with responding to the fire. Mary Proctor could not unsee the horror of her loved ones' burned dead bodies and treated in the most sacrilegious manner. Their bodies were dismembered, shoveled, and thrown out like garbage. Having internalized what she saw, her psyche was affected, as were her social relationships.

For the next year, Mary was inconsolable, depressed, and unable to accept the loss. During this phase of her experience, she was not in mourning but in an arrested state of extended melancholia—a state of withdrawal, most often from living loved ones, during which she was incapable of integrating the meaning and full impact of the loss. Such an inward retreat is often a desperate attempt to hold onto the figures who have shaped one's psyche and life who are now physically gone and cannot be replaced. To relinquish them to death, to accept the reality of their loss, was to experience a piece of oneself forever eviscerated. She withdrew into herself, and her interiority became the site where the traumatic vision resided. This subjected her to sustained exposure to the trauma. Her retreat into her interior world was also a place that haunted her. This is not the end of her story.

Her questions— "Lord, why?" "What now?" and "What am I to do?"— show that Mary knew her loss and grief would not have the final say in her life, though the long period of "depression" was grueling. Submitting to her grief was a part of her spiritual practice of attending to God's plans for her life. After the lessening of the intensity of her grief, she began to see that art was going to be crucial to her life and that this mission, to develop her creative self, was in process prior to the fire and depression.

TRANSFORMATION FROM "JUNK" COLLECTOR TO "ARTIST"

Mary's sensibility toward the artistic was evident prior to the death of her grandmother and aunt and uncle. She collected and stored a variety of things to sell in her "Noah's Ark Flea Market"[31] located in her yard at home but did not know have a vision for items she collected.[32] It was after she emerged from her depression in 1995 that the purpose of her life became clear.

All the junk was no more for sale. It's now become an art studio . . .

(people around here) they got angry with me and said what in the world do you are you doing? Well I just told them that I got a lot of painting in me and I couldn't stop.

As her inner transformation transpired, the way she viewed her immediate external world changed. This included reevaluating her "junk." She now claimed it as art and her junkyard was now her art studio. Her new sense of self was not immediately mirrored by her surrounding community. At one point, the city threatened to evict because Tallahassee rezoned the area. She was determined to find a home for her art and took to YouTube to raise funds. Viewers heard the desperation as she reported that she was "devastated. I have been here for 16 years and I have now been zoned out of my location in Tallahassee. I have thousands of pieces of art." Unlike her initial video, her voice quavers, and in place of excitement, is anxiety. She wore sunglasses throughout the filming.[33]

When someone or a group makes a new demand or changes the dynamics in interpersonal relating or imposes power in more restrictive ways, in psychoanalytic spaces, we ask, "Why now?" In this spirit, I ask, What was the meaning of the imposition of new zoning restrictions? Constance Perin offers an incisive perspective: "Why can threats to meanings evoke responses no less intense than threats to survival? How we make meaning is the key . . . our constructions of social and cultural worlds are dependent upon meanings."[34] Mary Proctor, who had always sold "junk" from her backyard, garage, and later, a small gallery, was threatened with eviction when her subjectivity had collapsed as she understood herself as "artist." Mary Proctor as junk collector was tolerable but for her to claim a new identity was to challenge the order of things. At this juncture, Mary's change was primarily internal because her art gallery was still located in the same space; her transformation is in the meaning the art had for her.

Mary's transformation from having a junkyard flea market to being an artist with a call and mission was so compelling that she could not stop, and this determination prevailed over her anxiety concerning her neighbors, zoning, and the need to support herself. In this transformation, we witness a shift in Mary's self and psychological makeup. She emerged with an artistic purpose that, unlike her junkyard sales, was mirrored by those who began to appreciate her art. She recalls, "When people started finding out about me, I knew I was painting." This shift was interior, but it was also social as well as communal.

As I have previously discussed, many who argue that mirroring is a developmental necessity, often do so without recognizing the many sociocultural ways in which mirroring for one's class, gender, racial, and sexual identity can be thwarted, and vigorously so, for Black women. This means that art-making be a means to resist non-affirming representations or negative mirroring. As such, outsider art is an expression of interior resources that serve to mirror Blackness as well as the complexity of being Black. Proctor's claim "I got a lot of art in me" is a claim about her developing self-affirming interiority and her public pronouncement of it. It also announces her disposition in relation to the vicissitudes of the world.

> If you look around me, everything that I do around me is positive. I don't much deal with negative negativism. If you deal with negative you become negative. Prayer's the key to having a positive mind.[35]

Mary believes we are not powerless in the face of difficulty. We choose to have a negative or positive mindset. The shift in her mindset comes through a spiritual practice of praying, but it is also embodied— "you have positive things that you can find, whatever you're doing if you can find something positive to do. You overcome" the negative.

BECOMING MARY: EARLY FORMATIONAL LANDSCAPE

Mary Proctor's narration of her early formational experiences begins with her mother, a preteen girl, pregnant and afraid, who did not know what to do when her newborn made her way into the world. Clearly desperate, she left Mary by the side of the road where Penny Cooksey, Mary's grandmother, would find her. Cooksey and her husband took Mary in, nourished her, and raised her as their own. Describing her life, Proctor begins with this early abandonment and recovery. Proctor never knew her father as a child but heard that he was an artist.

> It was my understanding that he was an artist, and was painting pictures in the church, and my mama was walking by. He was from Thomasville, Georgia. I went to meet him a couple of years ago. He was supposed to wait for me, but he left. He didn't want nothing to do with me 'cause his family didn't know about me. When I found them, they telling me, "you can't be. My daddy wouldn't have done this." This was tough for me.[36]

She also directs our attention to the way in which gender, sexuality, sexual abuse, race, and the reality of racism intersect in rural Tennessee:

> My mother was Pauline Cooksey, and she bore me at about age eleven. She got pregnant and was afraid, and tried to hide it from my grandmother. But my grandmother knew, and kind of followed my mother around. My grandmother tells me she found me out beside a road in a little ditch. She picked me up, took me in, nourished me, and kept me as her child. I was raised by my grandparents, a mixed-race couple. My grandmother was Black; grandfather, white.[37]

Her grandfather was hated by white locals because he married a Black woman and later suffered depression because he lost his land. Soon thereafter, her grandmother became depressed and alcoholic. Proctor's grandfather has not made his way directly into Mary's art; there are no paintings or sculptures of him, but he is there in her feelings about men and women and spirituality. Her grandfather's commitment to her grandmother is an abiding thread in Proctor's messages. And she readily recognizes that her grandfather also helped raise her and left a mark on her spirituality. He was "kind of a farmer. He had a garden. I never saw him do much. He was hated by his own peoples, but he was going to stick with his Black woman. He stayed with her, stood through the test." She adds that he was religious and wore Black all the time.

The art in her Church of Art is filled with teachings that bring this theo-ethical landscape taught to her by her grandparents to her understanding of the world and her presence in the public sphere. She has a painting that asks, "Am I my brother's keeper?" and it becomes clear, in her painting and what she says, that Proctor's sense of moral responsibility has depth and moves beyond her immediate relational milieu; it is intergenerational.

> If I can connect with [my grandfather] again in some way, I'll write a book about him. . . . As children, we were scared of his spirituality. He wore Black all the time, read his Bible, did not smoke, drink, or curse . . . I was raised by spiritually powerful people, raised with prayer night and day.[38]

INTERIORITY, LIMINAL, AND PUBLIC SPACE: THE GALLERY

In the second Mary Proctor video, she reveals a similarly driven quality to her art-making, a similar lifelong and sustaining spirituality, and a woman capable of deep interior reflection. However, in the second video,[39] six years after the Seehausen documentary, Proctor is now giving a tour of her American Folk Art Museum located in the Tallahassee Mall. We learn that Mary's calling has expanded: she now exhibits other artists' work as part of her call. Mary conveys direction, confidence, and a more explicit appreciation for Black history and culture.

In this video, filmed to introduce her new museum in Tallahassee, she is not wearing her dark glasses. She has a lilt to her laughter, and her sense of humor, often directed at herself, is evident. She communicates a sense of deep satisfaction with life, even though financial concerns continue. She laughs, sometimes at things that may be an inner source of humor or pleasure. She performs being a generous docent as she welcomes viewers to the museum. She embodies a unique and even quirky view of the world, and evidently models herself on tour guides she has seen. But Proctor's performance comes with a twist as she leads with an expansive stretch of one arm, and a smile that makes you as curious about Mary as the art. The whole presentation seems intentional and genuine at the same time. At moments, she may seem "off"—not quite of this world or fully in the moment, but then interrupts herself to direct the viewers' attention to a particular piece of art. She is never far away from art and its importance. There is an inner world that calls beckons Mary Proctor, and she stops and listens to it before continuing. She has a mission deep within her bones.

> Hi, this is Mary Proctor, this is my location at the Tallahassee Mall and I'm glad to introduce you to my new spot . . . these are some of my sculpture pieces I've done.

> . . . [A]s you come along further; you see that I have paintings all around here. I have mine, . . . and . . . other people's work not only my works . . . Kim Clayton. I have Pat Juno. This, . . . here is Ruby Williams from Plant City, Florida. I have [art] from other people like Eric Legge. And . . . my son's works. . . . His name is Christopher. This piece that is in the Smithsonian. I have this hanging in the museum and I am so proud.

Mary's shift in her sense of self and agency, the change in the public location of her art from front yard to her art gallery located within a building, and her art being exhibited in the Smithsonian suggest changes—interior and social—associated with the work of liminal spaces. Liminal spaces are spaces where inner change and social position reflect self-transformation. In other words, as Mary sees her art and vision as meaningful in the social context, her surround confirms this change in identity. Her calling to art extends beyond the act of creating art to bringing a variety of Black artists' art to the viewing public. This reveals an expanded vocation.

KINSHIP, TWINSHIP, AND RE-MEMBERING IN VOCATION

Mary's calling has expanded: she recognizes that other artists' works need to be known to her visitors, and that they will not likely encounter these artists in other galleries. But she also collects the art of friends whose work is now collectable: Ruby Williams and Eric Legge's work is now more widely known. Mary is not *in* the insider art world but she recognizes that the insider positionality of select art can contribute both to her investment in Black art and also to her financial future. Additionally, she and Ruby Williams are often at the same art festivals and have their art displayed in some of the same galleries. The experience of kinship and being part of a community of artists has clearly become important to her.

Mary also mentions her son, Christopher's art. Christopher is Mary's firstborn who died shortly after the fire. Mary allows visitors to see his work but not take pictures of it,[40] and this is important to note. Whereas Mary remembers her grandmother through artistic expression, suggesting a process of grief leading to a new internal relationship with the deceased, Mary has created a space, a psychological altar, by which to remember Christopher. Unlike her first conscious experience of loss and mourning, her mourning for her son is of a different sort—someplace between melancholia, celebration of his artistic gift, and mourning. Mary has mourned the loss of the artist he might have become. In this emotional twinship, we witness her struggle to acknowledge the finality of his death. The loss of one's child is, of course, excruciating and, even in the best of circumstances, takes some time to navigate.

However, alongside her unending experience of grief, Mary is changing in another important area. She now senses an expansion of her initial call to paint to one broader than that of an artist. This new calling emerged from an identification with an internalized idealized figure important to her.

> And this is Mary Mcleod Bethune Cookman, one of my favorite women. She's all, you know, just reading about her, talking about how she went out and sold things just to make a college Bethune Cookman. She did that.
>
> I feel she's a part of me, that I, I'm doing that same thing today, making things, doing things. So, that I [would have] my own museum . . . one day. People to see that Mary has made a museum, and if I can do anything, that you can do it too.

Mary Proctor sees herself as a mentor and educator; she wants people to learn about art and to provide spaces for them to express their own creativity, she has started offering classes to the public.

Mary has developed a twinship, not with another painter, but with Mary McLeod Bethune, a Black woman and an educator whose own vocation was the racial uplift of Black folks. This connection reveals that Missionary Mary's vocational calling is thoroughly connected to the enrichment of Black people through religion and art. This twinship, understood in self-psychological terms, is both an idealizing and a mirroring nature. As such, in the idealizing experience, Mary has taken Bethune's values and commitments into her inner life. She experiences herself as being of greater interest to the public. Her mission is to embody that enhancement for the betterment of others. In the mirroring function, Proctor feels that she and Bethune share aspects of personality, values, and resiliency, along with a vocational intention. Just as Bethune was determined to improve the life of other Blacks through education, so too does Mary.

THERE'S ALWAYS A MESSAGE

We witness in Mary Proctor's relationship with Mary Mcloud Bethune's story a process of self-transformation through idealization, twinship, and activism. Mary's new life suggests a significant change in her interior life that is communicated publicly in her gallery. The gallery is both a space to embody her expanded vocation and her religious vocation—one with a message to evoke transformation in those around her.

> I feel like I'm a message. Almost everything I do, there's a message beyond it.

Proctor wants the message to do its work of changing people but, like any minister, she also needs to sell her work and she does not deny this: "I want the work out there. I want people to see the message," she said. "I guess I want some money for it, too."[41] When I contacted her about incorporating her YouTube video in this project, she said yes and that she hoped I might become a collector of her work. The message in the art, however, seems to be primary.

Mary's messages are not just other-directed but also for her. She recalled a meditation where she spoke with God and expressed her desire to see an angel. Her meditation led her to look within.

> I was sitting there in 1996 and . . . I said, Oh Lord, I feel so good after meditation. I said, Lord, I want to see an angel.
>
> I looked up in the sky in a bright light shining down and all of a sudden there was a reflection. I looked in the mirror and at my face and said, look, and see, the angel is you.

These kinds of meditative experiences seem to bring about shifts within Mary and in her religious experience and sense of purpose. This would suggest a profound reworking or reframing of Mary's interior and psychological life—in other words, a reworking of interior content and processes much like we might expect in psychotherapy and spiritual guidance. The transformation of her interior is connected to an outward way of being and a message.

> It's the good to do every day. Every day I try my best. I try to put my hands to doing something good every day.

It is not surprising that Mary was empathically attuned to Joe's emotional state, given her own experience of depression, and that he was, metaphorically and physically, "down." She offered what she had to give: the truth, and a promise that signaled a prophecy. The truth—"I don't know what to do"; the promise—"but if I ever own a museum, I will hang your work"; and the prophecy—that his work would be collectable. Mary promises to take him, through his art, into the future—a space she senses that he, in his bodily form, will never see.

Mary did not let him die and leave. She conjures a future for him. "Joe is gone now but I love what he did." Because she loved Joe, she imagined a space where he will be remembered and his art acknowledged. She promised him, in essence, to create an altar in his memory and to remember him. Mary's space also remembers culture and history. Her art includes themes of race and history, and she looks for these themes in the art of others she exhibits. Mary's art is a form of cultural memory and remembering.

> Here's one of Dr. King; you know, how he was there.... There's a collection of my Black history people (who) have done great things. I have sold them to museums or given to people.... And here. I like these a lot. They are our soldiers. They're being made ... for ... Black history.

And in a religious visionary move, Mary makes a claim for her own divinity:

> That's what I do. And as you can see, I got all kinds of creations. Things I made out of nothing.

Mary Proctor's way of making something out of nothing relies on the intersection of interior and public spaces where each is infused with religious experience and language. In her videos, we see how the spaces of her front lawn gallery, YouTube, and the gallery are public social spaces where art is the message for mourning, healing, memory, and religious experience.

In her videos, we witness Mary Proctor documenting the relationship between her grief, mourning, and emergent vocational identity. The transformation of her desperate question to God, "What am I to do?" into her pronouncement of her artist identity and ministry was not without internal and social struggle. Art-making and economic struggle are often close companions in Proctor's life. She brings an urgency and determination to fulfill her calling. As she continues to live into this calling, recurring themes in her painting, sculptures, and sayings continue to speak to the needs beyond herself. Some of her earliest works, a series of signs, that she thought were lost during her move caused by the rezoning of her neighborhood, have been found in storage by Barry Courtney, a collector. When the Covid-19 pandemic began, he decided to display, not sell them, because he thought the paintings could inspire those struggling during this time of social upheaval. Mary Proctor agreed because "the message is needed forever. Not now—but forever."[42] Her religious sensibility, and experiences of loss, mourning, and healing, makes their way into her art. She recognizes that the purpose of her calling extends beyond her exhibitions because the confluence of interior and social spaces catalyzes her interior transformation and the religious message permeates the art-making process. In describing one of her early sculptures of Black woman dressed in a bright yellow pantsuit, she says,

> All the yellow represents the sunlight. I hope the light will shine through me and bring forth a message so powerful even a baby can understand it. It should touch the whole world. No matter their color, whatever their religion, I hope to touch their heart and make us all one.[43]

Where she anticipates a world where we are all one, it is a world populated by the particularities of Black women's experience. It is a Black woman, enveloped in bright yellow, who proclaims a message for the world. Proctor's vision is hopeful, spiritual, and universalist. She dreams of a world, not yet here, that art announces and creates.

NOTES

1. Phillis Isabella Sheppard, *Self, Cultures and Others in Womanist Practical Theology*, edited by Dwight Hopkins and Linda Thomas, Black Religion, Womanist Thought, and Social Justice (New York: Palgrave Macmillan, 2011); "Culture and Pastoral Psychotherapy: A Womanist Self Psychological Perspective," in *Transforming Wisdom: An Introduction to Pastoral Psychotherapy*, edited by Felicity Kelcourse and Bernie Lyon (Cascade, 2014); "Womanist Pastoral Theology and Black Women's Experience of Religion and Sexuality," In *Critical Trajectories in Pastoral Theology and Care: Theory and Practice*, edited by Nancy Ramsay (Hoboken, NJ: Wiley Blackwell, 2017); Stephanie M. Crumpton, *A Womanist Pastoral Theology against Intimate and Cultural Violence* (Palgrave Macmillan, 2014).

2. Heinz Kohut, "Idealization and Cultural Selfobjects," in *Self Psychology and the Humanities: Reflections on a New Psychoanalytic Approach*, edited by Charles B. Strozier (New York, NY: Norton & Company, 1985a); "On the Continuity of the Self and Cultural Self Objects," in *Self Psychology and the Humanities: Reflections on a New Psychoanalytic Approach*, edited by Charles B. Strozier (New York, NY: Norton & Company, 1985b).

3. Phillis Isabella Sheppard, *Self, Culture, and Others in Womanist Practical Theology*.

4. Ashton Cooper, "The Problem of the Overlooked Female Artist: An Argument for Enlivening a Stale Model of Discussion," Hyperallergic, January 2010. https://hyperallergic.com/173963/the-problem-of-the-overlooked-female-artist-an-argument-for-enlivening-a-stale-model-of-discussion. Accessed November 25, 2015.

5. Haley Coopersmith, "Black Performance Art as Black Feminism: Changing Perspectives in the Contemporary Art World." 2015. https://medium.com/Black-feminism/Black-perfomance-art-as-Black-feminism-changing-perspectives-in-the-comtemporary-art-world-e65aa238422. Accessed January 2018.

6. Alice Walker, *In Search of Our Mothers' Gardens: Womanist Prose* (San Diego, CA: Harcourt Brace Jovanovich, 1983).

7. Alice Walker, *In Search of Our Mothers' Gardens: Womanist Prose*, 233–34.

8. Alice Walker, *In Search of Our Mothers' Gardens: Womanist Prose*.

9. Alice Walker, *In Search of Our Mothers' Gardens: Womanist Prose*, 239.

10. Eugene W. Metcalf Jr., "Folk Art, Museums, and Collecting the Modern Self," in *Contemporary American Folk, Naive, and Outsider Art; Into the Mainstream?*, edited by Edna Carter Southard (Miami: Miami University Art Museum 1990).

11. Daniel Wojcik, "Outsider Art, Vernacular Traditions, Trauma, and Creativity," *Western Folklore*, 67, no. 2/3 (2008): 179–98, 180.

12. Christine Smallwood, "Outside In," *The New York Times Style Magazine* (June 1, 2015). https://www.nytimes.com/2015/06/01/t-magazine/outsider-art-essay-christine-smallwood.html. Accessed June 1, 2018.

13. Eugene Metcalf, "Black Art, Folk Art, and Social Control," *Winterthur Portfolio,* 18, no. 4 (Winter 1983): 271–89, 271.

14. Eugene Metcalf, "Black Art, Folk Art, and Social Control," 271.

15. Eugene Metcalf, "Black Art, Folk Art, and Social Control," 271.

16. For examples, see Caitlin MJ Pollock and Andrea L. Battleground, "A Gallery for the Outlaw: Archiving the Art of the Iconoclast," in *Association of College and Research Libraries* (Indianapolis, IN: American Library Association, 2013); Daniel Wojcik, "Outsider Art, Vernacular Traditions, Trauma, and Creativity," *Western Folklore,* 67, no. 2/3 (2008); Vera L. Zolberg and Joni Maya Cherbo, "Introduction," in *Outsider Art: Contesting Boundaries in Contemporary Culture*, edited by Vera L. Zolberg and Joni Maya Cherbo (Cambridge, UK: Cambridge University Press, 1997).

17. Roger Manley, "Outsider Art: Psychosis or Expression of Folk Art-Making?" *Folkstreams.* http://www.folkstreams.net/film-context.php?id=151. Accessed June 1, 2018.

18. Roger Manley, "Outsider Art: Psychosis or Expression of Folk Art-Making?"

19. Roger Cardinal, "Outsider Art and the Autistic Creator," *Philosophical Transactions of the Royal Society B: Biological Sciences*, 364, no. 1522 (2009): 1459–66, 1459.

20. Roger Cardinal, "Outsider Art and the Autistic Creator," 1460.

21. Roger Cardinal, "Outsider Art and the Autistic Creator," 1460.

22. Roger Cardinal, "Outsider Art and the Autistic Creator," 1460.

23. Pollock, "A Gallery for the Outlaw: Archiving the Art of the Iconoclast," *Scholars Works*, IUPUI. Proceedings of the 2013 Association of College and Research Libraries, Indianapolis, IN, 240–45, 240, April 10–13, 2013. https://scholarworks.iupui.edu/bitstream/handle/1805/4918/PollockBattleground_Gallery.pdf?sequence=1&isAllowed=y. Accessed July 6, 2020.

24. Elizabeth Alexander, "Preface," in *The Black Interior* (Saint Paul, MN: Graywolf Press, 2004), 56.

25. David Seehausen, "Mary Proctor: Tallahasee Florida." 2009. https://www.youtube.com/watch?v=AvH60zqcpyw. Accessed March 15, 2012.

26. William Arnett, "Mary Proctor," Souls Grown Deep Foundation, http://www.soulsgrowndeep.org/artist/mary-proctor/work/i-sho-nuff-brought-sunshine-my-life-when-i-picked-paint-can.

27. Mary Proctor, "Mary Proctor's Folk Art," 2015. https://www.youtube.com/watch?app=desktop&v=F8HcZtZbi-M Accessed September 20, 2015.

28. Katherine Webb-Heln, "Don't Ignore the Life and Art of Missionary Mary Proctor," *The Bitter South.* November 1, 2016. http://bittersoutherner.com/missionary-mary-proctor-southern-folk-art

29. Katherine Webb-Heln, "Don't Ignore the Life and Art of Missionary Mary Proctor."

30. William Arnett, "Mary Proctor."
31. Steve Kistulentz, "Mary Proctor's Vision: Steve Kistulentz Discusses a Powerful New Talent from Florida," *Raw Vision*, 29 (1999–2000).
32. Steve Kistulentz, "Mary Proctor's Vision."
33. Jennifer Kosherak, "Famous Folk Artist Mary Proctor Needs Your Help," https://www.youtube.com/watch?v=reTfpeqvkoE.
34. Constance Perin, "The Reception of New, Unusual, and Difficult Art." in *The Artist Outsider: Creativity and the Boundaries of Culture*, edited by Michael D. Hall and Eugene W. Metcalf (Washington, DC: Smithsonian Institute Press, 1994), 176.
35. Seehausen, "Mary Proctor: Tallahassee Florida."
36. William Arnett, "Mary Proctor."
37. William Arnett, "Mary Proctor."
38. Steve Kistulentz, "Mary Proctor's Vision: Steve Kistulentz Discusses a Powerful New Talent from Florida," 37.
39. Mary Proctor, "Mary Proctor's Folk Art," https://www.youtube.com/watch?v=F8HcZtZbi-M. Accessed July 15, 2015.
40. Katherine Webb-Heln, "Don't Ignore the Life and Art of Missionary Mary Proctor."
41. Katherine Webb-Heln, "Don't Ignore the Life and Art of Missionary Mary Proctor."
42. Jacob Murphey, "Painted Signs from Renowned Tallahassee Artist Provide Unexpected Source of Hope Decades Later," WCTV.TV. July 10, 2020. WCTV News, https://www.wctv.tv/2020/07/11/painted-signs-from-renowned-tallahassee-artist-provide-unexpected-source-of-hope-decades-later/. Accessed July 11, 2021.
43. Mary Proctor, "I Sho Nuff Brought the Sunshine in My Life When I Picked up a Paint Can," Souls Grown Deep Foundation. http://www.soulsgrowndeep.org/artist/mary-proctor/work/i-sho-nuff-brought-sunshine-my-life-when-i-picked-paint-can.

Chapter 3

Black Women Living Religion in Cyberspace

The Zen teacher Zenju Earthlyn Manuel offers a prayer for us to claim our identity in Black spirituality, "May we all abide in Daikoku, the great Blackness of prosperity and protection."[1] In this way, she stands in the lineage of Audre Lorde's recovery of divine entities who are Black and powerful and stand ready to reach into our everyday lives. I reiterate here that Black women and their religious experience not only require an engagement with class, race, gender, and sexuality—though this is crucial—but also expose the religious figures we carry inside. Such exposure reveals where we think spiritual power really resides in the life of Black people. I open this chapter with her prayer because Black power, Black religious power is about who our gods are and their efficacy for transformation in the interior and the material world, and in the world of cyberspace.

Octavia Butler, a Baptist-raised atheist, may be correct in saying, "Religion is everywhere. There are no human societies without it, whether they acknowledge it as a religion or not,"[2] but, is the Black interiority that breaks into religion, culture, and society, everywhere? How do religion, interiority, and culture show up, tethered, in the domain of cyberspace? In this chapter, I examine three Black women's engagement of religion in cyberspace. These spiritual teachers are Monica Roberts, a transgender woman and Christian, and author of the blogsite Transgriot, Zenju Earthlyn Manuel, a Sensei in the Buddhist tradition, and Leah V. Daily, who practices Islam. The nexus between their narratives is in the way the Internet has provided an environment to carve out a space as Black women who are religious leaders and spiritual teachers.

We would do well to be ever cognizant that the Internet is a linguistic, visual, rhetorical, and communal virtual web of connectivity created out of the same "stuff"—rituals, practices, and mores—that forms and, to our collective and individual detriment, malforms our social structures and psyches in the nonvirtual world. In his overly hopeful article "Cyberspace and the Changing Landscape of the Self," prophesizing the future of the self in the light influence of the Internet, Michael Strangelove wrote in 1994,

> The internet will have a dramatic effect on the cultures and individuals that interface with it due to the relationship between geography of their community and the physical shape of their bodies. The principle is simple: change the geography of existence and you change the nature of the self.[3]

And he was onto something when we consider the use of the Internet to express the various identities that individuals, as well as groups, hold. The Internet, probably more than any other technological advancement, depicts a malleable self that is far from the unified vision that has captured much of the Western philosophical traditions. Nonetheless, the alteration of geography does not obliterate the substance of the prior geography; this is primarily because the geographies coexist and second, the self is formed out of this previous context. Furthermore, in this instance, Strangelove failed to note that the interior of the self is something akin to a vortex and pulls into itself, as constitutive, values, norms, practices, ideologies, and affect that adhere as a collective part of the self. These are not easily separated from the self which means that entry into the Internet is with the self already formed. Hence, cyberspace is a cultural site much like a local religious setting, neighborhood, city, or ethnic institution. Questions concerning identity, especially race, gender, and sexuality, have been explored with varying levels of intensity since 1990s. Lisa Nakamura has argued that the "Internet is a place where race happens. In the early days of the Net, technological visionaries imagined the online world as a utopian space where everything—even transcending racism—was possible."[4] Frankly, I did not turn to the Internet to transcend race, its allure for me was the capacity to connect with Black people, the diaspora, and particularly Black lesbians, far and wide. So, yes, the Internet is a place where race, and racism, happens. It is also a place, a space, where gender, sexuality, class, and religion "happen." The very dynamics that make Black culture, Black religion, and Blackness emerge in collective lived experience occur in cyberspace and for those for whom the Internet is a space with the potential to become Black cultural space, we bring the thwarted and realized hopes and aspirations, the longings for Black we hold in the nonvirtual spaces. The cultural tools that make their way into, for instance, storefront churches, activism and community organizing, and political rallies[5] make their way into cyberspace. Ann Swidler's observation that culture "influences action not by providing the ultimate values toward which action is oriented, but by shaping a repertoire or tool kit of habits, skills, and styles from which people construct "strategies of action"[6] is helpful, however her two models of cultural influence, where she makes a distinction between settled and unsettled cultural periods, may not represent Black women's experience. Swidler argues that during

> settled periods, culture independently influences action, but only by providing resources from which people can construct diverse lines of action. In unsettled cultural periods, explicit ideologies directly govern action, but structural opportunities for action determine which among competing ideologies survive in the long run.[7]

Black women's actions operate, religiously and otherwise, in the United States and beyond, in a context that is continuously in a tailspin of cultural unsettledness. This is the nature, force, and effect of racism-sexism-heterosexism and cyberspace is no protected vacuum; it is, in fact, a conduit for these forces and reproduction of the rhetorical, visual, and strategic display of the macabre and death dealing that operates in other domains. These forces are felt by Black women in varying degrees depending on social location and identity even if, as in the case, for instance, of heterosexism, some marginalized Black women may not feel the full brunt of its weight or its effect because they identify as heterosexual. However, even in this instance, the rules of heterosexuality, which are linked to gender identity and representation, may not be felt because one has internalized the rules of being "woman" or "female" as normal, right, and even good for society, and religious expression. Rules of engagement, that is, the linguistic, behavior, feelings, thoughts, and dress that reflect social expectations of gender, race, class, and sexuality, are not static but when viewed through the lens of Black women's lives, they have a way of insisting on Black women's compliance and concurrently negative representations of Black women, and the presumed lack of agency and subjectivity. In cyberspace, religion is a site for complicating religion: it can communicate compliance while embodying by the very acts of teaching, preaching, and posting pictures the signification of strategic resistance to rules of constriction of identity and restriction of religious leadership. Thus, cyberspace can serve to mediate, shape, and create identity, religion, and culture.

Mary Pattillo-McCoy directed our attention to the means whereby Black religious codes of performance provide the cultural scaffold for other, seemingly nonreligious, sites of Black culture. She argues that Black religious experience is also the pattern one can observe in Black neighborhood public activities. The dynamic exchange is heard in

> prayer, call-and-response interaction, and Christian imagery are important parts of the cultural "tool kit" of Groveland's (the Chicago neighborhood she studied)

Black residents, and these cultural practices invigorate activism . . . Black church culture constitutes the taken-for-granted practices that put civic efforts into action.[8]

The tool kit comprising Black church practices is part and parcel to those whose religious identities are informed by Christianity or Christian spirituality. There is not, of course, a total blanket overlay onto Black civic life and activism because Black experience is much broader than Christianity; however, the Black tool kit's ethos has made its way into the fabric of Black culture such that it is familiar to many who not identify as Black protestant. We can hear the toolkit in cultural productions such as music, the imagery in literature, art, and activism. Black women's religious expression in cyberspace reflects this ethos, given the male centeredness of Black religious contexts, and can disrupt it. This means that whether adopting it or transforming it, Black women in cyberspace are in dialogue with Black religious cultural configurations because these configurations are internalized whether adopted or rejected. Within the interior, Black religious tropes, sounds, and cultural ways are operative and make their way into cyberspace.

Cyberspace has the potential to offer opportunities for being religious in new ways. However, we should note that cyberspace, as a tool of opportunity, has also proven to be a site for the surveillance and enforcement of religious and cultural rules—much like the panopticon designed by Jeremy Bentham in 1787 as a model for prison.[9] The ever-increasing global surveillance suggest that optic of "inspection" has transcended the architecture of brick and mortar in the creation of cyberspace. An example is individuals trolling for vicarious experiences, hidden spyware, and web cameras. A more dangerous example, and closer to his original idea, is government-sanctioned surveillance through infiltration, analytics research (think the Facebook/Cambridge Analytics scandal of 2018), and, to some degree, Amazon's Alexa feature of "always listening." The result can be living a Black life under siege, described by Townes as Black people living "within a panopticon in which people who often demonstrate meticulous illiteracy about Black lives watch them and judge them"[10] and then regurgitate images of worthlessness into the atmosphere as fact and truth. However, the panopticon can also be, and is, resisted by Black women in their use of their agency to create, to project onto and in cyberspace, their identity. Cyberspace then is created by, and is a facilitating environment and a container, for Black experience.

CYBERSPACE AS ARTIFACT AND CULTURAL CONTAINER

In ascertaining the potential of cyberspace, we will need to remember that the rhetorical strategies used in public spaces to preserve the hierarchies of race and gender, and sexuality and class, are appropriated in cyberspace even if they are not lived in the exact same way. There are no intersectional free zones—materially or virtually. Cyberspace is a place where intersectionality lives because it is an artifact of culture and, simultaneously, a discursive, expansive and fluid, container for cultural productions. Thus, culture shows up in many forms and it is pervasive. It stands to reason that religion shows up in many forms.

Black women, and Black experience in general, are noticeably underrepresented in the rapidly proliferating research literature on cyberspace and religion. When represented, such research often suffers from "the general failure to fully recognize people with intersecting identities as members of their constituent groups."[11] As a result, research highlighting marginalization based on, for instance, race without attention to class, gender, and sexuality. Such strategies may serve the limited needs of the framework of the researcher but fail to account for interlocking forces at play.[12] As a result, the intersection of race, genders, sexualities, and classes, as integral to religious experience and public practices, goes unrecognized and, therefore, not theorized. These facets of lived religion and spirituality are then rendered invisible. If taken at face value, the research profile would suggest that Black women as practitioners of religion have no place or impact in cyberspace or in the religious thought, formation of devotees, or the articulation of public theologies that may be discerned through an analysis of cyberspace.

The Internet is fertile ground for an intersectional ethnography of religion and culture. Cyberspace as a site for, and of, cultural production is still relatively new. The Internet was invented between 1962 and 1983, and Internet service providers, for a fee, began proliferating in the 1990s. So, in just 56 years, the Internet has become the force within the workplace, social lives, politics, news, religion, and spirituality. The Pew Research Center reported in 2000 that African Americans use the Internet to search for places to live and research major life issues and religious or spiritual information.[13] In spite of the research showing that higher income and education correlate with higher uses of the Internet, and that there is a wide gap between Blacks and whites in Internet usage corresponding to the asymmetrical income differences between Blacks and whites, the Internet has proven to be a site for cultural engagement among Black Americans in the United States. Pew also reported that in 2000, 47 percent of Blacks accessed the Internet for the first time in 1999, and that Black women were leading the surge and "represent 61% of the African-American Internet newcomers. . . . In just the past six months, about 1.2 million African-American women accessed the Internet for the first time, compared to approximately 750,000 African-American men."[14] Obviously, Black women are in virtual and nonvirtual spaces.

This chapter explores how Black women practice religion and spirituality in cyberspace and what we can ascertain about the intersection of interiority and the sociocultural in religious experience situated in the virtual world. This is an epistemological shift in womanist perspectives on Black women's lives. Womanist scholars, particularly pastoral and practical theologians, who are residents in cyberspace, have not given a robust examination of what religion in cyberspace might mean for Black women or our theorizing of self, community, culture, religious practice, or for Black women's experience in other, nonvirtual aspects of their public and private life. Focusing our attention on this requires the dispositional shift toward an ethnographic sensibility and perspective in our work. Carole McGranahan's approach to teaching students to develop an ethnographic sensitivity is helpful. McGranahan seeks to

> cultivate a concept, awareness, and practice of an ethnographic sensibility, that is, of a sense of the ethnographic as the lived expectations, complexities, contradictions, possibilities, and ground of any given cultural group. Such a view opens an . . . ethnographic approach to be an epistemological one.[15]

This is in keeping with a womanist epistemology that is grounded in real-life experience, with all the complexities of intersectional realities in being Black women. A womanist ethnographic sensibility means that we expect complexity and difference among Black women's experience of race, gender, sexuality, class, and relationship to religion.

As a womanist and psychoanalyst, there are several concepts that undergird the ethnographic sensibility I bring to my understanding of cyberspace. First is the idea that cyberspace is an interior construct; that is, cyberspace is an experience one has. Second, cyberspace exists as a place one visits (thus it has an existence beyond my presence). Third, cyberspace is a facilitating container for the formation of self and identity, and thus is a self-cultural object; fourth, cyberspace is a place for the experience, creation, and formation of community. Fifth, cyberspace, because of the preceding conceptualizations, is a site for the practice of religion.

These five descriptions collectively fall into the realm of interior-social space. Specifically, from a psychoanalytical perspective, they form a cultural selfobject milieu; that is, a site where cultural artifacts and actions are related to as both reflecting one's cultural identifications—and as an interior dimension of one's self. As such, these kinds of identifications provide opportunities wherein one feels mirrored, in kinship with others, or is exposed to idealizable aspects of culture. It is the artifact and the experience dimensions that signal the simultaneity of the interior-social. Julian M. Murchison and Curtis Coats have also turned to psychoanalytic theory to suggest that cyberspace is a "third space, hybrid, in between spaces of religious practice."[16] Third space has critically been more conceptualized by Randall Packer as those places distinct from home, designated as first space, or work, defined as second space.[17] Third space then is public space "where the individual can experience a transformative sense of self, identity, and relation to others." When viewed in cyberspace spaces, it is cultural, transformative, and social space. Packer argues that in this third space, boundaries are blurred and eventually crumple. In the crumbling, a new hybrid space emerges.

> Our new concept of the third space thus extends the model of the transformative social space into the online medium by suggesting a hybrid space that allows remote participants to transcend the limitations of spatial, geographic, and cultural differences as they engage with one another.[18]

This leads us to the notion of cyberspace as an emergent space wherein the nature of the space becomes as it is when engaged by particular parties. It is the engagement that creates the process for experience and the space as, for instance, religious space. Thus, Black religious experience does not just exist in toto but is more akin to the forming and movement of a whirlwind swirling into existence within cyberspace.

TRANSGENDER*ING* RELIGION IN THE BLOGOSPHERE

Unlike Alecia Brown, Monica Roberts's call to cyberspace was not to denominational pastoral ordination but rather to her public role as a griot. Roberts died, shortly after I completed the draft of *Tilling Sacred Grounds*, in October 2020. Her blogsite remains alive and available for the public to continue to benefit from the wisdom of her griot's voice. The griot is most often thought of as the storyteller who holds the culture, values, and hopes of the community, and reflects to the community the places where it needs to change. The griot relies on wisdom, multiple ways of knowing, and the telling of stories; for Roberts, her griot role was embodied in cyberspace and public social activism. Roberts was a transwoman and advocated for transpeople's right to exist and thrive. She did not reference her upbringing much on her blogsite, "Transgriot," but offered snapshots of her life as a transwoman, activist, and womanist in a misogynistic and sexist world. Religion was a crucial aspect of how she makes her way in the world. It was as important as a source of strength, comfort, and moral that influences her life and worldview. She resisted those who dismissed, in trans circles, Black religious experience.

Roberts was a true southerner and a Texan from Houston. She was born in 1992 to a mother who was a teacher and her father, a DJ. Houston was decidedly part of the segregated south. She grew up in a Black conservative church where her family was active and she, as expected, was baptized young. Her religious convictions and sensibilities permeated her approach to life even when she disavowed those religious beliefs that dehumanized those identifying as LGBTQ. She began the Transgriot blogsite in 2006 and continued to post regularly until her death. The message she articulated as the Transgriot resonates with womanist activist pastors in her attention to faith, interiority, gender, diasporic identity, and justice. Described as both generous and fierce, many in the LGBTQ, especially trans, communities continue to mourn her untimely death at 58.[19] Death, however, has not silenced her trans-loving, justice-centered griot voice. On the Transgriot blogsite, messages continue to speak to realize its mission.

> The Trans Griot blog's mission is to become the griot of our community . . . to speak truth to power, . . . from an Afrocentric perspective.[20]

Roberts's religious sensibilities existed as a constant in her life. In addition to addressing racism and homophobia as intersectional points of oppression, she critiqued anti-religious stance of many white trans activists and pointed out the difference race and social location make in regard to the importance of religious experience. She argued that a difference between white and Black trans people is how religion operates in Black lives; her perspective rested on the interiority of religion in that religion is a glue—a force that serves to give direction in life and a source of strength when obstacles and struggles arise. She needed religion in her life but also as an ingredient, as it were, of her evolving-transitioning self.

BORN GOOD: MORAL FORMATION AND FAITH

Roberts sustained her relationship to religion in contrast to many of the white trans folks that she encountered in the wider trans community.

> I have noted . . . the sometimes-outright hostility . . . in the trans community concerning faith and spirituality . . . I was baptized at my home church in Houston 40 years ago . . . faith has been an integral part of my life. I couldn't have made it without it.[21]

Roberts's Christian faith was her compass in life. Roberts's emotional and moral formation was tied to religion and activism. Unlike many white trans folk she encountered, who are suspicious of religion and reject religious people, for Roberts, religious practice made her a better human being. Drawing on the spiritual teacher Susan Taylor, who wrote that wisdom and power can be accessed through inner knowledge, and that "we are not powerless spectators of life. We are co-creators with God, and all around us are the gifts, the clay that we can use to shape our world,"[22] Roberts centered herself in the conviction that she, as a transgender woman, was born, and is, as a cocreator with God. This cocreator status provided her an anchor and ethical guide post, vocational frame, and her commitment to internal and social transformation. The nexus between this cocreator status and interior and social transformation was inextricable. The theological anthropology Roberts entwined in her teachings, however, took seriously the psychic damage inflicted on trans people in a trans-antagonistic society

> the problem . . . is the challenge of gender transition while dealing with the unholy trinity of shame, fear and guilt.[23]

Roberts interrogates Black trans interiority to evoke the power of self-agency as a crucial aspect to transforming psychic and social terrains. She demanded that Black trans people expel guilt and shame from within and recognize their own humanity among the "diverse mosaic of human life" and embrace their identity as "Black and trans" with pride.

> The shame, guilt and fear at times had such a power . . . that many people transitioned, melted away . . . never let anyone know they were trans.[24]

The next movement of transformation is to embody this assertion in Black spaces and collaborate in the work of Black liberation as full members. Roberts argued for a Black trans theological anthropology that critiqued the half-steps that settle for tolerance in place of dismantling Black heterosexism privilege. Her receptivity to religious experience emerged from her deep conviction that Black trans people are created in the image of God and, from this flat-footed position, she demanded other Black Christians to recognize Black trans Christians as full members theologically and in practice. She did not petition for a seat at the table; she presumed it, and where resistance to Black trans people emerges, she demanded it. She was not waiting for a place to be created for her humanity to be mirrored to flourish; she accepted herself, and her baptism guaranteed her place at the table. "Trans people . . . are part of the Kente cloth fabric of the African-American community."[25] Roberts arrived at this place after a long process, like many other Black women, without a roadmap or support, except religion. And it was this lack of roadmap that motivated Roberts to publicly claim a "mission is to become the griot" for the Black trans community.

CALL AND RESPONSE: TRANS PUBLIC RELIGION AND INTERIOR TRANSFORMATION

Roberts's work is an example of public theology and lived religion and the nexus between them. Her understanding of the place and function of religion was first, its ability to sustain people in the work for justice and, thus, address basic existential questions related to self-recognition by others. In this understanding, religion is the pulse that runs through private and public life and its intention or mission is social and political transformation. It is the force through which her call to serve as a griot to the Black trans community was heard.

Roberts turned much of attention to the murder of Black and brown trans women and men in her griot ministry because they were often ignored and under-investigated. In an audio interview on "Collections with Michelle Brown," Roberts's righteous anger about the continuing violence was evocative of a Black church preacher calling for repentance and change or face hell and damnation.

> Trans people . . . must . . . step up to leadership roles in our communities of faith. So, . . . find an accepting church.[26]

Roberts, still harkening Taylor, reminded readers that fear pervades a life without faith and situates trans people's experience in relation to those enslaved in the past. Enslavement, she asserted, was far worse, and it was faith that sustained those who survived its horror. In her own life, faith helped her fight against the hostility of transphobia outside the trans community, racism within the trans community, and the debilitating theologies that shame Black transgender people. Faith is necessary.

When Roberts was transitioning in the late 1990s, she did not have a template to follow. There was no Black transwoman to turn to for advice and guidance. The Transwomen of Color Collective did not exist. Janet Mock was not a household name. Lavergne Cox had not garnered her role on *Orange Is the New Black* Netflix series. Isolation during a process of consolidating her gender and public representation enforced the necessity of the spiritual practices she learned early in her religious life and her griot teachings admonishes the Black trans community to attend to the spiritual as they nurture gender and racial aspects of self. The failure to nurture one's spiritual life has negative implications for the individual's sense of self. An integral dimension to her griot spiritual teaching was the message that a spiritual life requires intentionality and consistency. The consistency not only counters negative messages about Black transgender embodiment, it reinforces Roberts's God image as one who stands with Black transgender people. This is a psycho-spirituality that works to dismantle the interiority of "shame, fear, and guilt" to be replaced by a deeper sense of one's humanity and in relation to one's God. "If we don't take that time to meditate, pray, and develop the spiritual sides of our humanity, ... doubt and the unholy trinity of shame, fear and guilt creep back into our lives."[27] Thus, the interior and God-talk are entangled. Where one experiences God as being on the frontlines of demanding a place at the table, shame, fear, and guilt dissipate. This engenders the internal space to experience oneself as good.

Roberts realized that Black trans folk who have given up on religion have done so because of the mistreatment and shame-inducing theologies they were subjected to in Black churches. For many, their churches preached negative messages about women, sexuality, and transgender experience. "It's understandable . . . you have major issues with organized religion" because "the bigots . . . wrap themselves in religious cloaks and use the Bible as a baton to beat people."[28] However, Roberts reminded Black trans people that they undertake the path of transition so that they can begin living authentically and that this authenticity is religious experience: The griot in her called the Black trans community to recognize that the interior, spiritual, and social combine as one attempts to live into a sense of being created by God, and living into an awareness of the imago dei transforms the interior tyranny of "internalized shame, guilt and fear"[29] and barricades one against the social messages that impose them.

Roberts's commitment to intertwining her theology and activism converged in a trans womanist identity—a move she described in 2009 as "coming out of the closet so to speak about being a womanist."[30] In the 12 years, Roberts maintained the transgriot.com blogsite, she only discussed in two, clear and cogent posts, her identity as a womanist. In her post titled "Journey to Womanist-hood," she underscored several reasons for her movement from feminist to womanist. The first was her critique of white feminists' racism. She traced one of the roots of this racism to 1870 when Black men one the right to vote before white women. She read the Democratic Party's 2008 path to the presidency as an example of white feminists' refusal to examine their biased attention to sexism. According to Roberts, white feminists defended Hilary Clinton at every opportunity but when Michelle Obama was under racist and sexist attacks, they, she argued, remained silent. Roberts wondered if they were unable to recognize Michelle Obama as a woman.[31]

The second impetus for Roberts to self-identify as womanist was the growing number of Black women in her circle who identified as womanists. The sense of kinship and belonging they effected stimulated her intellectual interests as well as her desire to belong with Black women who were challenging sexism and racism, and "fit her worldview."[32] Even so, she was reticent to publicly announce her identification as a womanist because she was anxious about some cisgender womanists, both latent and blatant, anti-trans attitudes, and whether these womanist would accept her as a woman.[33] Roberts's decision to finally name herself womanist was due to her sense of an interior transformation that buttressed her self-acceptance and led to her sense of subjectivity and agency. She recognized that she had the power to name herself a womanist even if some cisgender womanists were not ready to receive Black transwomen. Roberts's transformation was public, social, and interior and embodied in cyberspace intentionally.

The fluidity of cyberspace mirrors the interiority of Roberts's movement between self, community, and public spaces.

> I know my journey is far from over, but I intend to be a compliment to all that the pioneering womanist thought leaders have built. I want to continue taking major steps to bridge the knowledge gap between my cisgender sisters and my transsisters, and collectively work together.[34]

In her post "Womanists Have Not Disrespected My Humanity," Roberts expanded her identity to include womanism and expanded the context for womanist identifications.[35]

> We need clarification on what we African descended transwomen can do to help womanism seize on its golden opportunity to embrace their trans sisters, building on the inclusive principles that attract us to it in the first place and shape its ... forward momentum.[36]

Roberts levied a critique of US Black womanists' parochialism and limited perception of Black women:

> I'm more of an Africana womanist, ... I'm not only concerned about women of color here ... but across the African Diaspora.[37]

Roberts's movement from interior to social was marked by this major shift in her griot identity and occurred as her relationship to Black culture, Africana, and diasporic womanism expanded—in the third space of cyberspace. As her sense of kinship with Black women deepened, so did her religious leadership as a Transgriot.

In her blog report on the 2012 Transfaith in Color Conference, Roberts reported that

> we had seminars over the three days of TFIC 2012 that covered a wide array of topics from becoming a man or woman to *spirituality* while being trans. There was a fascinating *Afrocentric welcoming ceremony* Friday night and a *closing church service*.[38]

Roberts used this space to call Black trans folk to inner transformation through public activism and to confront negative representations of Black people in white spaces and anti-LGBTQI in Black religious spaces.

Roberts's Transgriot religious and cultural identity was diasporic and she increasingly pursued every opportunity to situate her work from a trans diasporic womanist particularity:

> I also found myself in . . . intergenerational conversations . . . with youth of Trini, Haitian and Nigerian heritage . . . we discussed . . . our . . . history, and where Black LGBT people fit.

Roberts enabled us to see how an appreciative sensibility (for language, practices, theologies, attitudes) *toward* Black religion, in cyberspace, generates, through iterative processes, can reveal Black cultural spaces where religion is operative. Furthermore, interiority, and sociality enact and reenact religion while also facilitating a religious social ethic:

> What happens to African descended trans people . . . *IS my business. I have a responsibility* to get those stories out . . . *We are all accountable* to each other.[39]

REMEMBRANCE AS COMMUNITY CARE

Monica Roberts's exhortation to herself and the wider digital trans community calls to mind a litany of the saints who are living and those who have crossed over. Her cyberspace presence is riddled with sites where she names the trans women who have died but were misnamed and misgendered by reporters, law enforcement, and even family. The women on the list were subjected to transphobia during and after their deaths through misgendering, poor investigative work, and blatant disregard for their humanity.[40]

In her role as the Transgriot, she continuously called out their names and created a digital space for litanies, a moment of reckoning, and an inviting space for those still making their way into their Black trans identity and trans pride. One such call out occurred when Roberts posted the story of Sadie, a young white trans girl. In reflecting on Sadie's story, Roberts admonished the community to remember that both the voices of the elders and the young have their own wisdom to share with the community—"We not only need to be paying attention to the wise words of our trans elders, but the wise words of trans kids like yourself as well."[41] She preached a theology centered on Black trans peoples' ontological and inherent worth. In true womanist form, Roberts privileged Black trans particularity, and Black trans women's lives, as the source and center of her transformative message. She marshaled the power of testimony and testifying as she creates space for the newly initiated and the elders. Cyberspace was her sanctuary, her altar, and pulpit, and she joined other cybergriots in making activism and transreligious experience visible.

BLACK ZEN BUDDHIST TEACHING IN CYBERSPACE

We each require a guide, who is internalized and held dear; one who challenges us and comforts. We require a guide who loves us. It matters not if she is across an ocean or has entered the realm of the ancestors and saints or that she may never have met you in person. Find you guide.[42]

I first encountered the teaching of Buddhist teacher Zenju Earthlyn Marselean Manuel, a Sensei,[43] in preparation for teaching a class on Black women and religion. I wanted students to understand that Black religious experience is not chained to Christianity and that Black Christianity is not locked into white Christian experience. She embodies the idea of Black women living religion in cyberspace. She teaches on her website zenju.org; she facilitates retreats, offers meditation, and conducts online tea rituals. She is the author of four books and each one emerged from her reflection on her lived experience and each one has also been the foundation for individual and group retreats. Among Black Buddhists in the United States, she is one of the most prolific. Her voice is strong, clear, and consistent. When teaching, her chestnut brown face can reflect a glow. She stands straight in Zen robes and her almost bald head leans back easily when she laughs, not infrequently at herself.

Having discovered her teachings and the path leading to her spiritual and cultural identities intrigued me. She offered, in two sentences, the multiplicity of spiritual and cultural influences in the development and sense of self.

> Zenju was raised in the Church of Christ where she was an avid reader of the Bible and adored the true teachings on Christ's path well into adulthood. She also participated in ceremony with Ifá diviners from Dahomey, Africa and studied Yoruba.[44]

This snippet does not convey all that converged in her life to form her into the spiritual teacher she is, but it depicts her teaching style—a brief paragraph reveals much about her disposition to life and spirituality. While she was born in Los Angeles, California, in 1955, her roots are Haitian Creole in rural Louisiana. Manuel's parents were born in the culture of Jim Crow sharecropping, lynching, and starvation Louisiana—her father was born in 1898 and her mother in 1910. She is the granddaughter of Marselean, a child slave and her father's mother. She is the daughter of Lawrence Manuel Sr. and Alvesta Pierre Manuel. She has two sisters, one younger and an older sister. Her mother named her Earthlyn, and Zenju was bestowed upon her Buddhist ordination.

Zenju recalls the Church of God as the place that held Black life as worth saving religiously and physically. Sanctuary space made an everyday living and survival was entwined with the religious and spiritual discourse.

> I remember how the church was our sanctuary . . . Church members helped . . . with gaining employment, sharing housing, and buy food, or . . . doctor bill. . . . The church grew us into ourselves despite the hatred against Black people. . . . So, sanctuary . . . was about sustaining sanity in a world that threatened our lives.[45]

Zenju takes her Blackness as inextricable from her Buddhist life but it was not just the Church of God that she took with her. She recalled that when her father was in the hospital and she went to visit him, she tried to ward off other peoples' illnesses entering her because she was a receiver. "I needed protection, talisman or juju, as I later found that my mother secretly wore."[46] Zenju brought this from her family's Haitian African spiritual beliefs that offered more than acknowledgment of suffering but directed them to beauty of Black spirituality.[47]

I had wanted to have her become my teacher and spiritual guide. She had somehow managed to integrate these spiritual paths in the life she lives as a Zen Buddhist of the Suzuki Roshi lineage. She is a drummer and a vision dreamer. A calligrapher, poet, and writer. She describes herself as Black, woman, lesbian, short, Buddhist. Her narrative is coherent where it could have presented as fragmented, painful where it could have been rageful, and rageful where it might have been sublimated into an insipid spirituality. She is complex, her life is complex, and her relationship with religion is complex. I resonated with her desire and determination to make meaning. I quickly learned that she was no longer accepting new students but she made her spiritual teachings available on her website and from this vantage, I began to not only learn from her but to interview her. If a teaching raised a question for me, I searched her responses on her website and other Buddhist sites. In time, the narratives of her spiritual life emerged.

Zenju, in many ways, presents as a "spiritual daughter" of Audre Lorde. Her spirituality is a bricolage of experiences. As with Lorde, her roots, by way of her paternal grandmother, are Caribbean though, specifically, Haiti. Unlike Lorde, her paternal grandmother was enslaved as a child, and Zenju's last name, Manuel, "is Haitian Creole passed down from slave owners (lest we forget)."[48] Like Lorde, her path to her spiritual home has been a process of integrating—again, a bricolage but one that reflects the teachings of Buddhism without renouncing other spiritual teachings she has encountered and internalized along the way. And like Lorde, Zenju's spiritual path was a path into her Blackness, sexuality, and gender but also class awareness. This awareness is acquired through practice and meditation:

> Meditation is a source of creative engagement, which means meditation is a total experience of life with each breath, each moment. When we sit in meditation, we turn the light inward with our breath. The light enables us to see how we engage with others, with life.[49]

Home[50] is a recurring theme in Zenju's teachings and writing. In teaching "Be Home, Be Still" she invites readers into her interior and social experience of homelessness as lived by a Zen Buddhist teacher. While attempting to buy a home in Oakland, California, in part because gentrification was making renting impossible, she and her partner experienced months of homelessness including a period where Zenju lived out of her car. When a Sensei becomes homeless, students can be anxious and project it onto the Sensei in intrusive ways, especially in the form of spiritual questions. "What lessons are you to learn around home? You have moved a lot." Zenju initially refused the "analytical" question because she was in the thick of suffering.[51] And yet, as a spiritual teacher she must hold, be a container for, students' anxieties as she offers a deeper Zen teaching.

> In some indigenous cultures and in Buddha's teachings, there is what is called initiation or time spent in life where one is constantly going through major life events that include loss and gain. These initiations are continuous.[52]

Zenju is a Black Sensei and must hear the spiritual in light of the socioeconomic and political context bearing down on poor, Black and brown people. And so, her spiritual teaching includes the interlocking structures of classism and racism. "Of course, my political stance rears its head and says many of us are being pushed out of our homes and the rental fees are meant for those making six figure salaries (despite their credit scores)." In so doing, she is highlighting the ways in which Oakland, California, is creating white affluent spaces by destroying working-class brown spaces. The threads of home/lessness, poverty, and racism are interwoven in her spiritual teachings in part because she never loses sight of her ancestral roots in Louisiana where her family went from enslavement to rural and then, urban poverty but where they also passed on their creole, Haitian, spiritual, and cultural teachings. For Zenju home is physical, spiritual, and cultural.

"CHOQUETTE" AND WOMANIST AUDACIOUS SENSIBILITIES

In the early phase of her cyberspace presence, Sensei was most frequently referred to as Zenju, a part of her ordination name.

> I was given the dharma name Ekai Zenju, which translates as Wisdom Ocean (Ekai), Complete Tenderness (Zenju). . . . my teacher told me that the second name is given as the path one is to explore, so I began to call myself Zenju in a quest to discover a lived experience of the name's essence.[53]

The movement to Sensei is most obviously connected to the transmission of the Dharma from her teacher, a process that allowed Zenju to teach and found a Sangha after her ordination. Becoming a Sensei also seems connected to the shift brought about by her deeper consciousness about herself as a diasporic, Black, lesbian, creole, Buddhist woman and the havoc society has wrought in her life. The deeper she engaged all the parts of her life, the stronger her Sensei voice emerges.

> It was clear at the beginning of my exploration that I had been hardened by the physical violence leveled against me. As a young child and the by the poverty with which my had to struggle as Louisiana migrants.[54]

> I had been hurt as a child when I discovered that others saw my dark body as ugly. And . . . I lived in fear of being annihilated for taking a woman as a lover . . . I had grown bound to feelings of injustice, rage, and resentment. . . . So how does someone who experienced deep hatred, . . . become Zenju?[55]

But it is also a result of her reflection on Black feminist and womanist cultural ways of being. After hearing a podcast interview where bell hooks (also a Buddhist) and Melissa Harris Perry called on the ancestral woman writers Audre Lorde, Pat Parker, and Zora Neale Hurston, Zenju experienced a sense of sisterhood with a womanist. During the interview, bell hooks described these writers as "as Black women voices of dissonance."[56] For Zenju, dissonance involves the refusal to ignore race, sexuality, and gender because "to investigate race, sexuality and gender is to go against the stream that the self is not dependent but interdependent of everyone and everything" to do otherwise "leaves out the emotional, empowering or positive effect of identity on those who are socially and politically objectified."[57] Harris Perry and hooks were embodying Black dissonance and Zenju aligned herself in the genealogy of Black women writers.

Zenju experienced a sense of kinship culturally and psychologically. As I have asserted previously, the cultural and psychological are fused in a womanist perspective on kinship, and conceptual schemas that separate them, do violence to Black experience. The cultural dimension is a repeated dimension of Zenju's spiritual teachings as well as her critical analysis. Harris Perry and hooks did not discuss Alice Walker's elaboration of the idea of "womanist," but the term immediately came to Zenju's mind.

Walker's term emerged from her reflection on Black southern women's cultural experience, especially those from southern rural agricultural contexts, but also urban Black southern women and those who migrated north with their southern ways fully internalized, embodied, and reflected in communal engagements. In other words, the term "womanist" held in its definition Black-gendered communal ethos, religious (mostly Protestant Christian) and spiritual practices, linguistic cadences and nuance, and Black women's responses to the sociopolitical surround. In epigrammatic prose, Walker described Black women's psychocultural development of becoming and being Black women. The intergenerational exchange, explicit and implied in Walker's definition, mirrored Zenju's sense of self—and we can see how her interior, cultural, and social converged:

> From womanist. (Opp. Of "girlish," i.e., frivolous, irresponsible, not serious ... outrageous, audacious, courageous, or willful behavior.[58]

For Zenju, there was an immediacy of an interior-social reverberation:

> The word and its meaning helped me to understand the reasons my mother called me the Creole name Choquette, which means sassy. I felt included.[59]

And she felt seen.

> Those of us whose ancestors would not let hatred rob them of life or destroy the possibility of future generations, are still part of who we are. We are still here and we are everywhere wielding the torch of prolonged audaciousness.[60]

Zenju was already a well-known presenter of Zen Buddhism for many years but her experience of the interview between hooks and Harris Perry reveals the complexity of the kinship. In addition to the similarity between Black southern women and Black creole women's relationship with their daughters, Zenju's kinship experience also suggests that the current and contemporary experience of being Black women reverberated for her. Her sense of being included was related to all of them being Black, embodied women.

CYBERSPACE SANGHA: THE PATH OF EMBODIMENT AND RAGE IN SPIRITUAL TRANSFORMATION

> The challenges of race, sexuality, and gender are the very things that the spiritual path to awakening requires us to tend to as aspirants to peace
> —Sensei Zenju Earthlyn Manuel

Whereas many teachers of Buddhism teach that rage is an impediment to spiritual life, Zenju, teaches a different Dharma. She sees the potential in rage to be "life-giving and illuminating" and a catalyst to "fuel a transformation toward awakening."[61] In her essay "Awakening Fueled by Rage," in the June 2020 issue of *Lion's Roar: Buddhist Wisdom for Our Time*, Zenju is writing in the maelstrom of the killing of George Floyd, Breanna Taylor, Rayshard Brooks, and Tony McDade at the hands of the police and the Covid-19 pandemic infecting and killing Black people at three times the rate of white people.[62] Her essay links rage, Dharma teachings, and responses to Black body:

> Many, because I interweave my experience of Blackness with Buddhist teachings, assume my teachings are limited to skin color . . . some students and teachers do not see me as a legitimate Zen teacher.[63]

As a Black Buddhist teacher, Sensei Zenju does not split off her rage evoked by racism but focuses on the work of transformation. She has closed the brick-and-mortar center, still breathing Zen Sangha, and has closed the open meditation meetings. She now focuses, primarily, on local Zen students of the African descent.

She does this because she knows that "we don't suffer that all lives matter; we suffer that Black and brown lives are not mattering. We suffer in the bodies that we have."[64] In some white Buddhist spaces, people of color are often expected to leave their Black cultural identities, and social location, outside the Sangha spaces. Such spoken and implied messages demand that Black and brown practitioners disavow their racial identity—as well as class, gender, and sexuality. The three Jewels of Buddhism—Buddha, Dharma (teachings), and Sangha (community)—are then whitewashed as a requirement for spiritual growth. In some settings, Sensei Zenju, in her teaching teacher role, is sought after because she is a Black Zen teacher and by having her teach announces the Sangha's interest in diversity. In reality, Blackness is rendered invisible in the process. As enraging as such expectations are, as a Dharma teacher she is expected to disavow and rise above her rage.

> Yet the rage persists. Tears fall. I know it to be the sacred fire of passion, a burning, from which I am able to speak on injustice from a place that includes the liberation of all beings.[65]

In her teaching "The Lived Experience as the Gateway to Freedom" posted to YouTube, Jan Willis, another Black Zen Buddhist and professor emerita of religion at Wesleyan University, agrees that Black people carry the trauma in "in the deepest recesses of our souls"[66] and is, in fact, the foremost issue to be faced. The intergenerational legacy of enslavement, often disavowed and split off from our awareness, is carried in psychic, spiritual, cultural, and communal processes. And it is carried in Black bodies, and cannot be "denied, forgotten, . . . suppressed. . . . Buddhism . . . provides methods . . . to get at those deep inner wounds and how to heal them."[67] Zenju, as well as other Black Buddhists, such as Willis, Angel Kyodo Williams, and Ruth King, asserts each in her own way that we do not avoid these painful experiences—"We must come through the fire of our lives to experience awakening."[68]

The awakening comes through or with one's body. The body is the path in which liberation rises and attempts to circumvent the body through spirituality is not possible. In fact, Sensei Zenju asserts in her teachings that our body is a requirement for engaging life and eschews the dualism that purports that the body must be renounced in pursuit of the spiritual life. "Given the relationship between awakening and the body, we must explore the surfaces of this body—it's race, sexuality, and gender—in relation to awakening at its heart."[69] The awakening of the heart, through a real awakening to the body and the hatreds directed at Black bodies, is, a way into tenderness, an orientation to the world and one's self.

> The way of tenderness is an experiential, nonintellectual, heartfelt acknowledgement of all embodied difference. It keeps alive the vow not to kill.[70]

For Audre Lorde, it was her prayers to Black female gods, especially in the form of poetry, that kept her from killing when overwhelmed by racist-induced rage, even though the desire to give rage license to strike was intense. Zenju teaches that it is the practice of meditation—in various forms (mind, heart, calligraphy, ritual, breathing) with attention to her Black body that sets her vow to not kill, in her heart and actions. She, like Lorde, teaches that rage can destroy or transform,

> rage, like fire . . . can be harmful, burning away everything in its path. But rage can also be life-giving, illuminating that which must be exposed before humanity can shift into a greater experience of interrelationship and love. . . . I've learned to use my rage to fuel a transformation toward awakening.[71]

Both are teaching about the slow process of transformation.

Zenju's spiritual presence on the Internet reveals the fluid nature of the container function of the Internet as well as understanding of the self as fluid and evolving.

The evolution of my life keeps me from saying I am this or that. My priest robe wraps around and embraces all the ways in which this life expresses itself. If it is the robe that you see, I bow to that. If it is the robe that you don't see, I bow to that. Aché.[72]

This fluidity is integral to the process of consciousness of struggle. Left in the realm of unconsciousness, the struggles we carry make their way into the path for liberation and we impose our suffering on those who are around us, including Sangha, activists, and family. Being conscious in our struggles is essential or will burn down the dream.[73] Zenju understands the complex nature of containers and recognizes this complex dimension in lived experience in the spiritual and political contexts of experience. This awareness, she teaches, comes from remembering the spiritual lessons of her ancestors.

When I entered the path of Dharma, I came with a collective sense of suffering. . . . In other words, spiritual awakening required attention to social injustices.[74]

Consciousness requires knowledge of the profound depth of experience. It is acquired through meditation and internalizing the Dharma, not for memorization, but for transformation. In all her teachings, she admonishes that true consciousness is pervasive and fosters deep interconnectedness beyond the immediate Sangha because in so doing "carve a path through the flames of our human condition. We must see it for what it is, and bow to it.[75] This courageous consciousness is countercultural to a society that avoids real introspection—soul-searching examination—and leaves in its wake more suffering especially in the forms of racism, sexism, homophobia, and colorism.[76] Consciousness helps us to know that the misrepresentations of Blackness, gender, sexuality, and queer being are not mirror images even though they inflict deep pain and distort the interior. The Sangha is to contain the suffering and heal the community, but in order for healing to occur, systemic oppression in Buddhist centers and society must be addressed, and the damage inflicted on the interior faced.[77]

That's where the hate is . . . I can feel the sadness . . . I'm not acceptable in this world as who I am. . . . Maybe because I'm short or a dyke ... I've had people run from me . . . I'm still the pariah. I had to have a practice to survive. Otherwise, ... I would have committed suicide.[78]

Sangha in cyberspace is a sanctuary, a container, and even a balm, but is not a place to hide. It is not some holy ground, well lit in the dark of skin and sky, with candles flickering on and off, burning sage wafting in the air, and Black bodies in absolute disengagement from affect. The healing Sangha does not hide from the world or from the internal scarring, hardened barnacles on our hearts, or feelings squeezed through the eye of a needle. The Sangha meditates together to know the feelings of "I am a pariah" and Black rage, and death-dealing thoughts alongside the cacophony of ancestors' voices reminding us of their legacy: to fight, resist, survive and not just change but to metamorphosize to loving Blackness. The Sangha reaches from the society we live into the interior we are unearthing to become Sangha, a healing community.

Jamerican Muslimah's Veranda: To Be a Black. Convert Muslim. Female—It's Been Rough

Jamerican Muslimah's blog[79] was written by a 32-year-old Black woman who converted to Islam at the age of 17. She began the site as a place to ask questions and vent about the experience of trying to find a place in the Muslim community for a Black Jamaican-American woman convert. For over a five-year period, Jamerican shared her joys and struggles of life as a Black Muslim woman convert. She argues with her communities even as she prays with them. She calls out the sexism, racism, colorism, and anti-convert sentiment she encountered. These forces, pervasive within and outside Muslim faith communities, are red threads in the narrative. She gives us insight into her interior longings for kinship—religiously, culturally, and relationally. In their absence, she wrestles and struggles, laments, and seeks them out almost relentlessly. The longing and seeking are part and parcel of development as a Jamaican-American convert into a religion and culture unknown to her; she is thrust into the complexity of relationships between Black converts from the United States and immigrant Muslims, both Black and Arabic. Sometimes, she bemoans and resists and sometimes falls into near despair. She is a Black woman who is accepted and rejected; she is told her hair is not right; her toes are not as they should be when she prays. Jamerican's life is a path of light and struggle. She is a woman seeking her spiritual and cultural home, and though she may lapse in its pursuit, she never fully eludes its claim. Ultimately, like the Black mothers, grandmothers, aunts, and cousins of her family neighborhood, she sits out on the veranda and tells her stories of her faith, struggles, loves, longings, resistance, and hope as a Black Jamerican woman Muslimah.

Jamerican does not include her actual name on the blogsite—maybe, she is every Black woman finding her way. She does, however, include her educational background. She earned a Bachelor of Art in African American Studies and is completing a thesis in African New World Studies. She wants to embody Islam practice that is "a . . . middle way . . .not too strict or too loose."[80] She created the blogsite as an offering to the Muslim readers, especially Black women, across the diaspora. In using the image of the

"Veranda," she draws on the picture of Black women's space on the front porch of their southern homes.

> (That is why I named the blog Jamerican's Veranda—imagine us sitting on the veranda discussing these topics). Insha'allah, hopefully, you can find some benefit in my writing.[81]

AN INSIDER-OUTSIDER MUSLIMAH

Jamerican's cyberspace presence is more religious autoethnography of the intersections of subjectivity in religious experience than explicitly identified as spiritual teacher or faith practitioner. Her path to a committed life as a Muslim has been difficult, and at one point she stopped practicing for five years and returned to the faith in 2000. After participating in the "Convert Truths blog carnival," Jamerican decided that she wanted to publicly share her experience.

> I wish I could tell you about the beauty. I wish I could tell you that I took shahadah[82] after being fascinated with Islam and seeing the goodness of Muslims.
>
> I wish I could tell you how I found a family, a community . . . I really wish I could. The reality is my convert experience has been a rocky one. It . . . with doubt and confusion.

We know very little about the factors leading up to Jamerican's process and decision to convert to Islam. She converted at 17 at an African American masjid, hoping that she would feel at home. She almost immediately experienced disappointment due to scandals and isolation.[83] What we do know is that her experience of conversion seldom shows up in conversion research studies. Lewis Rambo comes close when he defines the context stage in his seven-stage model of conversion (context, crisis, quest, encounter, interaction, commitment, and consequences). The context stage is split into two domains micro and macro. Micro context is comprised of those factors such as "family, ethnic group, religious community, and local neighborhood. These groupings play an important role in the creation of a sense of identity and belonging."[84] We see that in her conversion, belonging, family, and community are important to values but more salient, they are important selfobject needs and the disappointment in their absence in this new religion is painful. In particular, the context for this new religion has not provided her a sense of kinship and the scandals resulted in a rapid de-idealization of her mosque. When combined with the macro context of "social, cultural, religious, and personal environment,"[85] she has experienced doubt, frustration, and confusion. These dynamics shape both her experience of the religious context and her interior sense of wholeness as a Muslim. Given that the micro and macro create the milieu in which religious conversion occurs,[86] these are important features in the narrative she is sharing, and given that her purpose for creating Jamerican's Veranda is to sit and talk and to be of help, she wants the readers to know that the conversion process is fraught with longing, disappoint, and desire.

Jamerican's narrative is about more than adolescent conversion struggles. While distinct, Jamerican's narrative has overlapped with other Black adolescent girls, and Evelyn Parker argues that Black girls are beset struggles with, and negation of, colorism, racism, sexism, class, and heterosexism.[87] Jamerican joined members of the Tablight Jumat because she knew people there but eventually grew overextended and withdrew for a long period.

COLORISM, GENDER, AND MARRIAGE

> If you ask me what it has been like to be a Black, convert, Muslim, female, I will reiterate it has been rough. Having spent most of my Muslim experience in non-Black immigrant communities, I have faced a great deal of racism, sexism and colorism.

> . . . the reality . . . was and is far from the ideal. . . . I realized that being Black, a woman and a convert made me less than.

> I watched as my fair-skinned Latina friends were repeatedly asked for their hand in marriage. I watched as the White female converts were held in high esteem and absorbed into immigrant Muslim families (their babies will be so fair, *mashallah!*)

Jamerican's experiences of colorism and sexism combined are not uncommon. Another blogger Leah V. Daily lives in Detroit, Michigan, and grew up in a Black Muslim family. Her blogsite, "Beauty and the Muse," allows her to create a space where she proclaims her religious life by also reclaiming her curvy, large, Black body. Her posts are focused on resisting the religious patriarchal demands placed on Black Muslim women. But her resistance is necessary as a counter to the negative images of Black women. Her website is a demand for viewers to look at her as an embodiment of Black beauty, a large fashion model, a practicing Muslim, and a feminist. In the introduction to her blogsite, she writes,

> it encompasses all the different facets of my style and ideas. You'll see how I rock street style to vintage glam but this just isn't about beauty, every photo

is paired with meaningful content about feminism, social justice, divorce, and body positive activism. You get a front row seat to my life's journey. Pull up a chair.[88]

She forces us to remember that that the Internet is a linguistic, visual, rhetorical, and communal virtual web of connectivity created out of the same "stuff"—rituals, practices, and mores. That forms, and to our collective and individual detriment, malforms our religious and social structures, as well as our psyches, in the nonvirtual world. Her religious sensibilities and practice in cyberspace are never far from her feminist standpoint and this has made her a target of increased sexism, body policing, religious among some Black Muslims. In a post, "Am I Not Muslim Enough for You?" she reveals the interior struggle to feel under religious surveillance from men and women.

> I really hate the internet sometimes. Seems like in every crack and crevice is a someone lurking in the shadows to call you out on a misplaced period or find a sliver of your ankle meat showing so they can immediately tell you that you are soooo not a Muslim and to immediately remove your hijab because you are disgracing Islam.
>
> I had to block multiple Muslim sisters who felt the need to tell me that I'm *haram* (forbidden by Islamic law. . . I've been called *haram* for the most part of my life. . . . I get it. There are certain rules in Islam that I just don't abide by.
>
> One girl direct messaged me saying that men could "see me." That she was all for my Black Muslim empowerment but she thought I was taking my freedom too far.[89]

Leah's virtual and physical world overlap. Her website is filled with photos of Muslim feminist fashion style; here one also reads that after nine years, her marriage imploded. Her husband had a rather public and long affair. The divorce sent her spiraling into self-doubt, and while her relationship to Islam remains firm, she questions every aspect of its influence and authority in her life. She enters Muslim space as a feminist and body-affirming Black woman and admits the ambivalence with which she lives.

> It was revealed to me this year that I was much stronger than I ever thought I was. Because failing at a nine-year marriage made me feel so weak. So low. I questioned myself at every turn. Why this and why that? If you had only done such and such then you wouldn't be undesirable, single, divorced.

Leah is a self-identifying, strong Black woman who also wrestles with how being a Black Muslim woman should have meaning in her life and community.

> Some days I'm an OK Muslim and other times I drop the ball, fall . . . and land face first into a puddle of mud. I'm not the poster child for Islam. But then things got really confusing inside my head. Why wasn't I uncomfortable modeling with a male? What's wrong with me? Am I like half a Muslim or something? What kind of role model was I being for young Muslim girls?

Leah's brief narrative helps us in reading Jamerican's experience. Jamerican is not an individual Black Muslim woman wrestling solely with internal emotional dynamics. The difficulty Jamerican faced, as she entered religious life as a Muslim, highlights the convergence of the interiority, religious engagement, racial identity, and the sociopolitical as well as the trajectories and developmental hurdles that conversion in late adolescence brings.[90] Specifically, Jamerican's narrative raises questions about the effect of pervasive rejection on one's sense of self and within a community. Jamerican describes living with a sense of religious, racial, and gender dislocation, even prior to her conversion to Islam. In her adoption of Islam, she clearly longed for a sense of cultural and religious kinship.

> I was angry at myself because the Afrocentric movement was what had led me to Islam. Before becoming Muslim I was confident and proud of the color of my skin, the texture of my hair, the shape of my nose and of my slave ancestors. How did I move from that to being ashamed of taking off my hijab at sisters' only events? How could I sit silently as people insulted my skin?

Jamerican eventually left this community and found a new masjid, Muslim's place of worship and prayer, in a Black neighborhood. She recovered a sense of pride in being Black. The anticipation and excitement at having found a community where she belonged, however, was short-lived. Having spent years practicing with immigrant communities, she was unfamiliar with nuances and expectations of the Nation of Islam. Again, she felt ostracized and ignored but it was all the more painful because these were "her people." Unlike many, Jamerican continued to search for a religious home where she could experience kinship.

Jamerican began attending a Caribbean, Indian, and Indo-Pak community where she felt welcomed and accepted. However, this site for kinship and belonging is limited. Beyond the walls of religious community, she continued to feel she is "a foreigner at home" especially post 9/11. Almost overnight, she was not recognized as Black. "People assumed I didn't speak English."

They assumed she was "passive and docile" and that she was coerced to cover herself.

Furthermore, colorism, once a problem only among immigrant Muslims, was heightened.

> The strangest part of all was that Black people no longer recognized me as Black. My light brown skin (once considered too dark in Arab and Indian/Pakistani communities) combined with my hijab made people assume I was East African or a Black Arab. There were no head nods, complicit glances, or casual words spoken to me from other Black people.

Jamerican's displacement is religious, bodily, and cultural.

> Tonight, I was at the masjid praying . . . this sister came up to me and said . . . She wanted . . . me to know that my toes were not curled properly while sitting in Jalsa! . . . In broken English she asked if I was "sick" and unable to do it.

We see in this brief exchange the complex interaction between spiritual practice, socio-religious bodily disciplining, and anger-fueled, anti-immigrant sentiments in mentioning the sister's "broken English." Religious space is not free of the horizontal aggression among those who have similar interlocking sites of oppression—gender, color, class, and religion. Hierarchies of power can be evoked into practice at moment's notice as the aftermath of an affront or, as in this case, an imposition of religious bodily disciplining. The imposition of "broken English" is evidence of Jamerican's struggle to be in an elevated subject position in relation to the "sister" who confronted, or wanted to teach, her about her body's misplacement. Jamerican's confrontation reveals the stress points the strain that strain "sisterhood" between Brown women.

Jamerican's own family of origin has, over the course of her blogging, taken on deepened importance even though she still feels herself as partly an outsider religiously, she feels a part and welcomed by them as family. In part, it is because her mother was diagnosed with ALS and the symptoms progressed rapidly. Jamerican has been a primary source of assistance and care, and the family relies on her. After some time away from her blogging, she reported on her mother's declining health and newly revealed that their relationship has been strained and Jamerican hopes to repair some of the relational damage.

> When I last blogged my mom was in denial about having ALS—that has changed. She has fully accepted her condition now . . . and the pain is getting worse in her throat.

> My mother and I haven't had the best relationship and . . . I do hope that we can spend her last months or years mending this broken relationship. Allah knows best.

We again hear the longing for family in these posts, but they are intermingled with episodes of experiencing pleasure with family and imagining more in the future. In another post, we can see how she and the family are renegotiating their religious differences and are navigating religion and family.

> On Thursday my cousin had Thanksgiving dinner at his house. Initially I was opposed . . . my cousin wore me down when he talked about cooking halal so that I could eat.

> When I'm with my family I feel like I can truly be myself. It's not like being with the women from the mosque . . . I can be the old me with a new twist.

Given the discrepancy between being with her family and the sisters in the mosque, one must ask why she continues. Jamerican stays because Islam is her religious home and she can claim no other. Even when she writes that the year—not the week or month, but the last year—has been horrible, she declares that Allah is merciful.[91]

When Jamerican created "Jamerican's Veranda" to tell her story, she turned to cyberspace, rather than paper and pen and brick and mortar because she hoped some would "find some benefit in my writing." She embodies the Womanists' attention to particularity and contextualization. Specifically, as Debra Mageed contends in her article "Resisting the Veil of Universalism: Muslim Womanist Philosophy as a Lens for Authentic Representations of African American Muslim Women,"[92] she is part of the community of African American Muslim women who employ various tactics to negotiate the "categories of woman, African American, and Muslim." Their lives and "the sites of struggle" where they work toward the "consciousness integration of religion in their daily lives offer insight into the three worlds they traverse: the mosque, the Black community, and American society . . .(and) serve as a point of resistance to monolithic views of Black women and religion."[93] Sheppard supports this view when she argues that a "deep intersectional approach directs our attention to the fact that scant attention has been paid to . . . the complicatedness of Black women's religious engagement and practices," especially as discreet and separate from Christianity and church.[94]

These women curate their lives on the Internet as religious, social, and cultural space where their interiority intersects with the social and political, but they also transform cyberspace into spaces of resistance and of care. These narratives are not self-absorbed rants for all the World Wide Web to read for distraction or entertainment. There is a far more sophisticated aim here. Each offers her narrative as a critical reading of religious discourse to mirror Black women's lives, invite them into strategies of resistance, and spiritual practices that redefine religion as a site for the reconfiguration of self and cyberspaces. The Internet then is a container for dynamic engagement. The self and religion are not static, unitary, or solely interior. As such religious cyberspace is discursive and emergent and inextricable from the sociopolitical realm. As identity and subject location are experienced as foreground, the struggle to retain or bolster an interior sense of self, albeit a fluid self, becomes crucial to religious experience. The fluidity is apparent in moments of bodily and spiritual assertion—challenging, resisting, and in moments of rage, grief, dislocation, and depression. Hence, each time Jamerican is told she is an outsider as a Black woman convert, she must reengage the existential question, why be a Black Musalimah? Each time she asks this of herself, and her current community, she redefines her expectations of religious community and religious practice. She redefines herself and benefits from its therapeutic effects. Carol Rouse, in *Engaged Surrender: African American Women and Islam*, her research on Black women who have converted to Islam, argues that

> the power of conversion is the control one has over the recreation of a personal history. The history. . . .. Explains the contradictions between internal and external realities. Repositioning oneself within a personal and social narrative is usually very therapeutic.

But she also notes, from personal experience, that the therapeutic benefit does not alleviate the reality of cultural differences leading to exclusion. After attending a prayer service and joining the mostly Pakistani American women, she discovered they had relatively little in common.

> My outsider status was something I had never experienced at . . . predominantly African American masjids I had attended. Islam is supposed to be a religion that bridges cultural borders, that defies regional identities. While these cultural differences are bridged with respect to ritual practices . . . outside of those rituals, there are bridges yet to be crossed.[95]

Jamerican knows these uncrossed bridges well; she knows that borders, bridges, and regional affiliations and commitments create barriers between sisters and communities; she knows the way in which they exclude her and, simultaneously, reside within her. And yet, her faith in Islam is steadfast. Islam is self-defining for Jamerican. The communities in which she lives this out mirror this self or refract from it, but they do not obliterate it. Cyberspace is her religious space where she imparts this truth for other Black women.

CYBERSPACE AS BLACK RELIGIOUS SPACE

Cyberspace allows Black women to break through the frame of invisibility and silence. Their narratives are dismantling practices against the spectator sport that the Internet has contributed to in myriad of ways where Black women are fodder for stereotyped images and misrepresentations. These are rhetorical, homiletical, and bodily acts of resistance and formation.

Cyberspace is a religious space[96] constructed by Black women where they negotiate racial, gender, sexual, and class identity but also a space where they, in struggle and practice, rescript their religious practice while challenging its attempt to impinge and restrict their religious experience. Living religiously is a restructuring of religion where they legitimize Black women's voice as religious subjects capable of critiquing the oppressive and confining teachings, those authorized by religious power structures and often internalized by adherents, and reproduced in regulating practices. These Black women in cyberspace do not stop with critique but articulate counter teachings and narratives to subvert and transform the interior and social practices of religion that undermine them. These women take up subject positions—making themselves visible—asserting that their lived religious experiences are valid sources for epistemologies of Black women's religious practices. But they also make it apparent that religious experience, when understood through critical reflection, is disruptive. Each of these women in cyberspace not only names the ways that anti-Black, anti-woman, anti-body, and anti-queer permeate religious practices but how they take up residence in the psyche. Their counternarratives disrupt social and interior spaces and reclaim a religion and spirituality that sustains, rather than denies, Black experience. Moreover, these women are able to be in—are even called *to*—cyberspace as a religious space and to create in it spaces for Black women's self and communal care, religious formation as well as religion's reconfiguration and interpretation.

NOTES

1. Zenju Earthlyn Manuel, "Awakening Fueled by Rage," *Lion's Roar: Buddhist Wisdom for our Time.* June 1, 2020. https://www.lionsroar.com/awakening-fueled-by-rage/.

2. Octavia E. Butler, *Parable of the Sower Earthseed.*

3. Michael Strangelove, "Cyberspace and the Changing Landscape of the Self," http://project.cyberpunk.ru/idb/cyberspace_geography.html. Accessed September 4, 2018.

4. Lisa Nakamura, *Cybertypes Race, Ethnicity, and Identity in the Internet* (New York, NY: Routledge, 2002), xxii.

5. Mary Patillo-McCoy, "Church Culture as a Strategy of Action in the Black Community," *American Sociological Review*, 63 (December 1988): 767–84, 273.

6. Ann Swidler, "Culture in Action: Symbols and Strategies," *American of Sociological Review*, 51, no. 2 (April 1986): 273–86.

7. Ann Swidler, "Culture in Action: Symbols and Strategies."

8. Mary Pattillo-McCoy, "Church Culture as a Strategy of Action in the Black Community," *American Sociological Review*, 63 (December 1988): 767–84.

9. Jeremy Bentham, "Panopticon or the Inspection-House Containing the Idea of a New Principle of Construction." http://www.fcsh.unl.pt/docentes/rmonteiro/pdf/panopticon_%20jeremy%20bentham.pdf Accessed January 10, 2020.

10. Emilie M. Townes, "Cultural Boundaries and African American Theology," in *The Oxford Handbook of African American Theology*, edited by Anthony B. Pinn and Katie G. Cannon (New York, NY: Oxford University Press, 2014).

11. Valerie Purdie-Vaughns and Richard P. Eibach, "Intersectional Invisibility; the Distinctive Advantages and Disadvantages of Multiple Subordinate-Group Identities," *Sex Roles*, 59 (2008): 377–391.

12. An often cited example is the Daniel P. Moynihan Report, "The Negro Family: The Case for National Action," Office of Policy Planning and Research United States Department of Labor. March 1965. https://www.dol.gov/general/aboutdol/history/webid-moynihan. Accessed June 15, 2019.

13. Tom Spooner, *African Americans and the Internet Main Report* (Washington, DC: Pew Research Center, 2000). https://www.pewresearch.org/Internet /2000/10/22/main-report-24/ Accessed July 20, 2019.

14. Tom Spooner, *African Americans and the Internet* .

15. Carole McGranahan, "What is Ethnography? Teaching Ethnographic Sensibilities without Fieldwork," *Teaching Anthropology*, 4 (April 2014): 23–36.

16. Julian M. Murchison and Curtis D. Coats, "Ethnography of Religious Instants: Multi-Sited Ethnography and the Idea of Third Spaces," *Religions*, 6 (2015): 988–1005.

17. Randall Packer, "Defining Third Space," 2019. https://thirdspacenetwork.com/overview/defining-the-third-space. Accessed February 8, 2019.

18. Randall Packer, "Defining Third Space."

19. Pamela Lightsey, personal communication, July 6, 2021.

20. Monica Roberts, "Transgriot Mission Statement." https://transgriot.blogspot.com. Accessed August 23, 2019.

21. Monica Roberts, 2012 Transfaith in Color Conference Keynote Address. https://transgriot.blogspot.com/2012/08/2012-transfaith-in-color-conference_18.html. Accessed August 12, 2018.

22. Susan Taylor, *In the Spirit: The Inspirational Writings* (New York, NY: HarperPerennial, 1994), Back cover.

23. Monica Roberts, August 12, 2012. https://transgriot.blogspot.com/2012/08/tyra-hunter-17th-anniversary.html.

24. Monica Roberts, Trangriot.com. August 12, 2018. https://transgriot.blogspot.com/2012/08/transfaith-in-color-conference-day-two.html?m=0. Accessed August 12, 2018.

25. Monica Roberts, "2012 Transfaith in Color Conference Keynote Address."
26. Monica Roberts "2012 Transfaith in Color Conference Keynote Address."
27. Monica Roberts, "2012 Transfaith in Color Conference Keynote Address."
28. Monica Roberts, "2012 Transfaith in Color Conference Keynote Address."
29. Monica Roberts, "2012 Transfaith in Color Conference Keynote Address."
30. Roberts, 2009, "Journey to Womanist-hood."
31. Monica Roberts, "Womanist." https://transgriot.blogspot.com/search?q=womanist. August 12, 2018, 2009.
32. Monica Roberts, "Womanist."
33. Monica Roberts, "Womanist."
34. Monica Roberts, "Womanist."
35. Monica Roberts, "Womanist."
36. Monica Roberts, 2011, "Womanists Haven't Disrespected My Humanity."
37. Monica Roberts, 2011, "Womanists Haven't Disrespected My Humanity."
38. Monica Roberts, 2012 Transfaith in Color Conference—That's a Wrap." https://transgriot.blogspot.com/search?q=We+had+seminars+over+the+three+days+of+TFIC+2012+. Accessed February 8, 2019.
39. Monica Roberts, "What Happens with My Trans African Diaspora Trans Peeps IS my Business," 2016. https://transgriot.blogspot.com/search?q=diaspora. Accessed February 8, 2019. Italics added.
40. Samantha Allen, "Inside Monica Roberts' Mission to Identify Transgender Murder Victims," *The Daily Beast.* February 19, 2019. Accessed February 22, 2019.
41. Monica Roberts, "What Happens with My Trans African Diaspora Trans Peeps IS My Business," 2016. https://transgriot.blogspot.com/search?q=diaspora. Accessed February 8, 2019. Italics added.
42. Phillis Isabella Sheppard. Posted to FaceBook 11/9/18 9:27 a.m.
43. "Sensei means teacher. Zenju is her Dharma [ordination] name, which means complete tenderness." http://zenju.org/about/. Assessed October 18, 2016.
44. Zenju Earthlyn Manuel, "About." http://zenju.org/about/. Accessed November 11, 2017.
45. Zenju Earthlyn Manuel, "Remembering the Ancestors." http://zenju.org/category/dharma-notes/page/2/. Accessed June 1, 2020.
46. Zenju Earthlyn Manuel, "The Dance of Death." http://zenju.org/category/dharma-notes/page/3/. Accessed June 1, 2020.
47. Zenju Earthlyn Manuel, "Awakening Fueled by Rage."
48. Zenju Earthlyn Manuel, "About."
49. Earthly Manuel, *Tell Me Something About Buddhism* (Charlottesville, VA: Hampton Roads Publishing, 2011), 46.
50. See her books *Sanctuary: A Meditation on Home, Homelessness, and Belonging* (Somerville, MA: Wisdom Books, 2018) and *The Way of Tenderness: Awakening Through Race, Sexuality, and Gender* (Someville, MA: Wisdom Books, 2015).
51. Zenju Earthlyn Manuel, "Be Home, Be Still," 2015. http://zenju.org/blog/page/7/. Accessed November 30, 2016.
52. Zenju Earthlyn Manuel, "Be Home, Be Still."

53. Zenju Earthlyn Manuel, "The Wisdom in My Bones," *Buddhadharma: The Practitioner's Quarterly* (Spring 2015): 32–37.
54. Zenju Earthlyn Manuel, "The Wisdom in My Bones."
55. Zenju Earthlyn Manuel, "The Wisdom in My Bones."
56. Zenju Earthlyn Manuel, "The Dharma of Black Feminism: A Commentary on Black Women's Voices." November 20, 2013. http://www.buddhistpeacefellowship.org/the-dharma-of-Black-feminism-zenju-earthlyn-manuel-on-bell-hooks-and-melissa-harris-perry/. Accessed August 13, 2020.
57. Zenju Earthlyn Manuel, "The Dharma of Black Feminism."
58. Alice Walker, "Definition of a "Womanist," in *Search of Our Mothers' Gardens: Womanist Prose* (New York, NY: Harcourt Brace Jovanovich, 1983), xxiii.
59. Zenju Earthlyn Manuel, "The Dharma of Black Feminism: A Commentary on Black Women's Voices." November 20, 2013. http://www.buddhistpeacefellowship.org/the-dharma-of-Black-feminism-zenju-earthlyn-manuel-on-bell-hooks-and-melissa-harris-perry/. Accessed August 13, 2020.
60. Zenju Earthlyn Manuel, "Prolonged Audaciousness." http://zenju.org/category/dharma-notes/. Accessed August 12, 2020.
61. Zenju Earthlyn Manuel, "Awakening Fueled by Rage."
62. See William F. Marshall, "Coronavirus Infection by Race: What's Behind the Health Disparities?" https://www.mayoclinic.org/diseases-conditions/coronavirus/expert-answers/coronavirus-infection-by-race/faq-20488802; APM Research Lab Staff. July 22, 2020. "The Color of Coronavirus: Covid-19 Deaths by Race and Ethnicity in the U.S." https://www.apmresearchlab.org/covid/deaths-by-race. Accessed July 23, 2020.
63. Zenju Earthlyn Manuel, "Awakening Fueled by Rage."
64. Zenju Earthlyn Manuel, "Prolonged Audaciousness."
65. Zenju Earthlyn Manuel, "Awakening Fueled by Rage."
66. Emily Cohen, "An Interview with Jan Willis," *Journal of Feminist Studies in Religion*, 33, no. 2 (Fall 2017): 127–37.
67. Zenju Earthlyn Manuel, "Awakening Fueled by Rage."
68. Zenju Earthly Manuel, "Awakening Fueled by Rage."
69. Zenju Earthlyn Manuel, "The Wisdom in My Bones," *Buddhadharma: The Practitioner's Quarterly* (Spring 2015): 32–37.
70. Zenju Earthlyn Manuel, "The Wisdom in My Bones," 36.
71. Zenju Earthlyn Manuel, "Awakening Fueled by Rage."
72. Zenju Earthlyn Manuel, "Awakening Fueled by Rage."
73. Zenju Earthlyn Manuel, "Ouch! Systemic Suffering and the Second Noble Truth." July 14, 2014. http://www.buddhistpeacefellowship.org/tss-2014/2-zenju/. Accessed June 10, 2020.
74. Zenju Earthlyn Manuel, "Ouch! Systemic Suffering and the Second Noble Truth."
75. Zenju Earthlyn Manuel, *The Way of Tenderness: Awakening through Race, Sexuality, and Gender* (Boston, MA: Wisdom Books, 2014), 49.
76. Zenju Earthlyn Manuel, *The Way of Tenderness: Awakening through Race, Sexuality, and Gender.*

77. Zenju Earthlyn Manuel, "I Am Not My Hair." http://zenju.org/i-am-not-my-hair/. Accessed June 15, 2020.

78. Zenju Earthlyn Manuel, "Zenju Earthlyn Manuel in Conversation with Ann Marie Davis." August 29, 2017. https://journal.workthatreconnects.org/2017/08/29/zenju-earthlyn-manuel-in-conversation-with-ann-marie-davis/. Accessed June 20, 2020.

79. Jamerican Muslimah's Veranda: Can't stereotype my thing, yo. https://jamericanmuslimah.wordpress.com/who-am-i/. Accessed May 10, 2014.

80. Jamerican Muslimah's Veranda.

81. Jamerican Muslimah's Veranda.

82. Shahadah is the profession to Islam by declaring there is no god but Allah, and Muhammad is the messenger of Allah.

83. Jamerican Muslimah's Veranda. https://jamericanmuslimah.wordpress.com/who-am-i. Accessed May 10, 2014.

84. Lewis R. Rambo and Steven C. Bauman, "Psychology of Conversion and Spiritual Transformation," *Pastoral Psychology* 61, no. 5 (2012): 879–894.

85. Lewis R. Rambo and Steven C. Bauman, "Psychology of Conversion and Spiritual Transformation," 879.

86. Lewis R. Rambo and Steven C. Bauman, "Psychology of Conversion and Spiritual Transformation," 879.

87. Evelyn L. Parker, "Emancipatory Hope Reloaded." http://old.religiouseducation.net/proceedings/2009_Proceedings/23Parker_EmancipatoryHope.pdf. Accessed June 10, 2020.

88. Leah V. Daily. http://www.Beautyandthemuse.net. Accessed November 15, 2017.

89. Leah V. Dailey, "I am Muslim but I am Not Your Posterchild for Islam," http://www.beautyandthemuse.net/leahvdaily/2016/10/22/980e52hhbtz2zbo8m7mw28uqrx70i9. Accessed November, 15, 2017.

90. Phillis Isabella Sheppard, "Conversion Studies, Pastoral Counseling, and Cultural Studies: Engaging and Embracing a New Paradigm." Response to Lewis Rambo, *Ex Auditu: An International Journal for the Theological Interpretation of Scripture* 25 (2012): 17–22.

91. Jamerican Muslimah's Veranda: Can't stereotype my thing, yo. https://jamericanmuslimah.wordpress.com/2010/07/16/growth-allah-is-mericful/. Accessed May 10, 2014.

92. Debra Mageed, "Resisting the Veil of Universalism: Muslim Womanist Philosophy as a Lens for Authentic Representations of African American Muslim Women," in *Muslimah Theology: The Voices of Muslim Women Theologians*, edited by Ednan Aslan, Marcia Hermansen and Elif Medeni (New York, NY: Peter Lang Publishers, 2013): 247–65.

93. Debra Mageed, "Resisting the Veil of Universalism," 247.

94. Phillis Isabella Sheppard, "Womanist Pastoral Theology and Black Women's Experience of Gender, Religion, and Sexuality." in *Pastoral Theology and Care: Critical Trajectories in Theory and Practice*, edited by Nancy J. Ramsay (Hoboken, NJ: John Wiley & Sons Ltd, 2018), 125–47.

95. Carol Moxley Rouse, *Engaged Surrender: African American Women and Islam.* (Berkeley, CA: University of California Press, 2004), 211.

96. Morten Jojsgaard and Margit Warburg's edited volume, *Religion and Cyberspace*, is a useful volume on the broad topic. The Pew Research Center's 2014 report "Religion and Electronic Media: One-in-Five Americans Share Their Faith Online" indicates that in the United States, the Internet has become an important site for religious engagement.

Chapter 4

"Because I Am a Woman"
Vocation and Trauma

When the poet Pat Parker wrote Audre Lorde in 1985, in anticipation of a visit from Lorde, "If you don't give me too hard a time when you come, I'll even let you lose on my word processor,"[1] the world of the Internet was still new and personal home computers, especially owned by Black women, were barely a discernable reality. Alecia Brown, a second career Master of Divinity student at a southeastern seminary, decided, just ten years later, to develop a church congregation located solely in cyberspace. In this short-lived endeavor, she made use of the capacities of the Internet to integrate audio, texts, pictures, and participation via the comments section. After graduating from seminary, she returned to her hometown expecting to be called to pastor a church. Her narrative is what a Black woman does when her vocational call is stronger than the recurring attempts to deny her pastoral space. Hers is a story of longing and grief but also a story of self-authoring and authenticity.

Rev. Alecia Brown,[2] now 72 years of age, with nearly 30 years in ministry, is at a point where she is open to reflecting on her life in ministry. She grew up in southeastern Florida in a family of staunch Black Baptists with long-standing, intergenerational roots in the tradition and local area. They remain, in her description, "proud Baptists." The family church she attended stressed the importance of evangelization and the necessity of being born again and a personal relationship with God. Theologically conservative, they believed everyone should be able to come to church and experience God's grace through salvation, and to live a changed life as a result. This "everyone" attitude shaped her understanding of the church and how it should function in the life of individuals and communities. Rev. Alecia is a risk-taker in ministerial pursuits, not afraid to challenge the system, and though she has had some painful experiences in the ministry, she has a sense of humor and great empathy for the struggles of the everyday poor and Black people of her community.

Alecia Brown's idea for an Internet-based religious service originated out of an assignment for a Missiology class as part of a mission project. She created an online Bible Study to test the feasibility of the Internet to enrich the work of the church. The success of that assignment led her to expand the idea to build an Internet congregation with a full worship component. The website included a purpose statement, description of the church, information about the pastor, and weekly services were comprised of the same elements likely to be found in most Baptist churches. Alecia included audio files and text documents. Congregants and visitors could leave prayer requests in the comments section. The audio sermons, in addition to her preaching, included guest preachers. The digital bulletin contained a purpose statement, "The purpose of the church is to give an opportunity for the cyber-community to enhance their relationship with God."[3] The church was Christian in focus, ethos, liturgy, and resources. Given her Black Baptist roots, a clear emphasis on the life, mission, and death of Jesus was pervasive across the site, and in its vocational statement "to fulfill the call of Jesus Christ by offering on-line personal worship that require spiritual reflections that nurture and encourage Christ-like character."[4] As a religious leader, Rev. Alecia found a way to embody her role as pastor, spiritual guide, and worship leader.

WEBSITE AS CHURCH BULLETIN, BROCHURE, AND INVITATION TO DEEPEN SPIRITUALITY

The site served several functions, explicitly, it was the church bulletin—a cartography of how worship is done in a Black church in cyberspace. As such, it mapped out the liturgical means for visitors to enter the sanctuary for worship. In this regard, it was similar to the Sunday bulletin one might find in many other Black Baptist churches. A distinctive element rests in the brochure features to website. Here Alecia provides a list of links for spiritual resources that include a school of religion, biblical resources, resources for children, devotional guides, and search engines to find a church. She included just as many resources for humor, cooking, and computer clubs. Alecia exhibits a desire to influence her congregants beyond the worship service. The comment section on the site allowed parishioners to make request prayer but also to thank her for the spiritual work the Cyberspace Church is doing. "My spirit has been uplifted by this inspiring song and sermon." "May God continue to grant you strength to do His will in cyberspace as it is in heaven." "I thank you Rev. E for your pioneering spirit." The visitors to the church in cyberspace clearly affirmed Pastor Alecia's pastoral role in cyberspace.

Beyond Cyberspace Church, however, her vocation and pastoral identity were challenged.

The decision to explore cyberspace as a site to pastor a church was also likely fueled by two other factors. She had previously worked for five years for the state education department as a technology training specialist where she taught school personnel how to use computers in teaching and administration. She was an early adopter of technology, competent, and found the work fulfilling. Furthermore, Rev. Alecia quickly recognized that the Internet would become central for communication strategies including in the church.

The second reason was sexism in her Black church context. On the website, Alecia includes a seemingly contradictory notation. Under the heading "Church Membership," Alecia tells her visitors: "Cyberspace Church *was not* designed to support a 'physical membership.' The purpose was CMBC encourages each person to become active in a church of their in their own community." The very next heading is "PASTOR," where she includes information related to her professional experience and education. She emphatically announces that she is qualified to pastor her church. As such, on the one hand, she has assured her funding source, a local community church, that she is not interested in building her own congregation or competing for their membership; on the other hand, she has claimed her vocation. What we witness here, in her church in cyberspace, is Alecia's complex interiority negotiating gender, vocation, and sexism.

TRAUMA IN A CALL TO MINISTRY

In my ethnography on Black women and vocation,[5] I found there to be an array of narratives about vocation and call. Almost all have shared elements of resistance to the call to ministry, resistance from others, both women and men, to their call, and difficulty finding or deciding on the place to concretize their call. Alecia Brown is the only one to describe the internal struggle to heed a call to ministry as traumatic.

> I wasn't seeking a call to ministry. My call was traumatic. It was nothing I desired and nothing I ever envisioned. I was satisfied being a good church member in my Baptist church teaching a Sunday school class.
>
> I was at the height of my professional career. I liked my career, my job. I had the most beautiful house. God had blessed me with a job with a salary where I could pay my bills and go out to a movie.

Trauma is a destabilizing affective experience as well as a relational, cultural, and social experience. It disrupts who we understand ourselves to be and becomes integral to the stories we tell about ourselves and others. Trauma theorist Judith Herman argues that "unlike commonplace misfortunes, traumatic events generally involve threats to life or bodily integrity, or a close personal encounter with violence and death"[6] or psychic instability. Not as often discussed, events are experienced as trauma when one's sense of self, cultural location, and religious experience are disruptive such that we feel shaken to the core. Trauma runs between the interior life and the public and social spaces that generally support our sense of well-being or even humanity. For some, trauma is so repetitive that it can become the thread that runs through their life narrative even many years after the precipitant has been recognized and seemingly settled. Though negative in origin, in most regards, it may become an integral facet of the self. Thus, through narration, the trauma becomes a relational thread that creates and disrupts relational ties. The trauma to which Alecia Brown was subjected must be understood here as operating multiple levels. Kobena Mercer's observation that "the ugliness of the social and the way that Black psyches disintegrate in social relations is almost intolerable" is worth referencing here because Alecia's anxiety was, and remains, most assuredly connected to the social.

The themes of loss of social status and diminished self-esteem emerge in her narrative as she anticipates a change in her social position. What we witness is her struggle to respond affirmatively to this call without psychic and social disintegration. The instability of her equilibrium suggests that the sociality of her interiority predominates; in other words, her internal struggle about the meaning of her call is inextricable from her social relationships within a southern Black religious context. And class identity is integral to her sense of place in the world. She anticipated that the loss of income, a professional career, and the admiration and respect of those in her social surround will be unbearable. That is, she finds unbearable the prospect of losing her class footing and being relegated to a struggling class designation. Her economic security is located in the here and now: she owns a home; she had a job and a good salary "where I could pay my bills and go out to a movie." Note that Alecia's focus is not past oriented. She does not mention that she is planning for a vacation, or that she is able to contribute to her retirement, she does, it seems, imagine a future where she does not have to work. She is able to go to a movie. This close to the edge living, though she does not experience it as such, makes answering a call to ministry, for a time, nightmarish.

Discerning a pastoral vocation after an established career would likely incite anxiety in many if not most, for Alecia, however, having a professional job where her contributions are needed, affirmed, and are combined with "a good salary" have served as the source of her self-esteem and the glue to her sense of self. As such, in sensing a call to a pastoral vocation she astutely grasped that the costs to her would be deep and identity-altering because her self-esteem and self-image, her selfhood, were closely tied to money and professional position.

Thus, a downward shift in her financial security would expose her own feelings of vulnerability to a sense of depletion and loss. We might say that, in such a case, her interior would be experienced as inflicting suffering. This would make her own experience both as a threat and a part of herself.

> I did a lot of travel all over the state. A lot of travel. I trained thousands of educators at a time. And people kept coming up to me saying you teach these computer classes like you're preaching a sermon. The way you structure it and the images you use. I would laugh.

In her role as a technology educator, the context, the content, and role mirrored her need for affirmation and competency "and people kept coming to me" but they also saw a preacher in her style of teaching and participants would comment, "You teach these computer classes like you're preaching a sermon." Alecia engaged in a process. She both internalized their affirmation but verbally disavowed their perceptions through laughing until laughing was no longer effective as a means to avoid deflecting their admiration and her call. The result was less a disintegration, but rather, an overstimulated and easily agitated self that was also unbearable, "Suddenly I become increasingly dissatisfied with the job." Alecia became restless day and night. She could not sleep and found herself floundering in all areas. She came to experience a deep sense of isolation; her interior life was a cauldron of confusion; sensing a possible call to ministry, she turned to her mother for counsel, "I went to my mother and she said, don't come to me. That's between you and God." It was then that she heard specifically from God in her discernment.

> And then I heard God say to me, sell your house and go get your degree. Go to seminary. I said to God how am I going to live? I decided, okay, I will sell the house.

> I put a fleece before God. I put my house for sale and listed it in the little Penny Saver newspaper. It was about a ten-word ad. It was listed for 3 days. A woman called and they came by. And the woman said to her husband, "honey this is it. It's the right color and everything". They needed it immediately. The house sold in a week.

Alecia's approach to God, acceptance with conditions, was not unusual for her. Testing God for clarity and assurance and direction in her life are part of her understanding of listening to God. Like Gideon in the book of Judges, she prayed, "if you God want this," then make this thing happen. She explains her spirituality "I'm of the Baptist tradition. Born and raised, and so I check everything out with God." Such a direct line of communication with God reveals the sense of spiritual agency.

She describes a period of wondering if she was "crazy" for thinking of giving up the security of her job, selling her home, and striking out without knowing the future of ministry. The dissatisfaction in her current career was, as she understood it, God making her miserable so she would be obedient and faithful. Alecia had little support or women role models for navigating this early transition into her pastoral identity. Her mother agreed that God was speaking to her but did not suggest that Alecia was experiencing a call to ministry. Nor did her pastor or other religious leaders. Except for her discerning of God's intention and confirming it through the test, she was somewhat isolated and on her own. And she did not stop questioning God's intention or plans for the next step.

> Then I was off to seminary but how was I going to live? Well, it turns out that they had a computer lab but it wasn't being used because they had no one on campus who could run a local network. It came to my attention . . . I asked how many computers they had. It was about twenty-three and I said to myself, "I can do that with one hand behind my back." So, it came to the attention of the president of the school and he hired me.
>
> This was the first time they hired a student who was student/faculty. I taught computer literacy. In exchange, I paid no tuition and no housing. After I graduated, they . . . I guess because everybody got their own personal computers they closed the lab.

Once she created the plan for the Cyberspace Church model, she secured financial support from the Missionary Department from the church where she was an intern responsible for the evangelism efforts. The intention was for the cyberchurch to eventually become self-sustaining through "love offerings" and other contributions. Alecia pastored the Cyberspace Church from 1996 to 1999.

SEXISM AND THE LACK OF RECOGNITION IN THE BLACK CHURCH

Alecia was also motivated by the fact that she is "born and raised Baptist," and though she hoped she would be called to pastor a local traditional brick-and-mortar church, the sexism she had already experienced "in the Baptist church" meant that she would probably have to make her own creative way into a pastoral role.

> The most harming words have come from people in the Church. And most of them . . . most of my problems have come from the women. Now that I've been in the ministry a long time; it's over 25 years, I understand it's a threat; it's a jealously. I'm just saying straight up. . . . Most of the women in the Church they are secretly in love with the pastor, especially if he's male and most of them are male. They want what they see from the pulpit to the pew. They fall in love of the man who is in the pulpit. That physical personification.

There is no missing the anger and pain that Alecia experiences as a Black woman, often thwarted by sexism, in ministry. She emphasizes the strained and even hostile relationships with some women in the church. In fact, it is this hostility that predominates her discussion of women in the church.

> And they become the protective and jealous . . . and when a female acknowledges her call to ministry or is going to be called to the associate pastorate, they, the women reject you. It's just jealously. Only his wife really knows him so they don't really know the man.

Alecia sees this form of sexism as pervasive and that it explicitly erupts when a woman "acknowledges" her call to ministry. It is not the exercise of her gifts, but rather it is when she adjoins the skillful execution of them with vocational meaning, that a seismic shift, which occurs in her relational contexts, theological perspectives, and identity, is announced. At point that the power differential afforded Baptist clergy is exposed. The dynamic that erupts, in this case between Alecia and the other Black women in the church, signals a mechanism of boundary control. The women, it seems, feel acutely the possibility of being displaced, and they, in a move to protect their position and status in relation to the pastor, reject clergywomen. But it also signals that they have, in small and large measure, internalized the work of the actual boundary keepers; that is, Black male clergy who seek to enforce the line of demarcation between being called to ministry and being called to pastor—and ordination. The women who seek to preserve the boundary, seek to preserve their relationship to religious power brokers, and Alecia seeks to join the religious power brokers, and, as a result, is rejected by the male clergy and women parishioners.

Rev. Alecia was able to ward off this rejection, to some degree, when she began an online church. While supported by her local church, she designed the online presence of the church, chose the music, wrote or selected the prayers, wrote the sermons or invited guest preachers to provide recorded sermons, chose the music, and gave the benediction. She was the pastor of the church. She was not, however, in control of the cultural memory of groundbreaking Cyberspace Church.

In 1996, Alecia did a massive search of the Internet and found that after a search of "approximately 40 million Web sites,"[7] and her "Cyberspace Church," appeared to be the only Cyberspace Church offering a "traditional worship service." Her Cyberspace Church lasted a little over four years. Many who visited the church first became aware of it after Rev. Alecia was interviewed on a local news program[8] highlighting her innovative approach. She was happy to report that there was significant interest from the broader public. Also, in 1997, her seminary's Charles B. Copher Annual Faculty Lecture Series focused on the use of the Internet for religious formation. Alecia presented a paper on Cyberspace Church as did Drs. Anne Wimberly, David Rensberger, and Rosetta Ross. Beyond these published conference papers, I have yet to find the articles from the conference referenced in the plethora of research on religion in cyberspace or Black women and religion in cyberspace. If not for the conference at the seminary in 1997 and the publication of those papers, one would have to think that Black women are absent from the evolving dimension of religion and the Internet. This work, some small way, is a corrective.

CHURCH AS A THERAPEUTIC COMMUNITY

After graduating from seminary, Alecia returned to her hometown and area where she grew up. She returned home with the hope of receiving a call to a brick-and-mortar church. She described the core of her call as pastor, and her intention is to follow Jesus's "direction. I think that is Matthew 16:15 where Jesus says go you into all the world; trying to carry it out with the resources my church has available." Alecia has situated her ministry in a neighborhood where the congregants are often "ignored and invisible." They live on the edges of economic survival, making their way with limited resources, subject to police surveillance, and unpredictable violence. Alecia sees herself as pastor to the forgotten where she preaches a message of welcome and forgiveness. She does not want to pastor a church where the marginalized are shunned or made to feel unacceptable.

> Because we are an evangelistic ministry, we deal with people who not generally go into the church. The drug dealers, prostitutes, and people in recovery. The congregation is made up of people recovering from various addictions. Well, every church has people in recovery.

The power of religion is, for Alecia, its capacity to heal psychic and spiritual trauma in a communal context. She resists the idea that an individual should suffer alone or see a therapist for individual counseling. Given the poverty and economic instability of the neighborhood where she pastors, her congregants are not likely to seek counseling in a non-church setting. Church is the counseling setting and the congregation is a psycho-spiritual group.

> Our service is structured so that well we have testimonial time—not about how spiritual you are but about your struggles and how you fell off the wagon. No one is going to turn around and judge. We're going to hear you out. We encourage them to get back up. It's like a group therapy.

The church-based group therapy model Alecia adheres to is of a supportive "here and now" approach, and not psychodynamic in nature. She does not lead people to reflect on their past as a contributing feature of their current pain, or traumatic events, or to become familiar with their interior life. People's problems and issues that might cause distress are considered, primarily, to be individual realities needing a social context for healing. And even though poverty, racism, sexism, and poor housing are real structural issues, she offers little social analysis as to why her congregants suffer. She directs their attention to the power of a faith community to mitigate psychological and spiritual suffering.

Alecia is not alone in her perspective. Sociologist and womanist theorist Cheryl Townsend Gilkes argued for the therapeutic efficacy of Black church experience in her 1986 article "The Black Church as a Therapeutic Community: Suggested Areas for Research into the Black Religious Experience."[9] Gilkes writes,

> it is my informed suspicion that the social process of certain forms of Black religious practice act as a deterrent to specific psychiatric symptoms within the Black community and a depressant on rates of mental illness . . . the Black church is also a true asylum, a regular setting for group therapy, and an objective mediator between perceptions of experience of Black people and the messages of the wider social system.[10]

The wider social system and negative images of which Gilkes writes include segments of the broader Black church that have rejected those who make up Rev. Alecia's congregation. In the situation Rev. Alecia presents, the mediating value of the Black church is undermined by the class and economic disparity *within* the Black church, and the responses of those with more economic advantage not welcoming those who live at the edges of survival. It is Alecia Brown's proximity, first psychically, to the edges of the social and economic margins that make her acutely aware of the need for a therapeutic faith community, and because she takes interiority as a site for care, she believes that the Black Church needs to be a community that understands the daily assaults on Black existence. These assaults directed toward the most marginalized community members create internal and external challenges, and thwart their attempts to respond with life-enhancing choices. As the pastor of the street, Rev. Alecia's preaching and community care is aimed not just at interior transformation she thinks is needed, but it is also directed toward community formation and transformation. She hopes to spiritually form the community such that the community stands in solidarity with those suffering, prays for healing, and holds members accountable for the commitments they make to one another and themselves. Thus, interior transformation is tied to the social reality.

We can hear a similar argument for the therapeutic potential of the Black church in the preaching theology of Rev. Dr. Renita Weems, a womanist biblical scholar, former professor and administrator, who co-pastors a church with her husband. She is a popular speaker at conferences, women's retreats, and whose sermons may be found on YouTube. She is a regular poster to Twitter and Instagram. She is especially known for her blogsite "Something Within—Black women in the church." Her reach is wide. In her sermon "Come out of the Cave,"[11] posted on the Internet, Rev. Weems admonished listeners to come out from failed attempts at self-cure in the forms of isolation, withdrawal into interiority, and spiritual disengagement. Isolation, she tells listeners, leads us to nurse our anger and avoid the emotional demands of community participation. She argues throughout her sermon that pain and suffering are unavoidable but teach us what we need to know to survive the vicissitudes of life.

> Life is a series of lessons. Some of those lessons are obvious. Some of the lessons are not so obvious. We learn as we go, that dreams end. That plans get changed. That promises get broken.
>
> That people disappoint us, and that bad things can happen to good people. One thing time has taught me . . . despite years of hope of wanting to deny it. I know that there is no such thing as life without struggle.[12]

For Rev. Weems, unlike Rev. Alecia, engagement is almost a moral imperative. Withdrawal is not only not good for one's spiritual and emotional health, it is required of the Christian faith community. But Weems also realizes that the church itself can be a source and site of pain and discloses an example from her experience.

> I said life is not without struggle . . . I said life is a struggle. I'm talking . . . the church splits and I'm talking about walk-outs while the pastor's preaching. I said life is a struggle.[13]

Thus, the experience of struggle is not justification for withdrawal because, in Weems preaching theology, struggle and pain are a part of life. She normalizes struggle and pain not as right and good but as inevitable. Her read is a phenomenological one.

> You will struggle. I'm talking about when you were so depressed you didn't want to get up out of your bed. I'm talking when you're mad at the church and you're mad at God and you don't want to hear no gospel music. You don't want to hear no Scripture. You don't want nobody to pray for you. I'm talking about when you are in deep.[14]

In her careful exegesis of the text, the professor-pastor Weems brings a psycho-spiritual diagnoses to Elijah and congregants' response to the life of struggle. The diagnosis is that when one encounters the disappointments of life, the struggle leads some to isolate themselves and reject community. But Weems goes further when she asserts that the decision to seek isolation over community arises from an unexamined expression of narcissism:

> Cave-dwellers always think they are the only ones but the Lord said get up out of that cave and go to the mouth of the cave . . . when you are in the cave you isolate yourself from other people.[15]

As she preaches, Rev. Weems slowly begins to explain the context and cure for self-imposed for isolation and self-focus. The first is moving from the deepest place in the cave *toward* the front of the cave . . . "the Lord said get up of that cave and go to the mouth of the cave." Go to the mouth and look outward, not inward in a navel gazing withdrawal and not just to make yourself feel better, but, second, to be with community because your presence is needed by others. This perspective uproots any inclination to conflate withdrawal and disengagement with the move to interiority and introspection necessary for spiritual growth.

> What do you think we come to church for today, every Sunday, every Sunday? It is because we're trying not to isolate ourselves. I got to get myself to church. I need a community.

> So you're not in your cave by yourself. So, you're not crying by yourself. So you're not depressed by yourself.

> I know I need to get myself up from my house and make my way around the people of God. . . . When I see you come in here fighting through cancer I feel encouraged. Get out here and have some community.

This is where the anointing of God is. If I'm going to get out of my cave I need thee. Just to pull me out of the cave.

I need your voice to get me at the table. I need to get out of my cave.[16]

Both pastors, Weems and Alecia, make demands on their congregation as well. Rev. Alecia situates herself in close relation to the margins and Weems says, "Just pull me out the cave." Their pastoral ethics include the demand that the community, pastor, and the hurting accept responsibility for restoring the isolated and forgotten to fellowship with one another.

As the community's pastor Rev. Alecia discovered that she was being brought into a new community when the neighborhood congregation "the people, the drug dealers, and what have you" were watching out for her:

The police used to always come around, when my bus pulls up, to protect me. Just in case. But one day the drug dealers said, you tell the police that we are protecting you. Nothing will happen to you here. The people on the street gave us the church name: Church on Wheels. I would drive the bus up there, with six chairs, and a boon box. I would put the chairs out on the street. Eventually the people would come and help set them up. I would go through the whole worship like a fully contained worship that you would see in a building. Eventually some younger people in ministry started helping me. It's twenty years old now.

The community she sought to serve recognized her call to ministry to their neighborhood. Their commitment to protecting her revealed their ethic of communal responsibility. In the pastoral role, Rev. Alecia was also announcing her ethic of communal responsibility but, until the neighborhood drug dealers announced theirs, she had understood pastoral ethics as moving in one direction—from her to them. Once their commitment was established, they helped create the church by setting out the chairs, slowing down business so the street could be transformed into the movable faith community. This exchange between the ethics of communal responsibility and the creation of the church in the street is an exchange between the realms of interiority (pastor and individuals) and in the intersubjectivity (the neighborhood collective) to form a temporary realm of interior-intersubjective. This builds on Rev. Alecia's experience in cyberspace where the creation of the worship space was, ostensibly text based, however, her belief that the congregation existed in cyberspace with her was operative in the formation of her pastoral identity. She pastored a church where she did not see or hear her congregants. The regular process of creating the service, inviting speakers, selecting music, offering prayer—a ritual process—and reading the comments and responding to them, created, over and over, the pastor. These weekly encounters with the faith community, though unseen in cyberspace, were recreated with the Church on Wheels, and strengthened and firmed up an internal sense of her pastoral identity and vocational call as one side. The affirmation and internal satisfaction she experienced week to week was held alongside the reality that she was not affirmed by many of the Black male clergy in her area.

LAMINATIONS, REGRET, AND ACCEPTANCE: UNREQUITED VOCATIONAL DESIRES

For all her acceptance from her parishioners on the street, Pastor Alecia laments that she never received a call to a church. Race and gender combine in complex ways for her. Her experiences have resulted in a view of local white religious leaders as supportive and collegial. Their assistance very often centers around money, community resources, and as conduits of God's blessings and nearly miraculous acts God meeting a need. Black pastors, mostly men, on the other hand, have been the source of frustration, sexism, and disappointment. That racism and sexism, or what Linda Thomas describes as "racialized gendered sexism that becomes complexified when we add class, Queer, and heteronormativity to the recipe,"[17] may both be operative in her life seems not to be a question for her.

> After attending seminary and taking some preaching classes, I wanted to be able to preach across ethnic groups. I learned about and joined a ministers' association here because being a Black female I was not welcome in the Black pastors' area group and I was looking for a way to join. It is predominantly white but they accept that I am a woman pastor. It turned out to be a blessing and gave me information on resources I otherwise would not have.

The blessings of which Rev. Alecia speaks are access to people with money who support her ministry with gifts and those who use their reputation and access on her behalf. She recounted two examples that stand out as near miracles in her view. The first is that she needed a bus for her Church on Wheels but only had a $1,000.00 with which to purchase it. She prayed and then went to an auction where old school buses were available. The bids were starting in the $2,000.00–$3,000.00 range. She was about to give up when a

> white man said bid and I said I can't. All of sudden he raised my arm and the man said sold. I asked the white man, what just happened? And he said, you just bought a bus for 999.00 dollars. Can you believe it? But that's just how God works.

Her second example was a larger investment by a white man she barely knew. She was praying that she would be able to purchase a building because the bus needed so many repairs as to be unreliable. A white man said "come to the bank" and he got her the mortgage and it is paid every month. "Now see, he helped me." But the Black male pastors have not accepted her ministry.

> Church on Wheels is a small ministry but the amount of resources we receive are enormous. We serve food. We have earned the reputation that if we are given something we distribute. As a woman in the ministerial association, it turned out to be a blessing. Whereas the Black churches Black pastors would not help me. Our ministry has survived because of my white brothers and sisters.

"BECAUSE I'M FEMALE" THE TRAUMA OF SEXISM

> I try to take what I have learned and pour back into somebody else coming up. Be they male or female. I try not exclude just because I have been excluded. Most of the men, Black pastors hinder Black women. They hinder a strong Black female. And don't be able to write and spell your name! They're insecure.

> There was a mentee in ministry who had no formal training. A church was looking for a pastor so I told him to apply. I worked with him. Dressed his resume up. I told him what to preach on, and not on some topics. He got a call to that church. When they had the installation, you know . . . the pastor invites all his friends and other pastors. Guess who was not invited?

Rev. Alecia's exclusion from the installation, and particularly from the opportunity to be among the pastors precipitated a deep grieving denied opportunity. Not only could she not be accepted as a minister, she could not live vicariously through her mentee. Furthermore, he would not acknowledge her help publicly. He knowingly and intentionally exploited her and missed an "opportunity to counteract exclusion."[18]

> That really hurt. Been behind him every step of the way, I was mentoring him. Telling him what to say and do. Because see, **I** was living through him because that is the one thing that really hurt because, in my heart, I wanted to apply.

> I mean, you talking about hurt. I cried like a baby. That thing hurt me so much. I just wanted to go through the experience through him and he denied me that experience. He invited all the big dogs so he could have their approval. He would never tell them a woman helped me.

> That is the one thing to this day that I've always wanted. To be called to a church. To be able to apply to a vacant church and have the opportunity to go and preach in an interview. But because I am female. And he was called and forgot about me.

Three interior dynamics were operative in Rev. Alecia during this experience. First, she was trying to negotiate the effects of sexism through the process of vicarious experience. She knew they would not hire a woman but she wanted, if only through assisting this young man, to experience preparing for an interview. When he was called to the position she was gratified and bolstered in feeling that she knew how to prepare for an interview. However, when he failed to publicly acknowledge her mentoring, she was denied the initial feeling of success. Rev. Alecia was attempting to negotiate her anger about the sexism that prevented her from being considered as a candidate for the position. When these two attempts failed to protect her from fully, affectively, acknowledging the violence of sexism, she was deeply hurt by the betrayal and became depressed and temporarily bereft of solace, "I cried like a baby" because, again, fulfilling this aspect of aspirations were denied even when disguised.

Today, as pastor of the Church on Wheels, Rev. Alecia visits flea markets where she hands out sermons, speaks with people, prays with those in need, and offers concrete help to those who need help surviving on the streets. She describes this as a "market place ministry. This is where I am. And without a doubt I know I am where God wants me to me."

Rev. Alecia's relationship to race is more complex and reveals what gendered racism and racial sexism do to the psyche and relationships. In Rev. Alecia's sphere, race and gender experience are split where one side of the racial gender equation, sexism, holds most of her negative experience, and racism is split from her communications. The sexism she experiences renders Black male pastors suspect. When she speaks of pastoral disappointments, Black male pastors are the source of the disappointments she has faced throughout her career as a pastor in the nonvirtual world. While her identity as a pastor was solidified during her tenure as pastor of the Cyberspace Church, her self-esteem continues to fluctuate because of the way sexism has constricted the scope of her ministry. She does not have relationships with local Black pastors except for "the young people who help out." These young people in ministry are not peers and remain in collaboration with her until they eventually receive a call to an associate or senior pastorate. Alecia still longs to be "called" to a church; to be recognized and affirmed by the very male pastors who have repeatedly rejected her. The need for mirroring has not abated, and in its absence is lament, even as she says she has accepted that she will likely remain pastoring a small struggling church.

On the other hand, Rev. Alecia's deep appreciation for the white male pastors who use their influence and access to money, and other resources, to help her insinuates their "goodness" due to their "more accepting and supportive" response to her ministry. Embedded in this support are some assumptions connected to power and gender and the fact of her economic vulnerability. An underlying, and possibly undermining, message is that she needs someone to take care of her. This "taking care of her," making decisions on her behalf, or committing what would generally be bodily boundary crossings *seem* natural to her and the white men even if unexpected. For instance, when a white male, a stranger, noticed her reticence at an auction, he raised her arm at the appropriate moment and she bought a bus. There was no auction strategy on her part, or his, but rather the unnamed gendered, and likely racial, dynamic operating between them. Another white man used his access to help secure a mortgage. These are in contrast to her experience with Black male pastors. The lack of support of Black male pastors juxtaposed with white pastors set up an episodic process of splitting where recognition and mirroring adhere to whiteness and rejection to Blackness. White women, though they are part of the ministerial organization to which she belongs, do not seem to take up much of her psychic space. These dynamics of race, gender, and class are inextricable from religious experience or interiority. This suggests that the formation of her interiority has been shaped by experiences of sexism, class fragility, and white male privilege that are social, cultural, and individual in enactment. What is clear in her account, neither white nor Black males view her as an independent pastoral leader. And they are not alone. There are cultural aspects of the religious imagination operative in these exchanges.[19] To this point, Weems offers a helpful view. Shortly after Fox news began its tirade against Michelle Obama, Weems wrote in her online blog, "Something Within" about the interlocking reality of being Black and female.

> One thing experience has taught me. There's something about being Black AND female that drives some people insane. Being Black and female makes you the object of folks' worst fears and basest fantasies. People think that they can say and do whatever they want to you, because . . . they can. Black women may be praised for their strength and applauded for their courage. But none of that is the same as being respected. How does a Black woman get respect in this country is the question that deserves asking?[20]

It is this privation of respect with which Rev. Alecia has had to contend and it has exacted a cost. Therefore, unless critically and fully examined, the blatant and subtle encounters and effects of racism and sexism make their way into the interior such that they seem normal, as things "just are" and become integrated in one's life narrative. There is a powerlessness that can render one hopeless for change, and therefore resistance efforts become isolated and personal rather than structural. In Rev. Alecia's case, she has a triple jeopardy of gender, class, and race. The script of cross-racial encounter is read as spiritual encounters and is infused with an unconscious need for mirroring of her pastoral call and worth. These encounters affirm her unique and specific call in the eyes of God and serve to make her ministry meaningful particularly in light of the trauma of Black church sexism. This strategy of repair, so to speak, is an inadequate solution because Rev. Alecia still finds herself struggling with episodic fluctuations between the feelings of satisfaction and depression precipitated, in large part, by systemic and unrelenting failures to have her pastoral call recognized and affirmed. As a result, she has been unable to form the kind of professional relationships, in mentoring and support, through which her pastor self would be reinforced by Black male pastors. As a result, Rev. Alecia is subject to the irregular eruption of feelings of anger, regret, and loss as well as a deep sense of isolation.

These unmet needs for mirroring and kinship can lead to a sense of disintegration or, for example, Rev. Alecia's concern that she was going crazy. The need for kinship as it relates to a call to congregational ministry pertains to feeling a part of a community of pastors who are like you in essential ways where you are recognized and accepted, that you exist, as a pastor. Rev. Alecia has not experienced such a response from Black male pastors, which is where she seeks deep kinship (as opposed to white pastors who supply other needed experiences). Second, and closely related, is the need for mirroring or affirmation that the skills she brings to ministry are valuable, that she is a competent pastor, and a gifted preacher. The absence of a reliable and sustained community of Black pastors could have resulted in Rev. Alecia abdicating her pastoral aspirations and call. This clearly has not been the case.

> Ministry is a change agent. Because I started out wanted a nice church and big congregation. You know, being able to have a staff, a budget, and a mega church like mentality. But God has taught me over the years that everybody is not called to a megachurch.

> Somebody must be small. I have come to accept that. I struggled with that a long time, a long time, because, well, I didn't see myself as successful. God did not call me to be successful but he called me to be faithful.

MUST SOME OF US BE SMALL? VOCATION, TRAUMA, AND RELIGION

> Each person's life must be defined, nurtured and transformed, wherein the self is actualized, affirming the inward authority which arouses greater meaning and potential with each mystical experience.[21]
>
> —Katie Geneva Cannon

In attending to Alecia Brown's story, I think we would be advised to resist any inclination or pressure to separate the social context in which her religious experience occurs and her inner life. These "are not separate. In the world of experience," interior dynamics "become merged with (the) social."[22] This negotiation between interior and social is where meaning-making occurs. I maintain that because Rev. Alecia first pastored in cyberspace, without the immediate gendered and raced regulating of her call, and with the support of a local church, she had already made significant movement in negotiating her vocational call and identity as a pastor. However, this brief early experience as a pastor in cyberspace was during her graduate program in theological education while on a field placement. The church provided the financial support she needed to maintain the Cyberspace Church but she did have the option to continue the Cyberspace Church after graduating from seminary. This is why she returned to Florida to seek a pastoral call. The sense of vocation and pastoral identity was such that she initially believed that an opportunity would be forthcoming—in spite of her awareness that women, in her context, were not supported, or even recognized, in pastoral religious leadership. She could hold both the realities, her conviction that she was called to pastoral leadership and that she would not be affirmed, in her immediate social milieu, in this role.

As such, while Rev. Alecia cannot avoid these destabilizing episodes; at 72 years of age, she has internalized a religious value that "somebody has to be small," and in this case, it is her. She does not ask why sexism is the means by which she as a pastor in ministry must remain small. She grieves. Her grief is tied to the reality she has not been able to acquire those opportunities that would, internally and publicly, expand her sense of self as a minister. Her interior affective world is complex and even fluid. It is the fluidity and complexity of her interiority, related to, primarily, race and gender as well as mourning in the religious domain that shapes this phase of her life. Therefore, we should not be surprised that, over time, she has both forged a way forward and suffered from her grief:

> Mourning is not just about pain and loss, . . . Rather than promoting a view of what is normal, we should celebrate the diversity and passion of mourning and grief. We as a society are too eager to put an end to it, impatient with people who continue in their sadness, urging them to "move on" and "get over it" . . . (it) is painful, but it is also an opportunity for personal and social growth—it can't be rushed, or heaven forbid, discouraged.[23]

She is able, then, to continue in ministry, make her preaching available to her congregants and a broader public audience, and reflect on her ministry. Her authority extends beyond the practice of preaching to include her authority as a spiritual guide to those on the streets, whether living there or visiting. She is recognized as a spiritual leader on the streets and provides care through prayer with these who seek her out at the flea market and gives her sermon manuscript to those who are searching for a message outside a brick-and-mortar church. Ever cognizant of the trust placed in her, Rev. Alecia emphasizes that she "pulls them aside and prays quietly with them" so they have some privacy even though they are praying in public. In this small gesture, she recognizes and safeguards the interiority of the religious seekers who find their way to the streets in which she embodies her call to ministry.

As we think about Alecia Brown's experience of calling and trauma, we would do well to remember that she, and Black women everywhere, enters Black religious space from other aspects of Black culture. The social contexts in which Black women have been formed, according to the Beverly Greene, are "a social environment that is rich but also treacherous."[24] Alecia forces us to relinquish any reading of religious experience that tempers our awareness of the insidiousness, and ever pervasiveness, of the interlocking realities of classism, racism, sexism. One of the legacies and effects in her life is the asymmetrical valuing of experiences with white male clergy as a reaction to Black male clergy's devaluing of her pastoral gifts. The overvaluing of white male clergy, and whiteness, contributes to her experiences of grief because it does not mitigate her need and longing for recognition by Black male clergy. One side of her inner life affectively and communally attaches to white male clergy but another side is still attached to Black male clergy in a one-sided relationship.

What this tells us is that interiority and religious experience are shaped by, in part, the nature of our attachments to those whom we value and seek recognition and support as well as those who do not value us and deny longed-for sources of affirmation. These attachments, then, are not separate but are linked in ways not fully in our awareness, but emerge and take shape in everyday religious and social practices.

Closely related is Rev. Alecia's relationship with Black women in the religious community led by men. Again, there is sustained fluctuation between her disappointment and her disavowal of her longing to be received by them as a viable pastoral leader.

> The most harming words have come from people in the Church. And most of them . . . most of my problems have come from the women. Now that I've been in the ministry a long time; it's over 25 years, I understand it's a threat; it's a jealously.

> When a female acknowledges her call to ministry or is going to be called to the associate pastorate, they, the women reject you.

Black male sexism combined with women's internalized gender biases regarding women in positions of religious leadership, and therefore both subtle and blatant rejection, have produced an ambivalence, and even avoidance, toward Black relationships. In a discussion of similar concerns, Ana Flávia do Amaral Madureira speaks to the way in which interiority and socialization work together and are appropriated to maintain social hierarchies. Even those negatively affected by the hierarchies can be seduced into reproducing them because

> prejudices are affective, embodied through a constant and, often, implicit processes of active internalization and externalization of cultural meanings and values. Through the processes of socialization, individuals learn to recognize diverse kinds of symbolic boundaries present in the social world. . . . The transgression of these rigid symbolic boundaries, called cultural barriers, is perceive not just as undesirable, but as a real danger for society.[25]

These racial experiences in her Black community affect her interiority by comingling intermittent and quite ambivalence toward religious experiences associated with the brick-and-mortar Black church community and longing for an opening reflective of her capacities and call.

Black women's lived experience of religion complicates the picture of the religious in the interior-social realm. What is constant, or aspects of continuity, is in what flows through, and between, interiority and public religion. At the age of 72, Rev. Alecia's narrative reveals how religious experience is the ground through which major, lifelong themes of self, race, and gender are negotiated, both in the inner depths of one's being and the social and public domain. Alecia suggests that religious experience affords Black women a fluid space in which to be and become Black women. The fluid nature of religious space, interior and public, makes the engagement with religion an aspect of one's self-experience that it is simultaneously "religious" and a process for mediating the forces that shape one's being, and becoming, Black and female; this becoming Black, female through religion is a lifelong pursuit.

PRACTICES OF INTERIORITY AND MEANING-MAKING

Rev. Alecia has, to a significant degree, been able to claim her identity as a Black woman in religious leadership with a pastoral identity. Hence, she has been able to stave off and avoid the interior disintegration inflicted by religious soul murder. Soul murder, developed by Leonard Shengold, is defined by its deep and lasting effect on a person. Soul murder is

> a dramatic term for circumstances that eventuate in crime—the deliberate attempt to eradicate or compromise the separate identity of another person. The victims of soul murder remain in large part possessed by another, their souls in bondage to someone else.[26]

Womanist and Black feminist scholars have expanded the concept beyond the individual psychological experience to include cultural soul murder to uncover the debilitating and intergenerational effect of Black people's enslavement.[27] Both Patricia Williams and Stephanie Mitchum argue that "spirit murder," the collective form of soul murder, involves not only the individual psyche but the "social structures and institutions that enforce the cultural-psychic murder while simultaneously denying the pain inflicted."[28] The relational-cultural-psychic dimension is evident and relevant in Rev. Alecia's case because, as discussed previously, the effect of sexism in the church not only prevented her from *being* called to a church, but shaped her relationships with Black male clergy and Black laywomen in their congregations. These practices that produce soul murder have as their aim the annihilation of, in this situation, her pastoral self for the formation of a gendered self that supported Black male authority and leadership.

Religious soul murder emerges out of these same practices with similar effect and occurs in specifically religious settings. It is the process whereby sustained negative, and very often traumatic, experiences tied to the pursuit of religious aspirations and meaning-making experiences, deprive one of the capacities to reengage religion and spirituality in self, and communally enhancing ways because of the fear of the reactivating painful affects and emotional upheaval. In earlier work, I have written about the loss of religious cultural objects and the mourning required to recover.[29] Religious soul murder renders one unable to mourn the loss of religious meaning and deprived of religious aspirations. Pastor Alecia's conviction about her call, her capacity to mourn her losses and voice her anger, and her relationship with the parishioners on the street have buffeted her against the onslaught of religious soul murder.

The complex process of forming one's vocational identity is entwined with the lived realities of intersecting identities—class, gender, color/race, religion, sexuality as well as social location.[30] The process is interior and social. Womanist scholars remind us that Black women's lives must be centered in, and the center of, our work. The task is not without heartbreak. In listening to Black women's stories, we witness the many ways oppressive systems and social structures inflict debilitating harm on Black women; we hear how Black women's flourishing and authority to exist is hard-won. There is a cost levied on the psyche for *being Black women* in spaces that endeavor to deny Black women ground. The ancestor, womanist ethicist Katie Geneva Cannon, invites and implores Black women "to do the work their souls must have"[31] but it is not enough to pursue one's vocation or to resist those who would impede or diminish it. And Alice Walker, in observing her mother transform her flower garden noted that external and internal transformation are tethered: "It is only when my mother is working with her flowers that she is radiant, almost to the point of being invisible—except as Creator, hand and eye. She is involved in work her soul must have."[32] Cannon demands more than finding your soul's desire. Doing the work of your soul also means that Black women must ask "why things have gone wrong" and "why benefactors of oppression strive to maintain certain principles, values, and taboos as the center of social reality."[33] The praxeological intent here demands interior and public critical analysis.

Alecia engages in practices of interiority, such as prayer, devotion, and introspection, and public resistance. Her practices of interiority shape her public resistance. She preaches and prays from the pulpit of the Internet; she names her congregation and provides spiritual care to its members. She claims the Internet as neighborhood of her church—Cyberspace Church is as much about the space and the denominational identity and her ordained status. It is the movement from practices of interiority to public resistance to vocational invisibility to public practices of embodying her pastoral call, that Alecia's sense of authority as a pastor is made public, relational, spiritual, and obvious. She no longer doubts her call to ministry or her capacity as a religious leader. When the Cyberspace Church ended, and she did not receive a call to pastor a church, she started the church on Wheels. Again, she moves from the interior to public. She takes pleasure in sharing copies of sermons to those who request one. She is a pastor, available to offer spiritual and material support to those needing it. The churches where she has carved out a space to serve as pastor, both in cyberspace and on the streets, affirm her in this role. Her grief and disappointment are not completely abated but by insisting on the authenticity and authority of her pastoral leadership, she embodies her interiority as her Black woman pastoral self, and her interior and public are shaped and re-shaped by the exchange between two.

NOTES

1. Audre Lorde and Pat Parker, *Sister Love: The Letters of Audre Lorde and Pat Parker 1974-1989*, edited by Julie R. Enszer (New York, NY: A Midsummer Night's Press, 2018).

2. Alecia Brown is a pseudonym. "The author wishes to acknowledge grant support from the Louisville Institute for her "Womanist Ethnography and Black Women's Vocation," Faculty Research Project.

3. The archive of the church website may be found here: https://web.archive.org/web/19990202165851/http://www.cyberspacembchurch.org:80/index.htm

4. Cyberspace Church webarchive: https://web.archive.org/web/19990202165851/http://www.cyberspacembchurch.org:80/index.htm

5. Phillis Isabella Sheppard, "This is my Calling: Womanist Ethography and Black Women's Vocation," Conference, Vanderbilt University Divinity School, 2018.

6. Judith Herman, *Trauma and Recovery, With a New Afterward* (New York, NY: Basic Books, 2015), 33.

7. See also, Anne S. Wimberly, "The Faith Community as Listener in the Era of Cyberspace," *Journal of the Interdenominational Theological Center*, 25, no. 2 (1997): 13–71.

8. https://web.archive.org/web/19990202165851/http://www.cyberspacemb-church.org:80/index.htm

9. Cheryl Townsend Gilkes, "The Black Church as a Therapeutic Community: Suggested Areas for Research into the Black Religious Experience," *The Journal of Interdenominational Theological Center*, 8, no. 1 (1980): 29–44.

10. Cheryl Townsend Gilkes, "The Black Church as Therapeutic Community," 31.

11. Renita Weems, "Come out of the Cave," Sermon. February 20, 2011. http://jahasworld.blogspot.com/2011/10/dr-rev-renita-weems-2-20-2011-come-out.html Accessed May 24, 2012.

12. Renita Weems, "Come out of the Cave."

13. Renita Weems, "Come out of the Cave."

14. Renita Weems, "Come out of the Cave."

15. Renita Weems, "Come out of the Cave."

16. Renita Weems, "Come out of the Cave."

17. Linda Thomas, "Racialized Gendered Sexism is Complexified When We Add Class, Queer, and Heteronormativity to the Recipe," *Facebook,* 2018.

18. Forest Harris, "Called to Lives of Meaning and Purpose," Cohort Gathering, American Baptist College, August 17, 2018.

19. Emilie M. Townes, *Womanist Ethics and the Cultural Production of Evil* (New York, NY: Palgrave MacMillan, 2006).

20. Renita Weems, "Somethingwithin.com," Wednesday, June 18, 2008. Accessed June 18, 2016.

21. Katie Geneva Cannon, *Black Womanist Ethics* (Atlanta, Ga: Scholars Press,1988), 21.

22. Mark Joshua Gehrie, *Ethnography of Experience* (PhD Diss., Northwestern University, 1973), 9.

23. George Hagman, "New Models of Bereavement Theory and Treatment: New Mourning," a workshop at the Training and Research in Intersubjective Self Psychology. http://www.trisp.org/2016/05/19/new-mourning/. Accessed December 10, 2018.

24. Lilllian Comas-Diaz and Beverly Greene, "African American Women," in *Women of Color: Integrating Ethnic and Gender Identities in Psychotherapy* (New York, NY: Guilford Press, 1994), 10–29.

25. Ana Flávia do Amaral Madureira, "The Self-Control Ethos as a Mechanism of Social Exclusion in Western Societies," *Culture and Psychology*, 13, no. 4 (2007): 419–430.

26. Leonard Shengold, *Soul Murder: The Effects of Childhood Abuse and Deprivation* (New Haven, CT: Yale University Press, 1989), 5; See also, Irie Session, "Murdered Souls, Resurrected Lives: Post Modern Womanist Thought in Ministry with Women Prostituted and Marginalized by Commercial Sexual Exploitation" (DMin Diss., Colgate Rochester Divinity School, 2012); Leonard Shengold, *Soul Murder Revisited: Thoughts About Therapy, Hate, Love, and Memory* (New Haven, CT: Yale University Press, 1999).

27. Nell Irvin Painter, *Soul Murder and Slavery* (Waco: Markham Press Fund, 1995). The Public Broadcasting Service (PBS) also has a teaching resource page based on her book that is worth review. https://www.pbs.org/wgbh/aia/part4/4i3084.html. See also Michelle K. Scott, "A Perennial Mourning: Identity Conflict and the Transgenerational "Transmission of Trauma within the African American Community," *Mind and Human Interaction*, 11, (2000): 11–26.

28. See, Phillis Isabella Sheppard, *Self, Culture, and Others in Womanist Practical Theology* (Palgrave MacMillan, 2011); Stephanie Mitchem, "No Longer Nailed to the Floor," *Cross Currents*, 53, no. 1 (2003): 64–74. Patricia J. Williams, *The Alchemy of Race and Rights: The Diary of a Law Professor* (Cambridge, MA: Harvard University Press, 1991), 78.

29. Phillis Isabella Sheppard, *Self, Culture, and Others in Womanist Practical Theology* (Palgrave MacMillan, 2011).

30. Phillis Isabella Sheppard, "This Is My Calling."

31. A statement made by Katie Geneva Cannon and often referenced by womanist scholars. See https://muse.jhu.edu/article/723448/pdf

32. Alice Walker, *In Search of Our Mother's Gardens: Womanist Prose*, 241.

33. Katie G. Cannon, *Womanism and the Soul of the Black Community* (New York, NY: Bloomsbury Academic, 1998), 24.

Chapter 5

Tilling Sacred Ground

Meditation on Ritual and Resistance

BLACK WOMEN IN RITUAL SPACES

In ritual spaces, where Black women at the heart of process, Black women show up powerful. Ritual is always about the presence and use of power. Alice Walker's definition of womanist describes how Black women simultaneously embody cultural and spiritual power. Womanists, Walker writes, are

> serious . . . in charge. . . wanting. . . to know more and in greater depth than is considered good. . . for one. . . . Love music. . . . Loves the moon. Loves the Spirit. Loves love and food and roundness. Loves struggle. Loves the Folk. Loves herself. Regardless.[1]

Black women want to know more and produce religious, spiritual, and cultural knowledge through music, noticing lunar cycles, standing flatfooted in struggle and love, engaging the art of food preparation, practicing roots, and seeing the signs. They open themselves up to the Spirit to be let loose in the diaspora so that Black people can become a people who love their Black selves into healing, wholeness, and a future. This requires the wisdom and spirits of the ancestors and a commitment of the present, and a belief in a world most have not yet seen.

Black women's ritual processes are memory and reminders of the culture, history, religions, and families that the forces of racism, colonialism, and spiritual imperialism attempt to deny. Lama Rod Owens captures succinctly, "I have always felt touched by an unseen world; the world of ghosts, spirits, demons, and angels . . . these two worlds maintain a precious balance, continually rubbing up against one another."[2] This rubbing up against each other can take shape in ritual spaces and it holds the history of the community, both explicitly and implicitly. Malidoma Some´argues that ritual is to awaken us and make us conscious of the unseen world and the capacity to see or be aware of the unseen world helps in our transformation. More specifically, Malidoma speaks to the interior transformation that ritual yields. "Ritual can shake a person free from the rigidity of the that part of the ego that wants to limit growth and experience," and it is also the "crucible where this transformation and healing occurs"[3] so we dare not to take its efficacy or power lightly. Along this same vein, womanist anthropologist and theologian Linda E. Thomas, in her study of healing ritual in South African Indigenous churches, found that "rituals of healing blend worldviews (of the precolonial past and the present symbols of colonizers' religion) to form a cosmology that helps one to live with everyday challenges."[4] Ritual, she argues, helps because it promotes meaning. Such meaning-making is tied to the spiritual as well as the material and social contexts; in other words, womanist analysis of ritual, in matters of ritual processes, particularity matters. Particularity matters in research and analysis. Marla Frederick reminds us that in the social sciences, religion is sometimes reduced to its elements[5] rather than its meanings. As a practical theologian and psychoanalyst, I seek to resist these kinds of reductionistic productions of religion and ritual in the study of Black women's lived religion to a psychology of compensatory measures; adaptation to oppression in society; arrested development; or as confined to institutional life. Instead, I listen for, observe, and participate in meaning-making in public and psychic spaces.

In his study "Rituals of Healing in African American Spiritual Churches," Claude F. Jacobs reports that spiritual ministers place emphasis on the transformation of the mind and the congregant's "view of the self as the cause of problems."[6] This directs their diagnosis, rituals, and ritual objects. Jacobs reports that the spiritual ministers he encountered did not believe that ritual objects or ritual action had the power to change people but instead insist that "their problems are in the mind . . . people who believe they are hoodooed actually are hoodooed and the work of the Spiritual minister is to change such thoughts."[7] Malidoma Somé directs us to the interiority of suffering internally, "For the Dagara elder, pain is the result of a resistance to something new. . .Pain, therefore, is our body complaining about an intruder . . . It is possible then to say that pain is good, primarily because it is a call to growth."[8] While Jacob's description of spiritual ministers and Somé's understanding of pain argue that problems are interior and a cognitive transformation is required along with ritual objects for relief, they also confirm that ritual is a means for interrogating internalized caustic information previously transmitted as knowledge or reality. The interrogating of the interior is facilitated by counter mirroring acquired in the sociality of ritual. Even individual ritual practices hold a dimension that situates ritual action and meaning beyond the self, and bodily movement points toward the social and interior. The bodily actions of ritual work to interrogate and dismantle negative caustic messages about the meaning of Black life, and bodily actions pronounce counter messages and link the social and interiority to cultivate transform(ing) Blackness. Black women's ritual processes interrogate the interior and social but also interrogate ritual discourse around women, gender, and sexuality.

We see, for example, the need for interrogating ritual discourse related to Bruce Lincoln's study of women's rituals. While Lincoln could declare that women's rituals transformed the girl into an adult, restored society, and "renewed the cosmos,"[9] the ritual process seemed to be aimed at transforming a girl into a woman and renewing the cosmos for the existing social and religious structures. Such a womanhood does not resist the status quo; she reproduces it. In other words, ritual transformation seems more intrapsychic (how a woman feels about herself in relationship to the social) and symbolic rather than actual impact on the social-political, power-wielding world. Looking at Black women's everydayness of ritual processes, we see that transformation involves re/claiming the gendered, cosmological, sexual, and historical that is embedded in the interior and community, and this re/claiming is crucial for the present and future of the Black communities.

JANELLE MONAE AND RITUALS OF RECOVERY AND RESISTANCE

Janelle Monae's 2020 video "Turntables" is an oracle written for the documentary *All In: The Fight for Democracy* marking Stacey Abrams' rise in political significance in Georgia election and how the election was stolen from her, Monae prophesizes the turning of the tables on white supremacy. In characteristic bold and creative style, she presages an end to Black suppression, cultural dismemberment, and oppressive images of beauty. The video is replete with scenes of Black African-inspired culture: hair, art, acts of public resistance, everyday workers, history, and intergenerational relationships. In one scene, a young Black girl sits facing two dolls, one Black and one white. She chooses the Black doll. This scene revisits the historical "Doll Test" research undertaken by psychologists Kenneth and Mamie Clark[10] and points to the transformed Black interior's reidentification with one's Black self as good, desirable, and beautiful. The most powerful moment, at the end of the video, Monae pulls a large statue of Yemaya[11] from the ocean. Yemaya of the African Yoruba religion (Candomble in Brazil, Vodun in Haiti, Santeria in Cuba) is the "mother of the orishas and the Orisha of the sea."[12] Yemaya, also referred to as Yemanja, was an Orisha venerated by Yorubas transport from

Nigeria to Brazil, Cuba, as well as the United States during the slave trade. She continued to be venerated in ritual and religious ceremonies.[13] When Monae finally pulls it to make its full standing appearance, Monae's work is rich in ritual symbolism and signifies the inner spiritual recovery work we must engage to turn this unjust world, and ourselves around. Mikelle Smith Omari-Tunkara argues that rituals in Candomblès are "dynamic political entities in the sense that they . . . operate as centers of cultural resistance and power."[14] Ritual expresses and pulls together multiple multilayered public and historical meanings that become operative during ritual processes. In the video, Monae is enacting what Omi Osun Joni L. Jones describes as calling the orisa. Jones argues that the orisas are "inherently diasporic" and context shaped because "in fact, the orisa want to adapt to each region's needs so they can extend their own power and reach." This quality of contextualization and mobility meant that the orisas traveled with those stolen and sold into slavery in the West.[15] Furthermore, the orisas, when called in this new milieu, are done through the use of the local aesthetic and sounds. As such, "Spoken word, music, dance, oriki, drumming, and chanting are all employed as needed. . . . Yemonja gives an urgently needed stability to those who have had to reroute the legacy of enslavement and its subsequent, varied oppressions."[16] The stability that Yemonja gives to those needed it speaks to the interplay between the interior, material, and social dimensions of experience. It also reveals that ritual work makes evident the role of the ritual guide in the service of political and spiritual resistance, and that "Yoruba diasporic aesthetics" is "intimately linked with spirituality because Yoruba performance itself is linked to spirituality."[17] Practicing Yoruba spirituality became "a way of honoring Blackness, a critical survival tactic in racist environments."[18]

As powerful as the image of Monae pulling Yemaya from the ocean, Black women recovering and reclaiming an African ancestral spiritual practice is not without a struggle. As the spiritual retreat director for a group of Christian religious leaders, I prepared the space by creating a large African-inspired altar space including a Dan mask, elements for offering libation, candles, sage, and beautiful clothes. It was during the Christian advent season so there were four candles as well. We gathered in a large circle and offered libation as I asked each person what they wanted to recover from their ancestral roots. One participant, a woman, quietly left the gathering and entered the women's room. This part of the gathering lasts about 45 minutes and she was gone the entire time. She returned when we were discussing the ritual process and their experience of it. She told us she had been afraid to participate because of the masks. Initially hesitant to explain, she finally told us that she was from the Caribbean and had been told by the missionaries at her church, all white, that libation and masks were objects of the African continent, were evil, and should be avoided. As she spoke, she became emotional and even more so when she realized that had spent most of her life avoiding all things "African" including close relationships with most Black Americans. In another, similar instance, a Black mother brought her seven-year-old daughter to a womanist gathering. They arrived quite early and as I was preparing space, I noticed the young girl seemed to watch my every move. As I was about to burn the sage, I noticed her leaning forward from the front of her seat. I announced that I needed the help of a ritual assistant and asked her mother if her daughter could assist. The mother said yes and then said, "Wait, you not going to be calling demons up in here are you?" I explained that we were purifying the space and creating space to welcome the wisdom of the ancestors. We proceeded and the young Black ritual assistant entered spiritual role as if she had been born to it. I expected anxiety and caution; she had the confidence and demeanor of an ebomi. Turning Black material life and psyches around requires the retrieval and internalization of the Black spiritual wisdom that, for some, was buried at sea during the Middle Passage—for some hidden in the midst of colonizers' cosmology, and for some others, forgotten. Recovery is necessary to work in Black spiritual life, in spiritual practices, and in navigating the multiple spaces where Black embodiment is contested and denied.

Monae's video is dialogical art reflecting life. It recovers African spiritual sources and resists caustic negativity. A grandmother's ritual is as follows: Mrs. Batts, a grandmother, went to pick up her grandson, JB, after the first day of school and discovered that her grandson had proudly worn his new cornrows to his Catholic school. The principal told her they were unacceptable. Natural hairstyles were forbidden. They told the family the braids had to go. JB's grandmother refused, changed his school, and filed a lawsuit.[19] The ritual of recovering Black children's abused psyches and bodies from the claws of educational imperialism.

How do we love Black bodies when practices of Black hatred, denial, hatred, and violence, filled with ideologies of white supremacy, white beauty, and white omnipotence are so ingrained in psyches and the structures of society? JB was entering third grade at his parochial, religious, local school when he felt the full force of anti-Black embodiment pedagogy. JB as a third grader could affectively and intellectually follow the line of thinking related to his hair: if Black hairstyles are unacceptable, then Black people are unacceptable. Like Audre Lorde, he had to wonder if Black meant bad. Resistance to the infusion of anti-Black sensibilities requires an interrogation at the source of infliction. JB's grandmother argued this very point, "You're now making him feel like he's unacceptable."[20] His photo taken during a press conference revealed a supportive grandmother comforting her grandson who is near tears. His emotional response confirms her apprehension about his feelings.

It is safe to argue that the principal's behavior, first, rubbing JB's head as if in a demonstration of affection but it was, in actuality, an imposition of white power. This is especially so since intimate touch such as the touching of one's head is followed by verbal affection, acceptance, and affirmation. Instead, the principal informed Ms. Batts, in one sentence, that as principal, he was the arbiter of what and who is acceptable, and that her grandson could not return with his braids. Surely this negatively affected JB, but the embodied, ritual movement of his grandmother, a movement made by so many Black mothers, was an immediate counteraction to such psychic violence. But there is a ritual here.

Just leaving the house and neighborhood to stand in front of this white principal in full view of her grandson required something a walking meditation: notice where you plant your feet, deep inhale, exhale. Keep walking. Refute the lie. Deep Inhale. Exhale. Stand flatfooted. Show how much you love your Black grandson. Notice where you plant your feet. Keep walking.

We need our artists, our dreamers and interpreters of dreams. We need our historians, our warriors of truth and resistance. We need our ritual leaders, our children, elders, and future families. We need our prayers, chanters, and street corner preachers. We need our teachers of healing. And, so gathered, we need to see and love our Black selves, our Black "usness," and our Black communities.

BLACK LOVE

Historically, Black love has been the foundation upon which the Afro-American community has structured its ethical principles governing conduct in human relationships. Blues songs, folk tales, the civil rights movement (e.g., Martin Luther King's nonviolent movement built on principles of love), and Black preaching all emphasize the value of love for Black life and action. We hear this value in Zenju Earthlyn Manuel's teachings. In the preface to her classic *Sisters in the Wilderness*, Williams closes with the longing that Black women who "struggle . . . to bring dignity, hope, spiritual sustenance, economic well-being . . . to the everyday lives of Black people . . . that . . . in all their giving . . . remember to *love themselves*. Regardless."[21] The love of which she speaks is not the romantic and overly sentimental charade passing as entertainment in our media and entertainment-driven culture. As with the love between Audre Lorde and Pat Parker, this love is ethically principled, inspires conviction, courage, and fuels social action, and the activist voice we heard in Monica Robert's transgriot voice. Black love reminds us of the need to bring a loved self to our communities and commitments. Such a love moves in and toward the communal, and it rips back the claws of death dealing ways because it says, in the midst of Covid-19 and the wreckage and grief, it is leaving in Black and brown lives, in the midst of the violent brutality against Black bodies and communities, we will love our selves—our Black flesh—regardless, because, we are loveable.

In her essay on love and violence, Emilie M. Townes writes "Love is one more piece to the fabric of the universe, . . . one more sign that the Emmaus Road is not the end of the journey but it is the beginning. . . . It is a vital part of our journeys"[22] This love is not limited by the immediate, the past, or the imagined future; this love, this Black love is the thread that connects us, runs through us, across time, space, oceans, and cosmologies. This Black love links our lives to Blackness and Black people across the diaspora.

Monica Roberts, the transgriot, told us that she has an obligation to bring all Black transpeoples' narratives from across the diaspora to light because "we are each other's magnitude and bond."[23] When Black women enter a ritual process, we enter it as a slice of moral obligation to reach into all the spaces in need of transformation and healing. The process reshapes the interior in relation to the self and world. But it requires an arduous engagement with the past living in the present.

On some level, we, who are Black Americans, who are African Americans, people of the Black Diaspora, know that we have grief work, mourning work, and lamenting work to do. We often avoid it in social, communal spaces. Why? Because it is painful. We know it is important and crucial. We can trace grief, mourning, and lament in our literature, music, and art forms. Some of our most important literature is illustrative of the necessity of individual and cultural mourning and lament.

A return to Missionary Mary Proctor's mourning of family members burned in the fire is instructive here. While her husband dismissed the dream, Mary Proctor was convinced that she had received a message from her dying relatives, and this view was confirmed a few hours later. Proctor's interpretation moves dreaming from an interior psychodynamic process to the social life. Listening to predictive dreams is not a new phenomenon. We know that Harriett Tubman would dream the landscape and route to take freedom seekers.[24] Anthony Shafton quotes the writer Anne Petry where she writes that dreams handed down from generation, if traced, might lead back to Africa. In this ethnography, "African American and Predictive Dreams" found that Black people interpret dreams as spiritual phenomenon.[25] Jermaine Archer argues that these dreams are not only predictive and spiritual but that they are evidence of the link to African sociocultural life passed down through the generations and serves the community and validates the idea "that Africa and its traditions held firm in the memory of its people."[26]

Predictive dreams very often reveal an event that is forthcoming and the revelation is part of, and possibly sets in motion, a life-changing ritual process. Proctor's process begins with her dreaming of fire announcing death, followed by a withdrawal into an inexpressible grief, and a period of retraction from family and friends. She came to define this as a time where God allowed her to go through a period of depression for a year. She was in a period of public liminal potentiality. Proctor reemerged and returned to the emotional and social life she had temporarily left but as Karla Holloway argues, "Black death is a cultural haunting."[27] This haunting in Proctor's life infuses her art.

When Proctor returns, she first marked it in a way similar to how she began this process—she heard a new message. This message from God directed her to paint doors. As she painted the doors, she announced who she is in relationship to her husband, children, and community. She told us when and where she was born. She claimed her new identity as a painter, then as a missionary, and finally educator. Proctor communes with her grandmother and grandfather in her paintings and while painting and sustains a continuity between the ancestors and past and the present. She advises the living who seek her out, and she recovers Black history and a broader cosmological perspective. She is restored; her interior life is no longer paralyzed in her suffering her spiritual and social life deepens. Her experience suggests that ritual processes sets/resets in motion a life trajectory; as such, it is not an event.

The trajectory ritual sets in motion is not predictable. I keep a picture of one of my brothers walking down the middle aisle of a large Catholic church. He is wearing a Kente print hat and carrying a lit candle. At the front of the church, five large panels with symbols of Catholic Christianity and one with symbols borrowed from the Kwaanza celebration are hanging. As Phillip approached the altar, he bowed slightly and inserted the candle in the chamberstick. The ritual is not one specific to him. He is partaking in a ritual process in support of me.

At the age of 36, I participated in a ritual that would profoundly shape my life, identity, and my experience of myself as a religious person. I took first vows as a Roman Catholic sister in the community Sisters of Providence, Indiana. This was not an impulsive decision. It was not a singularly religious one either but I only came to discover this much later. Nor was it an individual one. Having entered the postulancy—the stage where a potential sister lives in the community as the sisters live—for a year of discernment. A postulant is, apropos Victor Turner, betwixt and between; in a liminal experience; not yet a sister but no longer un-vowed. For two years prior, for a period of discernment, a year-long novitiate, and a year as a mission novice—with each phase framed by powerful rituals of inclusion and becoming, and eventually, leaving and undoing.

This undoing of my vowed life, on the surface, seemed sudden: the ongoing power of those intertwined ritual processes still shape me as, in what I call, a post-Catholic. When I am speaking publicly of my spiritual formation; I am acutely aware that I must say something, even confess, about my decision to enter and leave vowed religious life. It exposes my hopes for deep community and may, depending on the audience, convey my convictions centered on pastoral ethical practice in the work of justice. But the greatest exposure is my leave-taking: announcing that I am no longer a vowed religious sister or a Roman Catholic in the capital "R" capital "C" exposes, if only to myself, an early failure to resist—as a teenager I began attending a small Baptist church, much to my parents' chagrin. At one point, my mother, concerned that I might want to become Baptist asserted: "You were born Catholic and you will die Catholic." She meant it. She was serious about her own ritual experience of "conversion" from the Free Methodists to Roman Catholicism as an adult. Such ritual, as far as she and my father were concerned, implicated the next generation and I had an obligation to live into this faith expression they had chosen for our family. During seven years of my early adulthood, I faithfully lived into it until I could not. By engaging in the ritual of joining the community, I embodied that spiritual hope of my mother as well as my own; by leaving I began a ritual process into a community beyond the parameters laid out for me. Ritual is space in which we become, are undone, and remember that we are always living into becoming. The struggle to do so was arduous and the path not always clear. But it is a path lived out in community.

RITUALS, ANCESTORS, AND RESISTANCE

A critical dimension of Black women's engagement in ritual should be read as resistance to the forces that conspire to deny Black women's self-worth, bodily integrity, spiritual knowledge, and quality of life. Womanist practical theologians, ethicists, sociologists of religion, and others, while deeply concerned with Black women's process of becoming, in the spiritual, psychological, and cultural realm, are just as concerned with the ways in which this process contributes to the communalism of Black life and what Marla Frederick discussed as the saliency of spirituality in Black women's activism.[28] She found that whether the Black Church takes up activism, members do. And that the work of the church resides in the spiritual and spirituality of its members.[29] Janalle Monae curated a video with a ritual arc of awareness in her "the tables 'bout to change,'" as a resistance to negative images of Black embodiment, gender, and sexuality, and recovery of diasporic spirituality. Monae declares. Mary Proctor resists the depression when she paints the doors; her family died in the fire because they could not get out of the house because the doors were blocked. The message she receives from God to paint doors is a directive for her to remember her family, in particular her grandmother and an oracle, a revelation, to remember that there is a spiritual door through which contact with the ancestors is possible. Her paintings are in fact, a continuation of the messages she receives and are to be shared.

Part of the ritual dimension of Black women's everyday lives of ritual and resistance is captured beautifully by Amina Wadud in her reflection "Hajar: of the desert." Hajar is the Arabic for Hagar. Wadud is a feminist, scholar of Islamic Studies, and Moslem. She was also the first American woman Iman. Her reflection reminds readers of the rightful place of Hajar in Hajj, the Islamic pilgrimage where devoted adherents to Islam retrace the steps of Hajar after she has been forced into the desert to die, most likely, of dehydration. Hajar is desperate to find water and goes back and forth seven times to save herself and child. The Quranic narrative says that she, at times, ran. The image is clear, she is a mother, who has resisted bondage and is now frantically trying to resist death. Finally, "the divine miracle intercedes and water springs forth, just at the heel of the child."[30] Wadud is one of the Moslems who make the pilgrimage to remember, bodily and prayerfully, follow in Hajar's footsteps, however, she notes, that today when the believers reach the places where Hajar is said to have run frantically, only the males are allowed to run. Somewhere along with the ritual and theological path, Hajar is rendered invisible or symbolic at best. Wawud is distressed by the sexism so apparent in the contemporary remembering of the pilgrimage but also by the "pristine" and consumerism attached to it.

> Something is amiss in our entire Muslim culture, and has been so for more than a few centuries now, when the central theme of this story is white-washed. Here is the ultimate expression of the intersectionality of race, class and gender made barren by our lack of commemoration.[31]

Wadud resists the obliteration of Hajar's narrative. She remembers and reminds believers that it was a woman escaping bondage running in the desert. She reminds us that Black women's ritual experience is embodied and lived intersectionally. When Wadud joins the pilgrimage, her aims are spiritual and sociocultural, and resists the silencing of Hajar the woman, mother, believer, and resister and future of a whole people. Delores S. Williams also takes up the Hajar/Hagar narrative from a womanist Christian perspective. Here Hagar is read through the lens of Black women's lives and Alice Walker's attention to spirit.

> The importance of this emphasis upon the spirit is that it allows Christian womanist theologians, . . . to identify and reflect upon those biblical stories in which poor oppressed women had a special encounter with divine emissaries of God, like the spirit. In the Hebrew Testament, Hagar's story is most illustrative and

relevant to Afro-American women's experience of bondage, of African heritage, of encounter with God/emissary in the midst of fierce survival struggles.³²

Williams reminds us that the Hagar was a woman who had no *little* over her body; she was in bondage to serve and, ultimately, reproduce for the sake of patriarchal goals. These goals were reinscribed not just by male authority and power but also by a woman, though under the weight patriarchy as well, in close proximately to that patriarchal power. Sara, in this narrative, benefitted from some patriarchal norms. The goal of impregnating Hagar was to save Sara from the social shame of not having born a son. Sara's name was to be rescued on Hagar's body. We have to interrogate the spiritual and religious narratives from those most distant from power and most vulnerable to its abuses. Alecia Brown experienced this when the women from her Baptist church, including her mother, would not mirror her call to ordination. Though women were allowed to participate in the church, preaching and pastoring were theologically and structurally denied them. After Alecia resisted these limitations on her call, attended seminary, pastored an online church, and returned home with the vision of receiving a call to a brick-and-mortar church, she was often ostracized and her calling ignored. It is important to note that she was specifically not recognized in liturgical spaces. Designated liturgical space is always contested space as are the cosmologies imbued in the space. But liturgical space is not only external so-named space; for a designated space to be entered as liturgical space, participants create the liturgical experience via an interior transformation; without such interior alchemy, the space is a room where groups gather. It is the dynamic between the interior, beliefs, and the actual public space that makes it ritual space. This is the case even when the liturgical space is designated as male space and women enter. Elaine Lawless observed that, in her field research in Pentecostal religious services, "Women are more likely to be 'filled' with the Holy Ghost, more likely to go into a trance, more likely to 'shout' and dance 'in the spirit,' and more likely to 'fallout,' . . . in a spiritual faint."³³ I would posit Lawless was also observing the convergence of spiritual and resistance to sexist control at work. Lawless argues, without explicitly interpreting the ritual experience as resistance, that "a woman who testified loud and long enough could actually gain temporary control of a Pentecostal service."³⁴ My own observation bears this out. In one service, I observed a woman take control of a service through the use of a tambourine. The tambourine was not hers, but one she "borrowed" during the service. She played it so hard and loud that all eyes rested on her as if she was conjuring the spirits from the depths, even though the male pastor was trying to resume leadership until the tambourine shattered across the floor. Then she collapsed. The ritual context is a fluid space where the expression of the spiritual is, in fact, intertwined with narrative and bodily forms of resistance to exclusion based on gender/gender expression, racial, and sexuality. Having never said a word, she contested Black women's invisibility and compulsory silence. She transformed the space, contested gender roles in liturgical space, and created space for woman in ritual.

Whether explicit or embedded, ritual space is permeated with gendered protocols for conduct and lexicons for the exercise of power—spiritual and political. Given the authority of these codes of conduct, it must be insinuated that the numinous is at work inside these oppressive forces, and that if the Holy Ghost, god or God, or spirits are operative in the ritual space, then power is always spiritual even when, as in sexism, it is misused or perverted. Overcoming its misuse requires transformation through interior awareness of having internalizing these lexicons and codes, interrogation in light of their impact on Black women's spiritual life and religious leadership, and bodily resistance. And, if these experiences of encountering the Holy are transformative, ritual is a space operative in the interior and social domains. These religious experiences are "underpinned by both psychical and social conditions that are at once inescapable and indifferent to the disruption they conjure and spread through the process of subject formation."[35] This change is crucial because, as Delores Williams argues, "the liberation of African American people cannot be effected until liberated womanist worship is the order of the day."[36] Liberated liturgy is the work of all the people where ever they embody religious and spiritual leadership. Monica Roberts, the transgriot in cyberspace, taught of the sacredness of Black trans women and men against the loud backdrop of the regular violence and murder of Black and brown trans people. Alecia Brown creates liturgical space on the street, and in the neighborhood where police surveillance is a constant intrusion, and survival against poverty and violence is a daily struggle. But the liturgical space is a weekly communally curated space. And Zenju Earthlyn Manuel shows up as Sensei in brown robes, offers deep bows, and leads a Sanghi into Blackness, lesbian, rage, tenderness, creole, activist, contemplative Zen Buddhism, and breathes compassion, and pours in a tea ceremony. She, like Audre Lorde, has traveled many spiritual practices to and she listens to the ancestors:

> Ancestors: We don't need you to be a good Buddhist, Muslim, Christian, follower of African Orishas, or whatever. We need you to remember the dust from which you came. We need you to remember a time before things went crazy, when they sold Africans like us. There was something before. It is still hidden from you. Find it.[37]

Black women in ritual space doing the work of liturgy and spirituality—transforming interior and public spaces such that those who have been wounded know the space is theirs and waiting for them. But the ancestors know that to find their space Black women must remember and resist. The message from the ancestors is one of interior re/formation and embodied public religious resistance.

> Lesbian Resistance: I learned my spiritual walk was not what I had traditionally grown up in.

Until very recently, Black women's spirituality and lesbian interlaced identities are quite often ignored in research on lived religion, spirituality, and psychology. Furthermore, when addressed, there has been a tendency to depict religious experience and sexuality as segregated due to heterosexism and internalized homophobia. Ahmad Greene-Hayes argues that this view is limited. Just as I have argued that Black women's religious experience is not limited to brick-and-mortar spaces, Green-Hayes also says that scholars have presented religious space as anti-queer and ignored queer people's religious agency and subjectivity. This limits what space is designated religious space and the actual lived religious experienced of LGBTQ persons historically, within religious traditions, and in public practices.

> While some scholars have traditionally thought of "religion" as being a category or lived practice that has *only* excluded queer, transgender, and gender nonconforming persons due to homophobia and transphobia, other scholars have shown how LGBTQ persons have engaged with religious traditions on their own terms, historically and in contemporary contexts.[38]

In Black lesbian women's everyday religion, the broader social landscape and religious cultural aesthetics run through ritual action and the claiming of one's self-identity. The religious and theological language provide the framework for how they interpret and explain *how* and *why* they are religious. The claims they make are not only about race, religion, and gender, but sexuality is dimension increasingly acknowledged as they give voice to their religious self.

SHELLA

Shella introduced herself, immediately, as 37-year-old Black lesbian and immediately began by flipping the ethnographer's script: "First, if you want to share a good bit about how you got into your current vocation and what it's like, that would be good." I spoke about the project, faculty work, my writing, and the divinity school in what seemed like, to me, a robust introduction of myself.

Shella prevailed and asked, "So where were you raised?" She set the terms by letting me know that this was to be conversational not a one-way monologue where she was a compliant interviewee. We began a conversation that required me to listen, be reflective, and reflexive enough to speak about myself as a lesbian womanist with Black Catholic roots, open to the wisdom of the ancestors; large family; northern, urban-rural. Happy. Nothing mind-boggling, but I felt exposed.

well, ok, about me. "Well, let me go back a bit. My people are from Mississippi and Alabama. They're like the second migration north. They went north to Detroit and worked in factories. Many are still there.

Not many of the folks went to college. I think a great uncle did. Two generations later, me and my cousin have graduated from college.

RAISED UP IN THE CHURCH

Um. Yeah . . . well I was raised by my great aunt. um. My mom asked her to babysit me and my sister for a week. She didn't come back for nine and a half years.

It wasn't wasted effort. It was a blessing. You know, in hindsight it was a blessing because my great aunt would always say, your mother will never be able to raise any children. Um, and so her goal was to instill in us, you know, values, work ethic.

You know, at five, five, and six, we could literally take care of our household and my sisters. We could take care of the household, which is like she said y'all have to be able take care of yourself. Also, we were, raised up in church . . .Me and my sisters, yeah, in the church, and we had to go up and sing in front of the church. (laughing) yeah, we were part of [this singing group]. I would have to get up every Sunday and be up there.

But we would get . . . well, we would break down and cry and we would never get through a whole song.

But I remember music; my aunt would take us to Value Village in the car and she would have Shirley Caesar playing with the windows down and I would be weeping. I would make an assessment, of myself, as a kid.

You know it was like as a kid, I could feel the weight of the world on my shoulders.

But you know Black families, what you crying for? Stop it.

But I wouldn't. I couldn't. I felt I had a heart for people.

And my mom came back into my life. She, was involved in her addiction. Yeah, A lot of pain there. Yeah.

But by 14, I was into my preaching, praise dance, prayer ministry but I grew up really fast. Started smoking weed and stuff. And I realized, I have got to stop. Got really involved in church. (Became) A leader. A prayer.

Shella's leadership put her in the limelight of the church. She was recognized for her capacity and spiritual gifts. In her community, her presence in the church and taking leadership roles were interpreted through a religious culture that reminds us of Clifford Geertz's notion that culture is "an ordered system of meaning and of symbols in which social integration takes place."[39] Her church assumed that their interpretation and Shella's interiority were in alignment. This interpretation of proffered in the religious culture and the attendant theology failed, ultimately, because Shella's mother returned and was a disruptive force psychologically and religiously. Her mother's brief return and insertion in her life caused her pain because her mother could not sustain her interest in parenting and the religious context could not adequately substitute for her mother's leave-taking; however, Shella had no alternative so her engagement in church became even more important as she navigated this loss and disappointment.

I MET A GIRL: TROUBLE IN A CHRISTIAN COLLEGE

And that's when the trouble started. My aunt could tell something was up. She started praying for me and then one day said, what's going on with you. You can tell me anything.

I felt relieved, so I told her I was in love with this girl who was in the church and we wanted to do ministry together.

My aunt, yeah, she went crazy. Said she wasn't going to have that up in her family and in her house. She said some things. So, at first, I tried to stop, you know, loving this girl. Wouldn't be alone with her. But my aunt she still didn't trust

126   *Chapter 5*

me and just kept at me. yeah. it was painful. I went to the altar again. This was, you know, a Pentecostal church. I was prostrate before the people.

Then 9/11 happened and I, I changed.

The social-political served as a catalyst for the transformation of her identity and spirituality. What is also apparent is the volatility she experienced relationally and internally. Shella felt relieved when her aunt offered to listen but then terror when her aunt rejected her, withdrew her trust, and affection. The effect initially disrupted Shella's sense of self and religious purpose. Pain and love converged. The response to her disclosure of emerging sexual orientation was disruptive spiritually because she could not disavow her attraction. In keeping with the religious culture of her context, she "went to the altar" to confess before the community. She exposed herself and subjected herself to their assessment of her spiritual readiness for leadership. The disruption to her life was pervasive and nearly unbearable. This disruption was only countered by the intensity and self-examination wrought by the cultural disruption of 9/11. Almost immediately Shella began a process of transformation marked by a new self-lesbian-affirming sense of self.

THIS IS MY JOY: BEING LESBIAN AND DOING THE SPIRITUAL POLITICAL WORK

I moved south and started doing ministry with the people. In the streets. I took my religion and spirituality with me. Look, I grew up in the church. It's part of me.

And I found political and spiritual teachers. That's where I found radical Black lesbians too. A lot of queer and trans folk who have had experiences like 'myself,' you know, been rejected out of faith institutions, we created a ministry base it's, it becomes the sanctuary to people.

So, and that's how I begin to nourish, to understand that my spiritual walk was not what I had traditionally grown up in.

This new path was one marked by a process of integration of the past and separation and reconfiguration from her previous theological teaching. Shella has not rejected the spiritual dimension of her religious upbringing or the emphasis on practice. She, like so many other Black women, has begun to integrate ritual and spiritual practices offering libation and reverence for the ancestors. Intertwined into her spirituality is her engagement with political action and resistance practices.

SPIRITUAL WORK AND SUBJECT RE/FORMATION

Black women's subject re/formation, then, via spiritual work and ritual spaces is achieved by re/transmitting revised and new codes to Black women across religions, sexualities, and spiritualities. This re/formation is aimed at the interior as deeply as the social. Sonbonfu Somé, argues that ritual is tied to the interior, spiritual and communal—not as separate entities but as integral to being human because "ritual allows us to connect with the self, the community and the natural forces around us. Ritual helps us to remove blocks between us and our true spirit."[40] Ritual is powerful because, in part, it gives expression and form to reality that

> people are embedded in their world, implicating a constant process of action and response. . . . A physical interaction of body and setting, a psychological interconnection of consciousness and culture, a dynamic harmony of sensory awareness all make a person inseparable from his or her environmental situation.[41]

Ritual interrogates, dismantles, and constructs the world and psyche. Black women enter into ritual space primed to counteract the suffering imposed on their minds, spirituality, and Black bodies and, when fully engaged in ritual action, commit themselves to the change religion and spirituality demand. The dynamic exchange between self, society, and religious practice cannot be overlooked.

> And I know, my work. I have to show up with my body, on the ground. Political. You know? Being in the work for justice; and it's my spiritual work. I am, I have to be a part, you know, of the resistance. I have to show up. And this is, yeah. This is my joy. Black joy. Showing up with my people.

Marla Frederick succinctly made this point when she argued that Black women confront and respond to the concerns and issues affecting their lives at the intersection of the institutional and personal. Black women's spiritual work is embodied in public spaces and directed at "unjust laws and practices" while also "creating communities of love and support."[42] They are living out their practical theologies, the practices that emerge from their convictions concerning self, community, love, and justice. These themes run through their mediations on their lives. The tethering of individual and public transformation is grounded in the spiritual. A critical analysis of the forces, operative in Black women's lives, centering their narratives in womanist ethnography, requires an engagement with Black women's interiority and public embodiment of resistance, love, religion. It is in the interstices between interiority and public, the past and the present, the body and psyche wherein religion becomes, emerges, and expands outward, as a lived practice. Thus, religion is a vehicle for social and personal transformation, the transmission of cultural meaning, and seeking the ancestors' wisdom.

Listen:

I hear the ancestors calling
telling me, it's time, it's time,
it's time, it's already time.
Their voices are rising,
directions becoming clearer:
meet at the border of north, south,
east, and west; inside outside
it's time; light your sage
purify your heart
recall your vows
know your teaching
strengthen your soul,
A shout will wake you,
thunder will guide you
anger will embolden you
courage will free you
the ancestors will hold you
in this time.[43]

NOTES

1. Alice Walker, *In Search of Our Mothers' Gardens: Womanist Prose*, xxi.
2. Lama Rod Owens, "Forum: Unseen Realized Beings," *Buddhadharma: The Practitioner's Quarterly* (Summer 2018): 57–74.
3. Malidoma Some´, *The Healing Wisdom of Africa* (New York, NY: Penguin Putnam, Inc., 1999), 30.
4. Linda E. Thomas, *Under the Canopy: Ritual Process and Spiritual Resilience in South Africa* (Columbia, SC: University of South Carolina Press, 1999), xv.
5. Marla Frederick, *Between Sundays, Black Women, and Everyday Struggles of Faith* (Berkeley, CA: University of California Press, 2003), 158.
6. Claude F. Jacobs, *Rituals of Healing in African American Spiritual Churches* (London, UK: Oxford University Press, 2005), 337.

7. Claude F. Jacobs, "Rituals of Healing in African American Spiritual Churches," 338.

8. Malidoma Somé, *Ritual, Power, Healing: The African Teachings of the Dagara* (New York, NY: Penguin Group, 1993), 22.

9. Bruce Lincoln. *Emerging from the Chrysalis: Studies in Rituals of Women's Initiation* (Cambridge, MA: Harvard University Press, 1981), 105.

10. See archived transcript of PBS interview with the Clarks. http://wayback.archive-it.org/8967/20171023214228/http://digital.wustl.edu/cgi/t/text/text-idx?c=eop;cc=eop;rgn=main;view=text;idno=cla0015.0289.020.

11. See image here: https://mysticsons.com/article/janelle-mon-e-turntables#.X2JHyy3Mxo4

12. Marta Moreno Vega, *The Altar of My Soul: The Living Traditions of Santeria* (New York, NY: One World Ballantine Books, 2000), 9.

13. Mikelle Smith Omari-Tunkara, *Manipulating the Sacred: Yoruba Art, Ritual, and Resistance in Brazilian Condomblè* (Detroit, MI: Wayne State University Press, 2005), 65.

14. Mikelle Smith Omari-Tunkara, *Manipulating the Sacred*, 8.

15. Joni L. Jones, "Yoruba Diasporic Performance: The Case for a Spirituality and Aesthetically Based Diaspora." in *Orisa Yoruba Gods and Spiritual Identity in Africa and the Diaspora*, edited by Toyin Falola and Ann Genova (Trenton, NJ: Africa World Press, Inc., 2005), 323.

16. Joni L. Jones, "Yoruba Diasporic Performance, 324.

17. Joni L. Jones, "Yoruba Diasporic Performance, 322.

18. Joni L. Jones, "Yoruba Diasporic Performance, 326.

19. Sarah Salvadore. "Catholic Schools to Accept Cultural Significance of Black Hair," *National Catholic Reporter*. 2020. https://www.ncronline.org/news/justice/catholic-schools-slow-accept-cultural-significance-Black-hair. Accessed March 1, 2020.

20. Michael Elsen-Rooney. "Queens Catholic School Told 8-Year-Old Student to Lose His Cornrows in Order to Stay in Class: Lawsuit," *New York Daily News*. https://www.Nydailynews.Com/New-York/Education/Ny-Catholic-School-Hair-Discrimination-20191030-Smfttve3mnhypbhskx6szbtjmu-Story.Html. Accessed March 22, 2020.

21. Delores Williams, *Sisters in the Wilderness: The Challenge of Womanist God-Talk* (Maryknoll, NY: Orbis Books, 1993), xix.

22. Emilie M. Townes, "Meditations on Love and Violence," in *Love and Christian Ethics: Tradition, Theory, and Society*, edited by Frederick V. Simmons with Brian C. Sorrells (Washington, DC: Georgetown University Press, 2016), 310.

23. Gwendolyn Brooks, "Paul Robeson," *Family Pictures* (Broadside Press, 1970).

24. Jermaine Archer, "Dreams in the African American Tradition," *Africa Unbound*, 2009, 2. https://africaunbound.org/index.php/aumagazine/issue-2/item/dreams-in-the-african-american-folk-tradition.html. Accessed July 10, 2021.

25. Anthony Shafton, "African-Americans and Predictive Dreams." https://asdreams.org/magazine/articles/african_prediction_dreams.htm

26. Jermaine Archer, "Dreams in the African American Folk Tradition."

27. Karla Holloway, *Passed On: African American Mourning Stories, a Memorial* (Durham, NC: Duke University Press, 2002), 3.

28. Marla Frederick, *Between Sundays and Everyday Struggles of Faith* (Berkeley, CA: University of California Press, 2003), 3, 219.

29. Marla Frederick, *Between Sundays,* 122.

30. Amina Wadud, "Hajar of the Desert," *Feminism and Religion.* October 17, 2013. https://feminismandreligion.com/2013/10/17/hajar-of-the-desert-by-amina-wadud/. Accessed March 15, 2027.

31. Amina Wadud, "Hajar of the Desert."

32. Delores S. Williams, "Womanist Theology: Black Women's Voices," in *The Womanist Reader*, edited by Layli Phillips (New York, NY: Routledge, 2006), 117–125.

33. Elaine J. Lawless, "The Night I Got the Holy Ghost" Holy Ghost Narratives and the Pentecostal Conversion Process," *Western Folklore*, 47, no, 1 (1988). For further discussion of Law's observation see Jermaine Singleton. *Cultural Melancholy: Readings of Race, Impossible Mourning, and African American Ritual* (University of Illinois Press, 2015), 75–76.

34. Elaine J. Lawless, "The Night I Got the Holy Ghost."

35. Jermaine Singleton. *Cultural Melancholy: Readings of Race, Impossible Mourning, and African American Ritual* (University of Illinois Press, 2015); 76.

36. Delores S. Williams, "Rituals of Resistance in Womanist Worship" in *Women at Worship: Interpretations of North American Diversity*, edited by Marjorie Procter-Smith and Janet Roland Walton (Louisville, KY: Westminster/John Knox, 1993), 222.

37. Zenju Earthlyn Manuel, *Sweeping My Heart.* https://www.lionsroar.com/sweeping-my-heart/

38. Ahmad Greene-Hayes, "Queering" African American Religious History," *Religious Compass,* 13, no. 7 (2019): 1.

39. Glifford Geertz, *The Interpretation of Culture* (New York, NY: Basic Books, 1973), 59.

40. Sonbonfu Somé, *Welcoming Spirit Home: Ancient African Teaching to Celebrate Children and Community* (Novato, CA: New World Library), 24.

41. Arnold Berleant, *Aesthetics and Environment, Theme and Variations on Art and Culture* (Philadelphia, PA: Temple University Press, 1992).

42. Marla Frederick, *Between Sundays: Black Women and Everyday Struggles of Faith* (Oakland, CA: University of California Press, 2003), 8.

43. Phillis Isabella Sheppard, "Ancestral Call," 2019. Presented as part of American Academy of Religion, Psychology, Culture, and Religion session.

Concluding Remarks

The womanist Catholic theologian M. Shawn Copeland captures the deep longing many Black women bring to their religious lives. About her own motivations, Copeland said,

> "You want to do some good in the world, you know? . . . You want to leave wherever you are better than when you found it. And you'd like to contribute to that betterment—not that you're solely responsible or that you can personally bring it about. It takes the work of many people, not just one person."

In essence, then, at its core, this work is about the religious impulses that inspire Black women to engage religion as part and parcel to impulse to leave the world transformed. Religion inspires and sustains them. It is about their hopes for themselves and for those with whom they travel this world. What, we might ask, are Black women teaching us in the telling of their stories of religious experience? What do Black women's lives tell us about the world and their place in it?

Womanist scholars argue that social location and particularity, along with race, gender, class, and sexuality, are lived simultaneously by Black women. As such, religion is the tributary through which experience runs. Bell hooks is representative,

> I live in . . . the Bible Belt . . . and in every way that I can, small and large, build a beloved community. . . . As a Buddhist Christian, . . . I'm challenging myself, "What are you doing, bell, for the creation of the beloved community?"[1]

Religion and their identities as Black women are powerful forces in their lives. Their interior identification with Black religion and Black life, quite broadly delineated, produces impulses toward public religious practice, social obligation to, and desire on behalf of justice for Black communities. That is, with this reading, we can apprehend the moral aims of Black women and the effects of living religiously and publicly.

This book was in formation long before Jessica Krug, a white Jewish woman and tenured professor, who claimed to be a Black Latina and a feminist admitted that she is neither Black nor Latina, and before she demanded that white folks at a protest rally "yield their time for Black and Brown indigenous New Yorkers."[2] Krug made her demands in the academy and the streets even as she stole Black Latina's time, space, and stories. Krug's deceit, misrepresentation, and misappropriation had a demoralizing effect on Black women in the university and guilds in which imposed her membership. She accepted positions and awards created for Black and Latina women, and in so doing, exercised a sense of entitlement that was aimed at obliterating Black women's scholarly vocation, silencing their critical voices, and claiming their space in the rituals of recognition and advancement. Krug's practices substantiated the hierarchy of whiteness by believing in, grasping it as one would be a religious creed, and publicly acting on the ideology of white superiority. So convinced was of her superiority that would stand before academic pulpits and activists' podiums to "explain" Black women's positionality in a racist sexist society, and she seemed convinced that she could do this more adequately than they could. This ideology was pervasive throughout her life. Under the name Jess La Bombalera, she claimed to be a Latina activist in New York City. Krug colonized Black and Brown spaces and would not yield. She stopped only when a courageous junior scholar reported her suspicions to two senior scholars with evidence and they intervened. When the junior scholar spoke up, she reinscribed Black women's ethical voice. Krug's story is important because she reveals the dangers of relying solely on a public performance of Black women's intersectionality. Krug became suspect when colleagues, in the academy and activists' communities, noted inconsistencies in her narrations of self. Krug's interiority increasingly revealed, no matter how hard she resisted, her whiteness. Krug's whiteness infused her interiority and public practice of racism. This vignette matters because in its full telling, we see that what is most important is the convergence of Black women's moral deliberations and resistance to racism and injustice.

WOMANIST ETHNOGRAPHIC LENS

This book, while recognizing the complexity involved in highlighting Black women's public practices of religion and interiority, strengthens the view that they cannot be extricated from each other. In taking them up simultaneously, religious space is reconfigured as interior, intersubjective, and public. How do we reach the depth of the interior in relation to the Black women's public engagement with religion? Throughout this book, I have maintained a womanist ethnographic disposition and approach to narratives.

Womanist ethnography is not just telling good stories. Womanist ethnographers report lives from Black women's perspective and the meaning they, very often through painstaking reflection, give them. Womanist ethnography reveals the complexities of Black women's lives in religion, community, and in the depths of their souls. These stories are portraits of Black life. Together they reveal the realities of Black life not noticed when focusing on the surface manifestations of experience. The women who sit with us, watching us as we record their lives, are griots.

Womanist ethnography involves the practice of listening to Black women's experiences and perspectives as a required, necessary, and valued basis of our research. It privileges Black women's social and cultural knowledge and their strategies for navigating the societal, religious, and relational complexities of being Black women. Womanist ethnography opens up spaces for conversation and shared knowledge to create new understandings of society, lived religion, and Black women. It is also subject to the ethical demands of the process because Black women who agree to share their stories and

> experiences also demand that womanist ethnographers come to the space not as an interviewer but as a Black woman who has experienced the same or similar encounters with suffering and resistance. The listening space that womanist ethnography demands is one of fluid mutuality, transparency, and care. It is . . . not just about acquiring "a good" interview or story.[3]

Womanist ethnographers are forced into a parallel reflection process thus making their interiority intersubjective, as when the interviewee inquires, "where are your people from?" The womanist ethnography is ethically required to deliberate and reflect on the demands embedded in research. As such, interiority and sociality of researcher and interviewees are intertwined, in varying degrees, in ethnographic narration.

NOTES

1. George Yancy, and bell hooks, "bell hooks: Buddhism, the Beats and Loving Blackness," December 10, 2015. https://opinionator.blogs.nytimes.com/2015/12/10/bell-hooks-buddhism-the-beats-and-loving-blackness/?mcubz=1. Accessed June 20, 2017.

2. "Jessica Krug White Professor Pretended to Be Black," September 3, 2020. https://www.theguardian.com/world/2020/sep/03/jessica-krug-white-professor-pretended-black. Accessed June 20, 2021.

3. Phillis Isabella Sheppard, "Womanist Gathering as Public Theology," in *The Gathering A Womanist Church: Origins, Stories, Sermons, and Litanie*, edited by Irie Lynne Session, Kamilah Hall Sharp, and Jann Aldredge-Clanton (Eugene, OR: Wipf and Stock, 2020), xiii.

Bibliography

Alexander, Elizabeth. *The Black Interior.* St. Paul, MN: Graywolf Press, 2004.
Allen, Samantha. "Inside Monica Roberts' Mission to Identify Transgender Murder Victims." *The Daily Beast,* February 19, 2019. https://www.thedailybeast.com/inside-monica-roberts-mission-to-identify-transgender-murder-victims.
Ammerman, Nancy. "Lived Religion as an Emerging Field: An Assessment of Its Contours and Frontiers." *Nordic Journal of Religion and Society* 29, no. 2 (2016): 83–99. doi: 10.18261/issn.1890-7008-2016-02-01.
Archer, Jermaine. "Dreams in the African American Folk Tradition." *Africa Unbound* 2 (2009). https://africaunbound.org/index.php/aumagazine/issue-2/item/dreams-in-the-african-american-folk-tradition.html.
Bentham, Jeremy. "Panopticon; or the Inspection-House: Containing the Idea of a New Principle of Construction." In *The Panopticon Writings,* edited by Miran Bozovic, 29–95. London: Verso, 1995.
Berleant, Arnold. *Aesthetics and Environment, Theme and Variations on Art and Culture.* Philadelphia, PA: Temple University Press, 1992.
Brooks, Gwendolyn. "Paul Robeson." In *Family Pictures.* Detroit, MI: Broadside Press, 1970/1971.
Butler, Octavia E. *Parable of the Sower.* New York: Grand Central Publishing, 2000.
Cannon, Katie Geneva. *Black Womanist Ethics.* Atlanta, GA: Scholars Press, 1988.
———. *Womanism and the Soul of the Black Community.* New York: Bloomsbury Academic, 1998.
Clark, Kenneth. Interview by Blackside, Inc., on November 4, 1985 for *Eyes on the Prize: America's Civil Rights Years (1954-1965).* Rolls 146–48, transcript. Film and Media Archive, Henry Hampton Collection, Washington University Libraries, St. Louis, MO. Last modified October 23, 2017. https://wayback.archive-it.org/8967/20171023214228/http:/digital.wustl.edu/cgi/t/text/text-idx?c=eop;cc=eop;rgn=main;view=text;idno=cla0015.0289.020.
Cohen, Emily. "An Interview with Jan Willis." *Journal of Feminist Studies in Religion* 33, no. 2 (Fall 2017): 127–37. doi: 10.2979/jfemistudreli.33.2.13.

Cole, Johnetta B. "Audre Lorde: My Shero, My Teacher, My Sister Friend." In *I Am Your Sister Collected and Unpublished Writing of Audre Lorde*, edited by Rudolph P. Byrd, Johnetta B. Cole, Beverly Guy-Sheftall, 231–37. New York: Oxford University Press, 2009.

Cooper, Ashton. "The Problem of the Overlooked Female Artist: An Argument for Enlivening a Stale Model of Discussion." *Hyperallergic*, January 10, 2015. https://hyperallergic.com/173963/the-problem-of-the-overlooked-female-artist-an-argument-for-enlivening-a-stale-model-of-discussion/.

Coopersmith, Hayley. "Black Perfomance Art as Black Feminism: Changing Perspectives in the Contemporary Art World." *Medium*, April 28, 2015. https://medium.com/black-feminism/black-perfomance-art-as-black-feminism-changing-perspectives-in-the-comtemporary-art-world-e65aa238422.

Comas-Díaz, Lillian, and Beverly Greene, eds. "African American Women." In *Women of Color: Integrating Ethnic and Gender Identities in Psychotherapy*, 10–29. New York: Guilford Press, 1994.

Cornwell, Anita. "Pat Parker – Black Lesbian Poet, Radical Pioneer. Readings/Appearances of *Movement in Black*. Interviewed by Anita Cornwell." *Hera* 15–18 (April/May – August/September 1975). https://www.amusejanetmason.com/Pat_Parker4.htm

Crumpton, Stephanie M. *A Womanist Pastoral Theology Against Intimate and Cultural Violence*. New York: Palgrave Macmillan, 2014.

Davis, Ann Marie, and Zenju Earthlyn Manuel. "Zenju Earthlyn Manuel in Conversation with Ann Marie Davis." *Deep Times: A Journal of the Work that Reconnects*. Last modified August 29, 2017. https://journal.workthatreconnects.org/2017/08/29/zenju-earthlyn-manuel-in-conversation-with-ann-marie-davis/.

De Veaux, Alexis. *Warrior Poet: A Biography of Audre Lorde*. New York: W. W. Norton & Co., 2004.

do Amaral Madureira, Ana Flávia. "The Self-Control Ethos as a Mechanism of Social Exclusion in Western Societies." *Culture & Psychology* 13, no. 4 (2007): 419–30. doi: 10.1177/1354067X07082751.

Dyson, Torkwase. "Black Interiority: Notes on Architecture, Infrastructure, Environmental Justice, and Abstract Drawing." Pelican Bomb. Last modified January 9, 2017. http://pelicanbomb.com/art-review/2017/Black-interiority-notes-on-architecture-infrastructure-environmental-justice-and-abstract-drawing.

Elsen-Rooney, Michael. "Queen Catholic School Told 8-Year-Old to Lose His Cornrows in Order to Stay in Class." *New York Daily News*, October 30, 2019. https://www.nydailynews.com/new-york/education/ny-catholic-school-hair-discrimination-20191030-smfttve3mnhypbhskx6szbtjmu-story.html.

Erinkitola, M. M. "A Church for the Cyberspace Community." *Cyberspace Missionary Baptist Church*, Atlanta, GA. Last modified 1998. https://web.archive.org/web/19990202165851/http:/www.cyberspacembchurch.org:80/index.htm

"Famous Folk Artist Mary Proctor needs YOUR HELP!" YouTube video, 1:33, posted by Jennifer Kosharek. October 3, 2010. https://www.youtube.com/watch?v=reTfpeqvkoE.

Fanon, Frantz. *Black Skin, White Masks*. New York: Grove Press, 1967.

———. *The Wretched of the Earth*. New York: Grove Press, 1963.
Frederick, Marla. *Between Sundays, Black Women, and Everyday Struggles of Faith*. Berkeley, CA: University of California Press, 2003.
Gehrie, Mark Joshua. "Sansei: An Ethnography of Experience." PhD diss., Northwestern University, 1973. ProQuest (302754253).
Gilkes, Cheryl Townsend. "The Black Church as a Therapeutic Community: Suggested Areas for Research into the Black Religious Experience." *The Journal of Interdenominational Theological Center* 8, no. 1 (Fall 1980): 29–44.
Greene-Hayes, Ahmad. "'Queering' African American Religious History." *Religion Compass* 13, no. 7 (2019): 1–17. doi: 10.1111/rec3.12319.
Griffin Ada Gay, and Michelle Parkerson Griffin, dirs. *Litany for Survival: The Life and Work of Audre Lorde*. New York: Third World Newsreel, 1996.
Hagman, George. "New Models of Bereavement Theory and Treatment: New Mourning." The Training and Research in Intersubjective Self Psychology Foundation. Last modified May 19, 2016. http://www.trisp.org/2016/05/19/new-mourning/.
Harris, Forest. "Called to Lives of Meaning and Purpose." Presentation delivered during cohort gathering, American Baptist College, Nashville, TN, August 17, 2018.
Henery, Celeste. "The Tears, Struggles, and Hopes of Black Women." African American Intellectual History Society: Black Perspectives. Last modified October 26, 2017. https://www.aaihs.org/the-tears-struggles-and-hopes-of-black-women/.
Herman, Judith. *Trauma and Recovery: The Aftermath of Violence – From Domestic Abuse to Political Terror*. New York: Basic Books, 2015.
Hine, Darlene Clark. "Rape and the Inner Lives of Black Women in the Middle West: Preliminary Thoughts on the Culture of Dissemblance." *Signs: Journal of Women in Culture and Society* 14, no. 4 (Summer 1989): 912–20. doi: 10.1086/494552.
Holloway, Karla F. C. *Passed On: African American Mourning Stories, A Memorial*. Durham, NC: Duke University Press, 2002.
Jacobs, Claude F. "Rituals of Healing in African American Spiritual Churches." In *Religion and Healing in America*, edited by Linda L. Barnes and Susan Starr Sered, 333–41. London: Oxford University Press, 2005.
Jamerican Muslimah. "Who am I?" *Jamerican Muslimah's Veranda* (blog). Last updated March 29, 2012. https://jamericanmuslimah.wordpress.com/who-am-i/.
John, Catherine A. *Clear Word and Third Sight: Folk Groundings and Diasporic Consciousness in African Caribbean Writing*. Durham, NC: Duke University Press, 2003.
Jones, Joni L. "Yoruba Diasporic Performance: The Case for a Spiritually- and Aesthetically-Based Diaspora." In *Orisa Yoruba Gods and Spiritual Identity in Africa and the Diaspora*, edited by Toyin Falola and Ann Genova, 321–31. Trenton, NJ: Africa World Press, Inc., 2005.
Kistulentz, Steve. "Mary Proctor's Vision." *Raw Vision* 29 (Winter 1999/2000): 32–37.
Kohut, Heinz. "Idealization and Cultural Self Objects." In *Self Psychology and the Humanities: Reflections on a New Psychoanalytic Approach*, edited by Charles B. Strozier, 224–31. New York: W. W. Norton & Company, 1985.

———. "On the Continuity of the Self and Cultural Self Objects." In *Self Psychology and the Humanities: Reflections on a New Psychoanalytic Approach*, edited by Charles B. Strozier, 232–43. New York: Norton & Company, 1985.

Lartey, Emmanuel Y. *Postcolonializing God: An African Practical Theology*. London: SCM Press, 2013.

———. "Report at the Society for Pastoral Theology Annual Meeting." Presentation delivered during the Post-Colonial Study Group, Atlanta, GA, June 14–17, 2018.

Lawless, Elaine J. "'The Night I Got the Holy Ghost...': Holy Ghost Narratives and the Pentecostal Conversion Process." *Western Folklore* 47, no. 1 (January 1988): 1–19. doi: 10.2307/1500052.

Lawrence-Lightfoot, Sara. "Portraiture." Last modified 2014. http://www.saralawrencelightfoot.com/portraiture1.html.

Lincoln, Bruce. *Emerging from the Chrysalis: Studies in Rituals of Women's Initiation*. Cambridge, MA: Harvard University Press, 1981.

Lorde, Audre. *A Burst of Light: And Other Essays*. Mineola, NY: Ixia Press, 2017.

———. *Cancer Journals*. San Francisco, CA: Spinsters Ink, 1980.

———. "Father, Son and Holy Ghost." In *Coal*, 4. New York: W. W. Norton and Company, 1996.

———. "From the House of Yemanja." In *The Black Unicorn*, 6. New York: W. W. Norton and Company, 1978.

———. *I Am Your Sister: Collected and Unpublished Writings of Audre Lorde*, edited by Rudolph Byrd, Johnetta B. Cole, and Beverly Guy-Sheftall. New York: Oxford University Press, 2009.

———. *Our Dead Behind Us: Poems*. New York: W. W. Norton and Company, 1986.

———. "Power." In *The Collected Poems of Audre Lorde*, 215. New York: W. W. Norton & Company, 2000.

———. *Sister Outsider: Essays and Speeches*. Trumansburg, NY: Crossing Press, 1984.

———. "Turning the Beat Around: Lesbian Parenting." In *A Burst of Light and Other Essays*, 30–39. Ithaca, NY: Firebrand Books, 1988.

———. *Zami: A New Spelling of My Name*. New York: Crossing Press, 1982.

Lorde, Audre, and Pat Parker. *Sister Love: The Letters of Audre Lorde and Pat Parker, 1974-1989*, edited by Julie R. Enszer. New York: A Midsummer Night's Press, 2018.

Mageed, Debra. "Resisting the Veil of Universalism: Muslim Womanist Philosophy as a Lens for Authentic Representations of African American Muslim Women." In *Muslimah Theology: The Voices of Muslim Women Theologians*, edited by Ednan Aslan, Marcia K. Hermansen, and Elif Medeni, 247–65. New York: Peter Lang Publishers, 2013.

Manley, Roger B. "Outsider Art: Psychosis or Expression of Folk Art-Making? The Functions of Outsider Art." Master's thesis, University of North Carolina Chapel Hill, 1991. http://www.folkstreams.net/film-context.php?id=151.

Manuel, Zenju Earthlyn. "About." *Zenju* (blog). Last modified 2021. https://zenju.org/about/.

———. "Awakening Fueled by Rage." *Lion's Roar: Buddhist Wisdom for Our Time*. Last modified January 8, 2021. https://www.lionsroar.com/awakening-fueled-by-rage/.

———. "Be Home, Be Still." *Zenju* (blog). Last modified 2021. https://zenju.org/be-home-be-still/.

———. "The Dance of Death." *Zenju* (blog). Last modified 2021. https://zenju.org/the-dance-of-death/.

———. "The Dharma of Black Feminism: A Commentary on Black Women's Voices." *Buddhist Peace Fellowship*. Last modified November 20, 2013. https://buddhistpeacefellowship.org/the-dharma-of-black-feminism-zenju-earthlyn-manuel-on-bell-hooks-and-melissa-harris-perry/.

———. "The Hunger for Home." *Tricycle: The Buddhist Review* (Spring 2018). https://tricycle.org/magazine/the-hunger-for-home/.

———. "I Am Not My Hair." *Zenju* (blog). Last modified 2021. https://zenju.org/i-am-not-my-hair/.

———. "Ouch! Systemic Suffering and the Second Noble Truth." *Buddhist Peace Fellowship*. Last modified July 14, 2014. https://buddhistpeacefellowship.org/tss-2014/2-zenju/.

———. "Prolonged Audaciousness." *Zenju* (blog). Last modified 2021. https://zenju.org/prolonged-audaciousness/.

———. "Remembering the Ancestors." *Zenju* (blog). Last modified 2021. https://zenju.org/remembering-the-ancestors/.

———. *Sanctuary: A Meditation on Home, Homelessness, and Belonging*. Somerville, MA: Wisdom Books, 2018.

———. "Sweeping My Heart." *Lion's Roar: Buddhist Wisdom for Our Time*. Last modified June 15, 2021. https://www.lionsroar.com/sweeping-my-heart/.

———. *Tell Me Something About Buddhism*. Charlottesville, VA: Hampton Roads Publishing, 2011.

———. *The Way of Tenderness: Awakening Through Race, Sexuality, and Gender*. Somerville, MA: Wisdom Books, 2015.

———. "The Wisdom in My Bones." *Buddhadharma: The Practitioner's Quarterly* (Spring 2015): 32–37.

Marshall, William F. "Coronavirus infection by race: What's behind the health disparities?" Mayo Clinic. Last modified August 13, 2020. https://www.mayoclinic.org/diseases-conditions/coronavirus/expert-answers/coronavirus-infection-by-race/faq-20488802.

Martin, John Angus, Joseph Opala, and Cynthia Schmidt. *The Temne Nation of Carriacou: Sierra Leone's Lost Family in the Caribbean*. Chattanooga, TN: Polyphemus Press, 2016.

"Mary Proctor." YouTube video, 5:31, posted by David Seehausen. April 23, 2011. https://www.youtube.com/watch?v=AvH60zqcpyw.

Mattis, Jacqueline S. "Religion and Spirituality in the Meaning-Making and Coping Experiences of African American Women: A Qualitative Analysis." *Psychology of Women Quarterly* 26 (December 2002): 309–21. doi: 10.1111/1471-6402.t01-2-00070.

Mattis, Jacqueline S., and Robert Jagers. "A Relational Framework for the Study of Religiosity and Spirituality in the Lives of African Americans." *Journal of Community Psychology* 29, no. 5 (2001): 519–39. doi: 10.1002/jcop.1034.

McGranahan, Carole. "What Is Ethnography? Teaching Ethnographic Sensibilities without Fieldwork." *Teaching Anthropology* 4 (April 2014): 23–36. doi: 10.22582/ta.v4i1.421.

Melville House. "Twenty-five Years after Her Death, What Audre Lorde Left Behind Most Definitely Has a Life of Its Own." Last modified November 17, 2017. https://www.mhpbooks.com/twenty-five-years-after-her-death-what-audre-lorde-left-behind-most-definitely-has-a-life-of-its-own/.

Metcalf Jr., Eugene W. "Folk Art, Museums, and Collecting the Modern Self." In *Contemporary American Folk, Native, and Outsider Art; Into the Mainstream?*, edited by Edna Carter Southard, 12–22. Miami, FL: Miami University Art Museum, 1990.

———. "Black Art, Folk Art, and Social Control," *Winterthur Portfolio* 18, no. 4 (Winter 1983): 271–89.

Mitchem, Stephanie. "No Longer Nailed to the Floor." *Cross Currents* 53, no. 1 (2003): 64–74.

Moreno Vega, Marta. *The Altar of My Soul: The Living Traditions of Santeria*. New York: One World Ballantine Books, 2000.

Murchison, Julian M., and Curtis D. Coats. "Ethnography of Religious Instants: Multi-Sited Ethnography and the Idea of 'Third Spaces.'" *Religions* 6, no. 3 (2015): 988–1005. doi: 10.3390/rel6030988.

Murphey, Jacob. "Painted Signs from Renowned Tallahassee Artist Provide Unexpected Source of Hope Decades Later." *WCTV* News. Last modified July 10, 2020. https://www.wctv.tv/2020/07/11/painted-signs-from-renowned-tallahassee-artist-provide-unexpected-source-of-hope-decades-later/.

Nakamura, Lisa. *Cybertypes: Race, Ethnicity, and Identity on the Internet*. New York: Routledge, 2002.

Omari-Tunkara, Mikelle Smith. *Manipulating the Sacred: Yorùbá Art, Ritual, and Resistance in Brazilian Condomblè*. Detroit, MI: Wayne State University Press, 2005.

Owens, Lama Rod. "Forum: Unseen Realized Beings." *Buddhadharma: The Practitioner's Quarterly* (Summer 2018): 57–74; 57. https://www.lionsroar.com/forum-unseen-realized-beings/.

Packer, Randall. "About." *Third Space Network* (performance platform and blog). Last modified 2021. https://thirdspacenetwork.com/about/.

Painter, Nell Irvin. *Soul Murder and Slavery*. Waco, TX: Markham Press Fund, 1995.

Parker, Evelyn. "Emancipatory Hope Reloaded." Paper delivered at the Religious Education Association Annual Meeting, Dallas, TX, November 23, 2009. https://old.religiouseducation.net/proceedings/2009_Proceedings/23Parker_EmancipatoryHope.pdf.

Parker, Pat. "Movement in Black." In *Movement in Press*, 86–93. Ithaca, NY: Firebrand Press, 1978.

Patillo-McCoy, Mary. "Church Culture as a Strategy of Action in the Black Community." *American Sociological Review* 63, no. 6 (December 1988): 767–84.

Perin, Constance. "The Reception of New, Unusual, and Difficult Art." In *The Artist Outsider: Creativity and the Boundaries of Culture*, edited by Michael D. Hall and Eugene W. Metcalf, 180–86. Washington, DC: Smithsonian Institute Press, 1994.

Pollock, Caitlin M. J., and Andrea L. Battleground. "A Gallery for the Outlaw: Archiving the Art of the Iconoclast." Paper delivered at the Association of College and Research Libraries Conference, Indianapolis, IN, Friday, April 12, 2013. https://www.ala.org/acrl/sites/ala.org.acrl/files/content/conferences/confsandpreconfs/2013/papers/PollockBattleground_Gallery.pdf.

Popova, Maria. "Audre Lorde on Poetry as an Instrument of Change and the Courage to Feel as an Antidote to Fear, a Portal to Power and Possibility, and a Fulcrum of Action." *Brain Pickings* (blog). Last modified May 6, 2018. https://www.brainpickings.org/2020/10/18/poetry-is-not-a-luxury-audre-lorde/.

Proctor, Mary. *I Sho Nuff Brought The Sunshine In My Life When I Picked Up A Paint Can*, mixed media installation, 1995 (photo: Matthew Arnett, 2001). Souls Grown Deep Foundation, Gee's Bend, Alabama. https://www.soulsgrowndeep.org/artist/mary-proctor/work/i-sho-nuff-brought-sunshine-my-life-when-i-picked-paint-can.

———. "Mary Proctor's Folk Art." YouTube video, 16:46. Posted January 4, 2015. https://www.youtube.com/watch?v=F8HcZtZbi-M.

Purdie-Vaughns, Valerie, and Richard P. Eibach. "Intersectional Invisibility: The Distinctive Advantages and Disadvantages of Multiple Subordinate-Group Identities." *Sex Roles* 59 (2008): 377–91. doi: 10.1007/s11199-008-9424-4.

Rambo, Lewis R., and Steven C. Bauman. "Psychology of Conversion and Spiritual Transformation." *Pastoral Psychology* 61, no. 5 (2012): 879–94. doi: 10.1007/s11089-011-0364-5.

Richards, Kimberley. "Pregnant Women in Ghana are Taking Skin Bleaching Pills for Their Unborn Babies." *The Atlanta Voice*, March 1, 2018. https://www.theatlantavoice.com/articles/pregnant-women-in-ghana-are-taking-skin-bleaching-pills-for-their-unborn-babies/.

Roberts, Monica. "2012 TransFaith In Color Conference Keynote Address." *TransGriot* (blog). Last modified August 18, 2012. https://transgriot.blogspot.com/2012/08/2012-transfaith-in-color-conference_18.html.

———. "2012 TransFaith In Color Conference – That's A Wrap." *TransGriot* (blog). Last modified August 20, 2012. https://transgriot.blogspot.com/2012/08/2012-transfaith-in-color-conference_20.html.

———. "TransGriot Mission Statement." *TransGriot* (blog). Last modified December 11, 2011. https://transgriot.blogspot.com.

———. "TransGriot: Search results for womanist." *TransGriot* (blog). Last modified March 31, 2009. https://transgriot.blogspot.com/search?q=womanist.

———. "Tyra Hunter 17th Anniversary." *TransGriot* (blog). Last modified August 7, 2012. https://transgriot.blogspot.com/2012/08/tyra-hunter-17th-anniversary.html.

———. "What Happens With My African Diaspora Trans Peeps IS My Business." *TransGriot* (blog). Last modified May 22, 2016. https://transgriot.blogspot.com/2016/05/what-happens-with-my-african-diaspora.html.

Rouse, Carol Moxley. *Engaged Surrender: African American Women and Islam.* Berkeley, CA: University of California Press, 2004.

Rowell, Charles H. "Above the Wind: An Interview with Audre Lorde." In *Conversations with Audre Lorde*, edited by Joan Wylie Hall, 52–63. Jackson, MS: University Press of Mississippi, 2004.

Salvadore, Sarah. "Catholic Schools Slow to Accept Cultural Significance of Black Hair." *National Catholic Reporter*, February 20, 2020. https://www.ncronline.org/news/justice/catholic-schools-slow-accept-cultural-significance-black-hair.

Schultz, Dagmar, dir. *Audre Lorde: The Berlin Years 1984 to 1992.* New York: Third World Newsreel, 2012.

Scott, K. M. "A Perennial Mourning: Identity Conflict and the Transgenerational Transmission of Trauma within the African American Community." *Mind and Human Interaction* 11 (2000): 11–26.

Sendejo, Brenda. "The Cultural Production of Spiritual Activisms: Gender, Social Justice, and the Remaking of Religion in the Borderlands." *Chicana/Latina Studies* 12, no. 1 (2013): 59–109.

Shafton, Anthony. "Dream Time Magazine: African-Americans and Predictive Dreams." International Association for the Study of Dreams. Last updated 2003. https://asdreams.org/magazine/articles/african_prediction_dreams.htm.

Shapiro, Ellen. "Audre Lorde." In *Conversations with Audre Lorde*, edited by Joan Wylie Hall, 18–25. Jackson, MS: University Press of Mississippi, 2004.

Shengold, Leonard. *Soul Murder: The Effects of Childhood Abuse and Deprivation.* New Haven, CT: Yale University Press, 1989.

Sheppard, Phillis Isabella. "Culture and Pastoral Psychotherapy: A Womanist Self Psychological Perspective." In *Transforming Wisdom: Pastoral Psychotherapy in Theological Perspective*, edited by Felicity B. Kelcourse and K. Byrnolf Lyon, 44–61. Eugene, OR: Cascade Books, 2015.

———. "Incantation." 2018. Unpublished.

———. "Response to Lewis R. Rambo." *Ex Auditu: An International Journal for the Theological Interpretation of Scripture* 25 (2009): 17–22.

———. *Self, Culture, and Others in Womanist Practical Theology.* New York: Palgrave Macmillan, 2011.

———. "This is My Calling: Womanist Ethnography and Black Women's Vocation." Paper delivered at Vanderbilt University Divinity School, Nashville, TN, 2018.

———. "Womanist-Lesbian Pastoral Ethics: A Post-Election Perspective." *Journal of Pastoral Theology* 27, no. 1 (2017): 152–70. doi: 0.1080/10649867.2017.1315791.

———. "Womanist Pastoral Theology and Black Women's Experience of Religion and Sexuality." In *Critical Trajectories in Pastoral Theology and Care: Theory and Practice*, edited by Nancy J. Ramsay, 125–48. Newark, NJ: John Wiley & Sons, Inc., 2018.

Singleton, Jermaine. *Cultural Melancholy: Readings of Race, Impossible Mourning, and African American Ritual.* Urbana, IL: University of Illinois Press, 2015.

Smallwood, Christine. "Outside In." *New York Times Style Magazine* online, June 1, 2015. https://www.nytimes.com/2015/06/01/t-magazine/outsider-art-essay-christine-smallwood.html.

Somé, Malidoma Patrice. *The Healing Wisdom of Africa*. New York: Penguin Putnam, Inc., 1999.

———. *Ritual, Power, Healing: The African Teachings of the Dagara*. New York: Penguin Group, 1993.

Somé, Sonbonfu E. *Welcoming Spirit Home: Ancient African Teaching to Celebrate Children and Community*. Novato, CA: New World Library, 1999.

Spooner, Tom. "African Americans and the Internet: Main Report." Washington, DC: Pew Research Center, 2000. https://www.pewresearch.org/internet/2000/10/22/main-report-24/.

Star, Susan Leigh. "Sadomasochism: Not About Condemnation: An Interview with Audre Lorde." In *A Burst of Light: And Other Essays*, edited by Audre Lorde. Ithaca, NY: Firebrand Books, 1988.

Strangelove, Michael. "Cyberspace and the Changing Landscape of the Self." *The Geography of Consciousness* 3 (1994). http://cyberpunk.asia/cp_pdf.php?txt=160&lng=us.

Strickland, William. "Frantz Fanon: His Life and Work." *International Tribute to Frantz Fanon*. 8 (1979). https://scholarworks.umass.edu/cgi/viewcontent.cgi?article=1007&context=afroam_faculty_pubs

Swidler, Ann. "Culture in Action: Symbols and Strategies." *American Sociological Review* 51, no. 2 (April 1986): 273–86. doi: 10.2307/2095521.

Taylor, Susan. *In the Spirit: The Inspirational Writings*. New York: Harper Perennial, 1994.

Thomas, Linda E. *Under the Canopy: Ritual Process and Spiritual Resilience in South Africa*. Columbia, SC: University of South Carolina Press, 1999.

———. "Womanist Theology, Epistemology, and a New Anthropological Paradigm." *CrossCurrents* 48, no. 4 (Winter 1998/1999): 488–99.

Townes, Emilie M. "Cultural Boundaries and African American Theology." In *The Oxford Handbook of African American Theology*, edited by Katie G. Cannon and Anthony B. Pinn, 480–89. New York: Oxford University Press, 2014.

———. "Meditations on Love and Violence." In *Love and Christian Ethics: Tradition, Theory, and Society*, edited by Frederick V. Simmons with Brian C. Sorrells, 303–12. Washington, DC: Georgetown University Press, 2016.

———. *Womanist Ethics and the Cultural Production of Evil*. New York: Palgrave MacMillan, 2006.

Vernon, Leah (Leah V Daily). *Beauty and the Muse* (blog). Last modified July 31, 2019. http://www.beautyandthemuse.net/.

———. "I am Muslim, But I'm not the Poster Child for Islam." *Beauty and the Muse* (blog). Last modified October 22, 2016. http://www.beautyandthemuse.net/leahvdaily/2016/10/22/980e52hhbtz2zbo8m7mw28uqrx70i9.

Wadud, Amina. "Hajar: of the desert." Feminism and Religion. Last modified October 17, 2013. https://feminismandreligion.com/2013/10/17/hajar-of-the-desert-by-amina-wadud/.

Walker, Alice. *In Search of Our Mothers' Gardens: Womanist Prose*. San Diego, CA: Harcourt Brace Jovanovich, 1983.
Webb-Hehn, Katherine. "Don't Ignore Signs: The Life and Art of Missionary Mary Proctor." *The Bitter Southerner*, November 1, 2016. https://bittersoutherner.com/missionary-mary-proctor-southern-folk-art.
Weems, Renita. "Come out of the Cave." Sermon delivered February 20, 2011. http://jahasworld.blogspot.com/2011/10/dr-rev-renita-weems-2-20-2011-come-out.html.
———. "Something within." *Somethingwithin.com*, Wednesday (June 18, 2008).
Wiggins, Daphne C. *Righteous Content: Black Women's Perspective of Church and Faith*. New York: New York University Press, 2005.
Wilcox, Melissa M. *Queer Women and Religious Individualism*. Bloomington, IN: Indiana University Press, 2009.
Williams, Delores S. "Rituals of Resistance in Womanist Worship." In *Women at Worship: Interpretations of North American Diversity*, edited by Marjorie Procter-Smith and Janet Roland Walton, 215–24. Louisville, KY: Westminster/John Knox Press, 1993.
———. "Womanist Theology: Black Women's Voices." In *The Womanist Reader: The First Quarter Century of Womanist Thought*, edited by Layli Phillips, 117–25. New York: Routledge, 2006.
Williams, Patricia J. *The Alchemy of Race and Rights: The Diary of a Law Professor*. Cambridge, MA: Harvard University Press, 1991.
Wimberly, Anne S. "The Faith Community as Listener in the Era of Cyberspace." *Journal of the Interdenominational Theological Center* 25, no. 2 (Fall 1997): 13–71.
Wojcik, Daniel. "Outsider Art, Vernacular Traditions, Trauma, and Creativity." *Western Folklore* 67, no. 2/3 (Spring–Summer 2008): 179–98.
Zolberg, Vera L., and Joni Maya Cherbo, eds. "Introduction." In *Outsider Art: Contesting Boundaries in Contemporary Culture*, 1–10. Cambridge, UK: Cambridge University Press, 1997.

Index

Abrams, Stacey, 113
activism: Anzaldúa on, xiv; and spirituality, 119. *See also* work
adolescence, Black, 74, 76
African religion: Lorde and, 3–4, 9–10, 13–14; Manuel and, 64; Monae and, 113–16
agency: Brown and, 92; Proctor and, 40; Roberts and, 59, 62; selfobject theory and, xix
aggression, horizontal, 77
Aido Hwedo, 9
Alexander, Elizabeth, xiv–xv, 35
Amaral Madureira, Ana Flávia do, 106
American Folk Art Museum, 42–43
ancestors: Manuel and, 71, 122; rituals and, 1–2, 113–16, 119–23; Shella and, 127
anger: Brown and, 101; Lorde and, 15; Manuel and, 69–72
anthropology, Roberts and, 59–60
Anzaldúa, Gloria E., xiv
Archer, Jermaine, 117
art: and mirroring, 27–29; valuing of, 31–32. *See also* outsider art
art brut, term, 32
art collecting: issues in, 31; Proctor and, 39
authenticity, Roberts and, 61

Baptists: Brown and, xxi, 87, 92; Butler and, xii
Battleground, A. L., 35
Batts, Mrs., 115–16
beauty, Daily and, 74–76
belonging. *See* home
Bentham, Jeremy, 54
Bethune, Mary Mcleod, xx, 44
Blackness: Brown and, 105; Lorde and, 5–7, 12, 18; Proctor and, 40
Black Panther Party, 19
Black power movement, Lorde and, 8
Black women: and art, 27–49; and rituals, 111–13, 119–23; use of Internet, 55
blogs, 79; Daily and, 74–76; Jamerican and, 72–79; Roberts and, 57–64
Bobo, Jacqueline, 27
body, Black: Daily and, 74–76; Fanon and, 17; Lorde and, 7–10, 16–17; Manuel and, 69–72; ritual and, 112–13; Willis and, 70
boundary control, Brown and, 93
Brooks, Rayshard, 69
Brown, Alecia (pseudonym), xxi, 87–110; background of, 87; and ritual, 122
Brown, Michelle, 60
Buddhism, Manuel and, 64–72

Butler, Octavia, xii–xviii, 51

call/vocation: Brown and, 89–92, 99–100, 103–6; and outsider art, 29–32; Proctor and, 36–37, 43–44, 46
cancer, Lorde and, 10, 18, 22
Cannon, Katie Geneva, 103, 108
Cardinal, Roger, 32–34
care: Brown and, 95–96; Jamerican and, 77; Roberts and, 63; Shella and, 124
Caribbean culture: Fanon and, 10; Lorde and, 2–3, 10–11
cartography, colonialism and, 11
Catholicism: Lorde and, 3; Sheppard and, 118–19
Cesaire, Aime, 11
change, Butler on, xii, xvii
church: in cyberspace, 88–89, 98–99, 104; sexism in, 92–94; Shella and, 124–25; as therapeutic community, 94–99; women in, Brown and, 93, 102, 105–6
Church of God, Manuel and, 64–65
Clark, Kenneth and Mamie, 113
Clarke, Cheryl, 3
class: and artistic judgment, 27, 33; Brown and, 90; in cyberspace, 55; Manuel and, 66; Parker and, 20–21
Clayton, Frances, 13
Clayton, Kim, 43
clergy, male, Brown and, 93, 99–102, 105
Clinton, Hillary, 61
Coats, Curtis, 56
Cole, Johnetta, 21
collaboration, Roberts and, 59
colonialism: and Caribbean, 11; Fanon and, 12, 14
colorism: Daily and, 74–76; Jamerican and, 72, 74–79; Lorde and, 5–7, 13; Manuel and, 71
community, 119; Brown and, 94–99; hooks and, 131; Jamerican and, 72, 76–77; Lorde and, 3; Manuel and, 69–72; Proctor and, 43; therapeutic, 13; Weems on, 97
compensation: artists and, 32; Brown and, 99–100; Proctor and, 45
connection, in cyberspace, xxii, 52, 55
consciousness, Manuel and, 71
consistency, Roberts and, 60
containers, Manuel and, 66, 71
context stage, in conversion, 73
conversion, 119; Jamerican and, 72; Lorde and, 12
Cooksey, Penny, 41
Cooper, Ashton, 29
Coopersmith, Haley, 29–30
Copeland, M. Shawn, 131
cosmology, Lorde and, 10
Courtney, Barry, 46
COVID-19 pandemic, 46, 69, 116
creativity: Proctor and, 37–39, 44, 46; Roberts and, 59; Walker and, 30
cultural tools, in cyberspace, xxiii, 52–53
culture: Geertz on, 125; Manuel and, 68; Monae and, 113; and self, 14; as selfobject, xviii–xix, 28; Thomas on, x
cyberspace, xi, xxii–xxiii, 51–85; Brown and, xxi, 87–110; Daily and, 74–76; Jamerican and, 72–79; Manuel and, 64–72; nature of, 51–52, 54–57, 79; religion in, xi, xxi, 80, 85n96

Daily, Leah V., xxii, 51
death: Holloway on, 118; Lorde and, 4, 19, 22–23
De Veaux, Alexis, 15
diaspora community, African: Jamerican and, 72; Jones and, 114; Lorde and, 9–10; Roberts and, 62–63
difference, Lorde and, 7
dissemblance, xv
dissonance, hooks on, 67
Doll Test, 113
dream space, xiv–xv, 17–18

Index

dualism, Lorde and, 22
Dubuffet, Jean, 32
Dunham, Mary, 19
Dyston, Torkwase, xv
dystopia, Butler on, xiii

economic issues, Brown and, 90, 99–100
elders, Roberts and, 63
engagement, Weems on, 96
Enzer, Julie R., 19
epistemologies, Black, 10–15
erasure/invisibility: of Black/brown interiority, xiii; of Black experience in cyberspace, 55; of Black women's cultural work, 27–28; Krug and, 132; Lorde and, 18; Manuel and, 69; Wawud and, 120. *See also* scholarship, lack of
erotic: Lorde and, 4, 8, 16–17, 20. *See also* sexuality
ethnography. *See* womanist ethnography
evil, Townes on, xiii–xiv
examination. *See* self-examination
eyes: Lorde and, 18; Proctor and, 37, 39

faith: Jamerican and, 79; Roberts and, 58–59
family: Jamerican and, 77–78; Lorde and, 2–3, 22; Manuel and, 64–65; Proctor and, 38, 41, 43–44; Roberts and, 57–58; Shella and, 124
Fanon, Franz, 5, 10–15
fear, Lorde and, 17–19
feminism *vs.* womanism, 61–62
Floyd, George, 69
Frederick, Marla, 112, 119, 127

Gail, xxiii, xxiv
Geertz, Clifford, 125
gender: in cyberspace, 55; Jamerican and, 74–79; Lorde and, 6, 8; Manuel and, 69; rituals and, 121–22
ghosts, Lorde and, 8–10

Gilkes, Cheryl Townsend, 95
God, communication from: Brown and, 91–92; outsider artists and, 29; Proctor and, 39, 45
Greene, Beverly, 105
Greene-Hayes, Ahmad, 123
grief. *See* mourning
griot, Roberts as, 57, 59–61, 63
group self, 28

Hagar/Hajar, 120–21
Hamer, Fannie Lou, 10
Harris Perry, Melissa, 67
healing, Manuel and, 71
Henery, Celeste, xiii
Herman, Judith, 90
heterosexism: in cyberspace, 53; Fanon and, 12; Shella and, 125–26
Hine, Darlene Clark, xv–xvi
Holloway, Karla, 118
home, homelessness: Brown and, 104–5; Daily and, 76; Jamerican and, 73; Lorde and, 17, 22–23; Manuel and, xxi–xxii, 66
homophobia: Lorde and, 13; Manuel and, 71; Shella and, 125–26
hooks, bell, 67, 131
Hooper, Annie, 33
Hurston, Zora Neale, 67

idealization, xviii; in cyberspace, 56
identity: and conversion, 73; Internet and, 52; Lorde and, 5–7
Ifá diviners, 64
image of God, Roberts and, 59, 61
imagination, Townes on, xiii
imagoes, 9
immigrants, Jamerican and, 72, 77
incantations, 1
initiation, Manuel and, 66
intentionality, Roberts and, 60
interiority, ix–xxx, 131–34; aspects of, xv–xvi; Brown and, 95–96, 105–8; Butler and, xii–xviii; Fanon and, 10–

15; importance of, xiii–xvi, 131–32; Lorde and, 4; outsider artists and, 32–36; Proctor and, xx, 40, 42–43, 45; and public religious experience, xvi–xvii; racism and, xxiii; rationale for study of, xxiv–xxv; ritual and, 112–13
Internet. *See* cyberspace
intersectionality, in cyberspace, 55
introspection. *See* self-examination
isolation, Weems on, 96–97

Jacobs, Claude F., 112
Jamerican, xxii, 72–79
John, Catherine, 22
Jones, Clyde, 33
Jones, Omi Osun Joni L., 114
Joseph, Gloria, 4, 22
Juno, Pat, 43

King, Martin Luther, Jr., 46
King, Ruth, 70
kinship, xviii; in cyberspace, 56; Daily and, 76; Jamerican and, 72; Lorde and, 8–9; Manuel and, 67–68; Proctor and, 43–44
knowledge, Thomas on, x
Kohut, Heinz, xviii–xix, 28
Krug, Jessica, 132

Lartey, Emmanuel Yartekwei Amugi, 9
Lawless, Elaine, 121
Lawrence-Lightfoot, Sarah, xvii
leadership, Roberts and, 60
Legge, Eric, 43
lesbians, Black: Lorde, 1, 3, 22; Parker, 19–21; Shella, 123–27
LGBTQ individuals: cyberspace and, 57–64; and religion, 58–63, 123–27
liminal space, Proctor and, 43
Lincoln, Bruce, 113
listening, in womanist ethnography, xii, 133
litanies, 1, 67; Lorde and, 10; Roberts and, 63. *See also* rituals

literary criticism, and Black women's cultural work, 27–28
liturgy: in cyberspace, 88; liberated, 122
Lorde, Audre, x–xi, 1–26, 70; character of, 2, 21; Manuel and, 65–67
love, Black, 116–34; Lorde and, 12, 21; nature of, 116

Mageed, Debra, 78
Mandela, Winnie, 10
Manley, Roger, 33
Manuel, Zenju Earthlyn, xxi–xxii, xxiv, 51, 64–72, 122
marriage, Daily and, 74–76
McDade, Tony, 69
McGranahan, Carole, 56
McMillan, Terry, 27
meaning, finding/making: Brown and, 106–8; Daily and, 76; Proctor and, 40; religious practices and, xvii–xviii
meditation, 111–30; Manuel and, 71–72; Proctor and, 45; Roberts and, 61. *See also* rituals
melancholia. *See* mourning
mental health, and outsider art, 32–34
mentoring, Brown and, 100
Mercer, Kobena, 90
Metcalf, Eugene W., 30–32
methodology: Shella and, 123–24; womanist ethnography as, xii, xvi–xviii, xxv, 27, 55–56, 132–33
ministry. *See* call/vocation
mirroring, xviii; art and, 27–29; Brown and, 102; in cyberspace, 56; lack of, xix, 3, 60; Lorde and, 3, 18; outsider art and, 40; Proctor and, 45; ritual and, 112–13
Mitchum, Stephanie, 107
Monae, Janelle, 113–16
moral nature: Lorde and, 6; Roberts and, 58–59
mother: Lorde and, 5–6, 11, 18; Proctor and, 41; Shella and, 124; Walker and, 108

mourning: Brown and, 100, 104; Proctor and, xx, 37–39, 43–44, 46; soul murder and, 107
Murchison, Julian M., 56
museums: nature of, 31; Proctor and, 42–45
Muslim women: bloggers, xxii–xxiii; Jamerican, 72–79; Wadud, 120

Nakamura, Lisa, xxii, 52
names, naming: Lorde and, 4, 9; Manuel and, 67–68; Roberts and, 63
Nation of Islam, 7, 76
negativity: Monae and, 115; Proctor and, 40

Obama, Michelle, 61, 102
Omari-Tunkara, Mikelle Smith, 114
Orishas, 113–14
outsider art, xix–xx, 27–49; classification of, 31; definition of, 33–34; and interiority, 32–36
outsider status: Jamerican and, 73–74; Lorde and, 2–3
Owens, Lama Rod, 111

Packer, Randall, 57
panopticon, 54
Parker, Evelyn, 74
Parker, Pat, 3, 5, 19–21, 67, 87
Pattillo-McCoy, Mary, 53–54
Pentecostal religion, xxi, 121
Perin, Constance, 40
Petry, Anne, 117
poetry: Lorde and, 9; Parker and, 5, 20–21
Pollock, C. M. J., 35
Popova, Maria, 19
poverty: Brown and, 94–95; Manuel and, 66–67; Proctor and, 46
power, 122; Brown and, 93; Lorde and, 15; Roberts and, 62; spiritual, 51
practices, religious, xvii–xviii, 54, 119; Brown and, 106–8; Jamerican and, 72; Lorde and, 13; Proctor and, 40; Roberts and, 60–61. *See also* rituals

Proctor, Christopher, 43–44
Proctor, Mary, xix–xx, 34–49, 117–18; background of, 36–37, 41–42; reactions to, 34–35
psyche, Black: damage to, Roberts and, 59; Fanon and, 10–15
psychoanalysis. *See* therapy
public religious experience, and interiority, xvi–xvii

race: in cyberspace, xxii, 52, 55; Manuel and, 69
racism: Brown and, 99, 101; in church, xxiii; in cyberspace, 52–53; Fanon and, 11–12, 14; Jamerican and, 72; Lorde and, 13, 15–16; Manuel and, xxiv, 66, 69, 71; and religious experience, xxii–xxiv; Roberts and, 60–61; Weems and, 102
Rambo, Lewis, 73
rape, and interiority, xv–xvi
recognition, lack of, Brown and, 92–94
rejection: Brown and, 93, 100, 105; Daily and, 76
religion: Brown and, 103–6; Butler and, xii–xviii, 51; in cyberspace, xi, xxi, 80, 85n96; Fanon and, 14; importance of, 131–32; LGBTQ individuals and, 58–63, 123–27; Manuel and, 64–65; outsider artists and, 29, 35; Proctor and, xx; Roberts and, 57–64; as selfobject, xviii–xxiv. *See also* African religion
religious experience, Black, ix–xii, 131–34; Brown and, 87–110; complexity of, xvi–xviii; in cyberspace, 51–85; Gilkes on, 95; Jamerican and, 72–79; Pattillo-McCoy on, 53–54; Proctor and, 34–49; Roberts and, 57–64; selfobject theory and, xix
remembrance: Proctor and, 43–44; Roberts and, 63–64
Rensberger, David, 94
resistance, 54; Batts and, 115–16; Lorde and, 18; rituals and, 119–23; Shella, 123–27

respect: Brown and, 99–100, 102–3, 105; Roberts and, 63
responsibility: Brown and, 98; Proctor and, 42
rituals, 1–2, 111–30; Lorde and, 9–10; Manuel and, 51, 64, 67; Shella and, 126–27; and work, 127–28
Roberts, Monica, 51, 57–64, 117, 122
Rollins, Ed, 3
roots practices, ix–x, 111
Ross, Rosetta, 94
Rouse, Carol, 79

Sadie, 63
sanctuary space, Manuel and, 65, 71
Sangha. *See* community
scholarship, lack of: on Black experience in cyberspace, 55; on conversion, 73; on folk art, 32; on interiority, xi–xii, xxiv; on religion, xii
Seehausen, Dvaid, 36
self: Brown and, 104; cohering sense of, xix; and culture, 14; group, 28; Internet and, 52, 79
self-esteem, Brown and, 91, 101
self-examination: Lorde and, 8–9; Manuel and, 71; Shella and, 126
selfobject, 28; definition of, xviii, xxxn24; religion as, xviii–xxiv
Sendejo, Brenda, xiv
September 11, 2001, and self-examination, 126
settled cultural periods, 53
sexism: and Black religious experience, 54; Brown and, xxi, 89, 92–94, 99–103, 107; in cyberspace, 53; Daily and, 74–76; Fanon and, 12; Jamerican and, 72; Lorde and, 7, 13; Wawud and, 120; Weems and, 102; Williams and, 121
sexuality: in cyberspace, 55; Manuel and, 69. *See also* erotic
Shafton, Anthony, 117
Shakur, Assata, 10

Shange, Ntozake, xiv
Shengold, Leonard, 107
silencing, Lorde and, 18
Smallwood, Christine, 31
social: Brown and, 104; ritual and, 112–13
Somé, Malidoma, 112
Somé, Sonbonfu, 127
soul murder, definition of, 107
space, sacred, xv, 121; Manuel and, 65, 71
spirit murder, definition of, 107
spirituality: and activism, 119; Lorde and, 2–4, 12–13, 16–17, 22; Manuel and, 69–72; outsider artists and, 29; Parker and, 20–21; Proctor and, 34–49; Shella, 123–27; Walker on, 30; Yoruba, 113–14
status: Brown and, 103–6; of outsider artists, 34–35; of women artists, 29
Strangelove, Michael, 52
struggle: Brown and, 90; Hine and, xv; Jamerican and, 72; Manuel and, 71; Proctor and, 46; Weems and, 96–97
subjectivity, Roberts and, 62
suffering: Brown and, 91; Manuel and, 71; Somé on, 112
Sullivan, Mecca Jamilah, 19
surveillance, 54; Daily and, 75
Swidler, Ann, 52–53

Taylor, Breanna, 69
Taylor, Susan, 58–59
testifying, Roberts and, 64
theology, Roberts and, 59–61
therapy: church and, 94–99; Lorde and, 13; and outsider art, 32–33
third space: cyberspace as, 56–57; definition of, 57
Thomas, Linda E., x, 99, 112
Toomer, Jean, 30
Townes, Emilie M., xiii–xiv, 54, 117
transformation: Manuel and, 69–72; Proctor and, 45; ritual and, 112,

121–22; Roberts and, 59–63; work and, 127–28
transgender individuals: cyberspace and, 57–64; and religion, 58–63
transphobia, Roberts and, 60–61
trauma: Brown and, 89–92, 100–106; definition of, 89–90; Lorde and, 8; Proctor and, 38; Willis and, 70
Tubman, Harriet, 117
Turner, Victor, 118
twinship, xviii; Proctor and, 43–44

unconscious, x, xiv
unsettled cultural periods, 53

violence: Fanon and, 14; Lorde and, 14–16; Manuel and, 67; Parker and, 19; against transgender individuals, 63
vocation. *See* call/vocation
vulnerability: Brown and, 91; Lorde and, 19–20; Proctor and, 37

Wadud, Amina, 120
Walker, Alice, 30, 68, 108, 111
Webb-Hehn, Katherine, 37
websites, Brown and, 88–89

Weems, Renita, 96–98, 102
Wiggins, Daphne, xxiii
Williams, Angel Kyodo, 70
Williams, Delores S., 116, 120, 122
Williams, Patricia, 107
Williams, Ruby, 43
Willis, Jan, 70
Wimberly, Anne, 94
Wojcik, Daniel, 31
womanism: definition of, 111; Manuel and, 67–68; Roberts and, 61–62
womanist ethnography, xii, xvi–xviii, xxv, 27, 55–56, 132–33; Shella and, 123–24
work, of Black women, 108, 126–28, 131

X, Malcolm, 7–9

Yaa Asantewaa, 10
Yemaya/Yemanja, 113–14
Yoruba, 64, 113–14
youth, Roberts and, 63

Zen Buddhism, Manuel and, xxi, 64–72

About the Author

Phillis Isabella Sheppard is the E. Rhodes and Leona B. Carpenter Associate Professor of Religion, Psychology, and Culture at Vanderbilt University Divinity School and Graduate Department of Religion and the director of the James Lawson Institute for the Research and Study of Nonviolent Movements.

She is a womanist practical theologian, ethnographer, and psychoanalyst whose scholarship focuses on the intersection and interstices of interiority, culture, and religion. She hosts an annual Womanist Ethnography conference at Vanderbilt University Divinity School.

Sheppard has received several grants to fund her ethnographic research including three Randall Mason Research Awards, a Louisville Institute Faculty Research Grant, and a Research Grant from the Center for Practical Theology at Boston University.

She is the author of *Self, Culture and Others in Womanist Practical Theology* (2011). Her current research concerns Black women's multireligious involvement.

www.ingramcontent.com/pod-product-compliance
Lightning Source LLC
Chambersburg PA
CBHW020123010526
44115CB00008B/946